Oxford Modern Britain

The Mass Media and Power in Modern Britain

John Eldridge
Jenny Kitzinger
Kevin Williams

OXFORD UNIVERSITY PRESS

OXFORD
UNIVERSITY PRESS

Great Clarendon Street, Oxford OX2 6DP

Oxford University Press is a department of the University of Oxford.
It furthers the University's objective of excellence in research, scholarship,
and education by publishing worldwide in

Oxford New York

Auckland Bangkok Buenos Aires Cape Town Chennai
Dar es Salaam Delhi Hong Kong Istanbul Karachi Kolkata
Kuala Lumpur Madrid Melbourne Mexico City Mumbai Nairobi
São Paulo Shanghai Taipei Tokyo Toronto

Oxford is a registered trade mark of Oxford University Press
in the UK and in certain other countries

Published in the United States
by Oxford University Press Inc., New York

British Library Cataloguing in Publication Data
Data available

Library of Congress Cataloging in Publication Data
Eldridge, J. E. T. (John Eric Thomas)
The mass media and power in modern Britain / John Eldridge
Jenny Kitzinger, Kevin Williams.
(Oxford modern, Britain)
Includes bibliographical references (p.   ) and index.
1. Mass media—Great Britain. 2. Mass Media—Audiences.   Mass media—
Influence. I. Kitzinger, Jenny. II. Williams, Kevin. III. Title. IV. Series.
P92.G7E43 1996   302.23'0941—dc20   96–32233
ISBN 0-19-878172-5
ISBN 0-19-878171-7 (Pbk)

10 9 8 7 6 5

Typeset by Hope Services (Abingdon) Ltd.
Printed in Great Britain
on acid-free paper by
Selwood Printing Ltd,
West Sussex

Foreword

The Oxford Modern Britain series is designed to fill a major gap in the available sociological sources on the contemporary world. Each book will provide a comprehensive and authoritative overview of major issues for students at all levels. They are written by acknowledged experts in their fields, and should be standard sources for many years to come.

Each book focuses on contemporary Britain, but the relevant historical background is always included, and a comparative context is provided. No society can be studied in isolation from other societies and the globalized context of the contemporary world, but a detailed understanding of a particular society can both broaden and deepen sociological understanding. These books will be exemplars of empirical study and theoretical understanding.

Books in the series are intended to present information and ideas in a lively and accessible way. They will meet a real need for source books in a wide range of specialized courses, in 'Modern Britain' and 'Comparative Sociology' courses, and in integrated introductory courses. They have been written with the newcomer and general reader in mind, and they meet the genuine need in the informed public for accurate and up-to-date discussion and sources.

John Scott
Series Editor

Acknowledgements

We are grateful for the support of our colleagues in the Glasgow Media Group, whose work and influence is evident in this text: Greg Philo, Jacquie Reilly, David Miller, and Lesley Henderson. Claire Heard who spent the session 1995–96 on work placement from Middlesex University has also been of great assistance. Joanna Yuill has been a tremendous help in preparing the manuscript and we thank her for her contributions and unfailing good humour.

We have appreciated the opportunity to write this book in the Oxford Modern Britain series and in that connection thank John Scott, the series editor, Tim Barton, the Chief Editor, and Jenni Scott, Assistant Editor, College Books. We particularly want to thank the copy editor, Tim Bartel, for his meticulous reading of the text.

Although this book is not the product of a particular research project, the Glasgow Media Group has received a number of grants from the ESRC in recent years and we would like to thank the ESRC for its support in enabling us to develop our work.

For permission to reproduce images we thank the following: the *Guardian* for Figure 6.1; Sygma for Figure 6.2; Martin Rowson for permission to publish the cartoon in Figure 7.1; *The Ecologist* for permission to publish their cover in Figure 9.1; and the Hulton Deutsch collection for permission to publish the photograph in Figure 10.1.

On a personal note, we would like to thank Diana Mutimer and Christine Reid for their support.

Contents

List of Figures

Part I

Communication and Media Power

Chapter One

Introduction

There are two terms which crop up again and again in our field of study. Sometimes they are used interchangeably. They are 'communication' and 'media'. In modern times they have often been prefixed with the word 'mass'. These terms are used so often they are like familiar objects that we take for granted. Yet in reality they point to a variety of processes and activities and part of our concern at the outset is to disentangle these.

As human beings we make contact with one another. This is an essential part of what it is to be human since it makes us social individuals. There is a physical dimension to this. Contact is possible through shared settlements. Contact between settlements (rural and urban, coastal and inland, international) becomes possible through means of communication: roads, rivers, canals, sea-routes, trains, and airways. We can still speak of these as means or systems of communication, but more often refer to them in terms of modes of transport. Without these physical developments, which have both promoted and responded to the process of urbanization, what we now know as the modern communications industry would not have emerged.

But making contact with each other involves the capacity to create symbols and imbue them with meaning. This constitutes a collective shared activity although the boundaries may vary from the local to the global in different times and places. In any event, one crucial way of doing this is through language. Born into a world with the potential for learning a language, most of us are socialized into the learning of one language, sometimes called our 'native language' for that reason. Some of us may learn more than one language early on, as when the two parents speak different languages, or when the language of an ethnic minority group is different from that of the society in which we live. Thus in Britain, where English is the dominant language, some children will learn Gaelic, Punjabi, Urdu, Welsh, or Chinese, as the case may be. Through language we learn to think in categories and concepts about the world and our immediate place in it. We learn to classify things. We learn to give meaning to what is said to us. It quickly becomes a two-way process. Through language, messages of all kinds are imparted. Language itself becomes a resource which enables us to identify things and people and gradually form our own sense of self and identity. Because there are different languages, we may even think about this in terms of different linguistic communities. This link between communication and community suggests the notion of something in common. Language, then, as a form of communication is something that enables ideas, beliefs, understandings to be made common to many. But we can notice this also: communication in the form of language constitutes an action, but a communication, let us say a written communication, can be recognized as an object.

Language is a means of communication. Through it, a myriad of messages are transmitted day by day. The medium in which language is communicated can vary from the spoken word, in the physical presence of those with whom we are speaking, to satellite television linking people in different parts of the world. The written form of language can likewise vary from the letter, the newspaper, or the book through to the latest form of interaction through computer networking. Written forms of communication can outlive the writers and, in that respect, represent a cultural resource through which earlier generations can speak to those who come after them, even beyond their own societies. We in turn can use such materials for pleasure or instruction. The interaction that then takes place is not with the author but with the text, although this may be done with others as in a group meeting to study the Bible, Shakespeare, Beatrix Potter, or whatever. We may wrestle with what the author intended or meant without the opportunity of asking them direct, let alone arguing with them. We should note, in anticipation of later discussion, that simply studying the text without other materials that can help to provide a context may limit our understanding unnecessarily. In our day, since the development of recording techniques, the spoken word can also be kept beyond the lifetime of the speaker.

It is not difficult to see that a medium of communication in the modern world can require very considerable resources, skills, organization, and sophisticated technology. Thus we talk in overall terms of the communications industry or, more specifically, of publishing, the press, broadcasting, film, and telecommunications industries. Although they change, sometimes with great rapidity, they can be seen as organized constellations of activity and they are regarded as significant enough to be studied as objects in their own right. Thus, we may read about the history of broadcasting, the economics of publishing, technical change in telecommunications, and so on.

We have taken language as an example of communication. Crucial though it is, communication can take other forms although, interestingly, the idea of language can be invoked. Thus, we can refer to body language, to the language of gesture, of music, and of mathematics or, for that matter, the grammar of film. In the case of visual imagery, written material is by definition visual and we can recall as an instance the iconic and pictorial representations of the Bible in the Orthodox Church, which have explicitly served as a means of telling the Christian story to peasants who cannot read. When it comes to modern forms of visual communication such as photography, film, television, and video, in very many instances the image does not exist unsupported. The photograph has a caption, the film has commentary or dialogue and sometimes subtitles. And filmic material is very commonly permeated with music, whether as background or foreground. But just as we can think of a linguistic community in terms of shared codes which enable us to understand what is being said, so we can extend this in terms of other forms of communication. Thus, we recognize the music that introduces television news or a soap programme like *Neighbours*. We also recognize music in a film thriller that is designed to intensify our sense of fear. What is experienced as a subjective feeling is something shared with the rest of a cinema audience. We can even say it contributes towards a structure of feeling.

Sociologists sometimes try to get to grips with a problem by identifying elementary forms or structures. One of the more determined attempts to do this in relation to communication is to be found in an early work of Umberto Eco (1976). Even the most elementary form of communication will be structured in terms of a message, a sender, and a receiver. Even so, as we know sometimes to our cost, not all messages arrive; some are sent in hope rather than certainty, as with the proverbial message in a bottle thrown into the sea, some end up in unforeseen or unintended places. And the possibility of misunderstanding exists even with the simpler forms of communication. Stevie Smith's well-known poem speaks of a misinterpreted sign—the person who was drowning not waving. The happier, if more complex example, is the story of the police who were called to a flat in Bournemouth after cries of 'Help!' were heard by a passer-by, only to discover him in the shower singing along to the Beatles record (*Guardian Society*, 6 September 1995). In these cases, the mistake can be understood with the benefit of hindsight or further information. Human communication is intrinsically symbolic in character and this carries with it

5

possibilities for conflict and confusion as well as co-operation and comprehension.

If society is impossible without communication and, through communication, socialization takes place (for example in the settings of home, school, work, religious activity, leisure activity), it follows that through communication the possibility exists for influencing the attitudes and behaviour of others and of being influenced ourselves. This leads us to ask about the communication process: who is communicating with whom, by what means, for what purposes, with what effects, and in whose interests? The answers to such questions tell us much about the kind of societies we live in and the ways in which power and control operate. We cannot assume that the process of communication is always benign. That is why, in the lexicon of communications research, we encounter such terms as 'propaganda', 'indoctrination', 'manipulation', 'ideology', 'distortion' and 'deception'. If, for example, from time to time, those in positions of power take Machiavelli's advice, then things will not always be what they seem. 'Occasionally,' he wrote, 'words must serve to veil the facts. But this must happen in such a way that no one becomes aware of it; or, if it should be noticed, excuses must be at hand, to be produced immediately' (in Koestler: 1947: 135).

We come now to the troublesome word 'media', which is the plural of 'medium'. Language is a medium of communication. But language is transmitted in many ways: through the voice in direct person-to-person encounter, through the printed word, through the instruments of radio, film, television, telephone, fax, e-mail, and so on. These instruments of communication, grounded in specific and often complex technologies, represent different means of communication. Each can be differentiated as representing a distinctive medium of communication, but it is the socially organized clusters of activities that are described as the media. That is our main concern in this book. But we can at least recognize other common usages. We can see a work of art exhibited in a gallery described as mixed media, referring to the co-existence of different materials in the composition. We will see advertisements for multimedia computers, meaning that they have the capacity, for example, to give and receive printed messages, as well as provide spoken messages, play music, and show films and pictures.

It was Marshall McLuhan who, in what became a famous phrase, told us that 'the medium is the message' (McLuhan, 1973). This is how he began the essay:

In a culture like ours, long accustomed to splitting and dividing all things as a means of control, it is sometimes a bit of a shock to be reminded that, in operational and practical fact, the medium is the message. This is merely to say that the personal and social consequences of any medium—that is, of any extension of ourselves—result from a new scale that is introduced into our affairs by each extension of ourselves, or by any new technology. (McLuhan, 1973: 15)

Interestingly, McLuhan takes physical means of communication as an example. Thus, the railway was not the first kind of transportation in human society, but it served to accelerate and enlarge the scale of previous human functions and, in the process, create new kinds of cities, work, and leisure. He argues that new technologies (and not only technologies of communication) add something to what we already are. This is a very generalized notion of what constitutes a message. Thus we might say, in the spirit of McLuhan, that the message of television is that we have become televisual people. Put like that it is a tautology. A little more specifically, he states that we should not concentrate on the content of messages without having regard to the character of the medium. To drive the point home he uses the example of electric light as a medium of communication without content:

For it is not till electric light is used to spell out some brand name that it is noticed as a medium. Then it is not the light but the 'content' (or what is really another medium) that is noticed. The message of the electric light is like the message of electric power in industry, totally radical, pervasive and decentralised. For electric light and power are separate from their uses, yet they eliminate time and space factors in human association exactly as do radio, telegraph, telephone and TV, creating involvement in depth. (McLuhan, 1973: 17)

The phrase 'the medium is the message' does bring us up with a jolt, as was no doubt intended. For our part, we resist the determinist connotations here, since the question of how the media are organized and the actual messages that are transmitted remain important. And, while it is relevant to consider the character of the medium in relation to message content, questions about that content and the way it is produced remain, in terms of education, culture, and politics. Eco (1994) offers an intriguing example which explicitly challenges the assertion that the medium is the message. In the 1930s and 1940s, the Chinese were exposed to British and American comic strips such as *Tiffany Jones*, *Mickey Mouse*, and *Little Orphan Annie.* When the Communist Party came to power in China in 1949, they put out their own comic strips. At first they were for entertainment with low ideological content. But a decade later, they were being used with anti-colonial and anti-American content as an instrument of revolutionary education. Not only was the comic strip used when it might have been condemned as a form of Western decadence but the graphics were in the style of British and American graphics or, in another case, of Hergé's *Tintin.* Moreover, the representation of the narrative sequences was similar to the Western comics although, of course, the content and purpose of the message was very different. In a clear reversal of McLuhan's statement, Eco concludes his analysis with this comment:

the comic form is not an ideological cul-de-sac. It allows for multiple manipulations and articulations and even a narrative model very probably borrowed from Western culture has lent itself to opposing communicative aims. It is untrue that the medium is always and utterly the message. Sometimes *the message becomes the medium*. (Eco, 1994: 166; italics in original)

What about 'mass media'? The invention of printing made possible the distribution of material, books, pamphlets, journals, books to a far wider readership than earlier forms of communication. The great European movements of thought in the Reformation and the Enlightenment provoked and responded to these opportunities. 'Mass' implies something about the extent of the communication process. The rise of the newspaper industry in the nineteenth century, of radio and later television in the twentieth century have brought us to the place where millions of people in a country like Britain read the press, listen to the radio, and watch television. In the history of such industrial societies, we observe the co-existence of the label 'mass' to depict various dimensions of their development: mass education, mass production, mass consumption, mass meetings, mass media, and even mass society. One of the noteworthy things about the term 'mass' is that it has been used on both the left and the right of the political spectrum, albeit with different concerns. On the right, the contrast has been made between elites and masses, with the implication that there is a threat to tradition and to all that is best in a culture from the masses. This is profoundly anti-democratic in sentiment. The masses have to be kept at bay since they are equated with the mob who want to overthrow the cherished values of the elite, so debasing the culture. According to the left, the masses have to be mobilized and organized to overthrow the ruling class. Essentially, they exist as a battering ram. The leaders, the party vanguard, are the strategists in this conflict. It is the masses who have to be educated to see this and then to act.

The cultural critic Raymond Williams understood this very well, which is why he put a question mark over the use of the term 'mass':

There are in fact no masses; there are only ways of seeing people as masses. In an urban industrial society there are many opportunities for such ways of seeing. The point is not to re-iterate the objective conditions but to consider, personally and collectively, what these have done to our thinking. The fact is, surely, that a way of seeing other people which has become characteristic of our kind of society, has been capitalised for the purposes of political or cultural exploitation. What we see, neutrally, is other people, many others, people unknown to us. In practice we mass them and interpret them, according to some convenient formula. Within its terms the formula will hold, but it is the formula, not the mass, which it is our real business to examine. It may help to do this if we remember that we ourselves are all the time being massed by others. To the degree that we find the formula inadequate for ourselves, we can wish to extend to others the courtesy of acknowledging the unknown. (Williams, 1961: 289)

This is a matter we want to keep in view since it touches precisely on questions of power and control, including concerns with manipulation and surveillance.

Power is the central issue addressed by this book. The next chapter, Chapter 2, places debates about media power in historical context. It explores ongoing attempts to control films, the press, radio, and television and examines concerns going back to debates in the nineteenth century about the influence of music halls. Chapter 3 introduces the issue of media ownership. Chapter 4 documents the history of the BBC and the struggle for public service broadcasting. Chapters 5 to 9 explore the media coverage of 'scares', the uses of photo-journalism, the perennial fascination with the royal family, and the role of advertising and propaganda.

The final section of the book introduces themes about media audiences. Chapter 10 outlines the development of audience reception theory. Chapter 11 examines how people use media technologies. Chapter 12 explores how audiences take pleasure from the media and the different ways in which audiences interpret the same film or television programme. The final chapter, Chapter 13, returns to the key question of media effects and discusses the role of the media in shaping public understandings.

Chapter Two

Reflections on Media History

Today we are saturated by media of different forms, shapes, and sizes and every day the average citizen spends a large amount of his or her time in the consumption of media products, whether as readers, listeners, or viewers. The dominance of the mass media in our lives has led people to blame the media for a range of social ills. Whether it is increased violence in society, the growth of juvenile delinquency, football hooliganism, riots, terrorism, permissive behaviour, falling educational standards, political apathy, or any other social problem we are ready to attribute 'fabulous powers' to the mass media. As Connell says, it is commonplace to blame the mass media for 'the spread of this or that social problem by being carriers of all manner of distortion or misunderstanding' (Connell, 1988: 88). This is a view of media power as total and all-embracing. Such a view of the power of the media is often couched in the assumption that this is something new. It is associated with the conditions of modernity. However, the history of mass communications shows that the emergence of every new medium of mass communication or popular amusement has been accompanied with great claims about the power of the medium to change the behaviour of men, women, and children as well as the values and mores of society.

Pearson (1984) demonstrates a long tradition of complaint against the influence of popular media and entertainment forms in Britain. In the 1950s, there was an outpouring of concern about the corrupting and depraving influence of American comic book magazines and rock and roll music. In the 1930s, the worries were over the cinema which, according to cultural critic F. R. Leavis, involved the 'surrender, under conditions of hypnotic receptivity, to the cheapest emotional appeals' (quoted in Pearson, 1984: 93). One psychiatrist, as Pearson points out, could assert in 1938 that '70% of all crimes were first conceived in the cinema.'

Earlier, at the turn of the century, the music halls were seen as encouraging lawlessness with their glorification of violence and immorality. The 1840s and '50s witnessed the 'penny gaff' theatres and 'twopenny hop' dancing saloons singled out for peddling immoral and criminal behaviour among the young. An editorial in the *Edinburgh Review* in 1851 stated that

> one powerful agent for the depraving of the boyish classes of our towns and cities is to be found in the cheap shows and theatres, which are so specially opened and arranged for the attraction and ensnaring of the young. When for 3d a boy can procure some hours of vivid enjoyment from exciting scenery, music and acting . . . it is not to be wondered that [he] . . . then becomes rapidly corrupted and demoralised, and seeks to be the doer of infamies which have interested him as a spectator. (quoted in Root, 1986: 19)

At the end of the eighteenth century, people talked of the harmful impact of newspapers with the depiction and discussion of villainy and depravity in their columns. Even the emergence of the first newsbook or corantos, at the beginning of the seventeenth century, was greeted with hostility from members of the educated classes. For dramatists such as Ben Jonson the news industry was a 'dereliction, a degradation of the proper function of a writer' and references to the 'contemptible trade' were common in Jacobean drama (Gerard, 1982).

These complaints have been motivated by a fear of the masses and what they represent. Prior to the nineteenth century, the words used to evoke this fear were 'multitude' or 'mob'. It is only in the late nineteenth and twentieth centuries that the term 'mass' has been used to refer to what the historian Claredon called those 'dirty people of no name' (quoted in Carr, 1971: 50). The growth of the media and communications industries has provided increasing visibility for the masses. Intellectuals, moral guardians and politicians, and those in positions of power, have always been deeply suspicious of the people, the masses of society. As Sorlin (1994: 2) points out, the term 'mass', when added to other words, provides a depreciative nuance. Thus, mass-circulation newspapers are full of trivia and gossip; mass art is cheap and lacking refinement; and mass production is aimed at satisfying the lowest common denominator. The growth of the mass media for intellectuals has been accompanied by cultural debasement—for Nietzsche the 'rabble vomit their bile and call it a newspaper' while T. S. Eliot was more restrained in expressing his view that the effect of Sunday and daily newspapers on their readers was 'to affirm them as a complacent, prejudiced and unthinking mass' (quoted in Carey, 1992: 7). For moral guardians, the growth of the mass media has been the root cause of the moral decline of the nation and the rise of permissiveness; and for politicians it has sullied the conduct of politics by making them respond to what the people want rather than what is best for the nation. Such fears, whether real or imaginary, have led to the attempts to control and regulate the mass media.

Freedom and Control

Traditional interpretations of the development of the mass media in Britain portray a struggle by the press to gain its freedom from the state and political interests in society. The struggle is regarded as having been won in the middle of the nineteenth century with the repeal of the 'taxes on knowledge': taxes on newspapers and periodicals which raised their prices beyond the reach of the vast majority of the British people. Following their repeal, the press is seen as being a check on government—the 'fourth estate'—and, through the provision of information, enabling a discussion on public affairs which eventually made possible the growth of democracy (see Curran, 1977*a*, *b*; Curran and Seaton, 1991 for a discussion of the traditional view of press history). New media, according to this view of history, further develop the ways in which the media and communications industries can contribute to the extension of democracy. Thus, the birth of the cinema and the wireless in the first half of the twentieth century and the post-war emergence of television helped to expand and deepen mass democracy and the democratic process.

This view of the development of the media does not sit comfortably with the fears expressed about the impact of mass communication. For critics of the traditional history, the development of the mass media is not a steady and inexorable march toward more freedom but a history of changing forms of control. They see the media as acting as agencies of social control, in the hands of established authority or a dominant class, and used to manage and manipulate the emergence of mass opinion and mass democracy to serve their ends. In terms of this analysis, the middle of the nineteenth century did not see the establishment of the freedom of the press, but rather a change from state to market control of mass communication. Curran (1977*b*), in his account of the struggle for the repeal of the taxes on knowledge, highlights this as the main objective of many of those involved in the campaign against the press taxes. One of the leading voices of the campaign, Bulwer Lytton, wrote in 1832 that

at this moment when throughout so many nations we see people at war with their institutions, the world presents us with two impressive examples. In

Denmark, a despotism without discontent—in America, a republic without change. The cause is the same in both: in both the people are universally educated. (quoted in Curran and Seaton, 1991: 26)

The stress was on the role the press could play in the engineering of social consent. Nearly seventy-five years later, the birth of the wireless was accompanied by similar concerns about the power of the media on the masses. For the Committee for Imperial Defence, the emergence of broadcasting had 'incalculable significance for political stability' (quoted in Pronay and Spring, 1982: 13). The Committee was wary of the power of the new medium to act as an instrument of propaganda and argued strongly against allowing any private individual with sufficient funds to broadcast. It was, as Pronay and Spring note, a risk that the 'CID felt was impossible to take'. The preferred solution was again that the new medium should be placed in trusted hands. The General Strike in 1926 proved that in 'the hands of experts and under firm political control, radio could give the government . . . a most powerful weapon'. The fear of those in power of the masses led them to see the mass media as a potential instrument for social control.

The conceptualization of the mass media as being either the 'fourth estate' or 'agencies of social control' is an oversimplification. The role of the mass media at any time is shaped by factors particular to the period under consideration as well as the medium under study. More detailed examination means that such conceptualizations become more complex and qualified. However, history does show that central to any debate about the power of the media is an understanding of the countervailing pulls on the mass media as the representatives of the public, public opinion, and the masses *and* as the agents of control exercised by the state and the dominant institutions in society. And this has raised questions throughout history about the impact of the mass media on their audience, the nature and extent of censorship, the power of owners to influence the content of the media, and the relationship between the media and their audience.

The Impact of the Mass Media: Fears and Reality

The birth of every new medium of mass communication has been accompanied by concern about the impact of that medium on its audiences. Take one example—the cinema. The new medium of film developed in the first decades of the twentieth century. There were concrete fears about the impact of the moving images on the health of early cinemagoers. The flickering images were responsible for causing many viewers to have violent headaches, while the penny gaffs and sideshows in which they viewed the films were unhygienic places as many people transfixed by what they saw would relieve themselves in their seats (see Dewe-Mathews, 1994: 9). The combustible nature of early celluloid material also meant that there was a possible risk of fire and, in 1909, these health and safety hazards were used as the pretext for the state to become involved in the regulation of the content of films when the Cinematograph Act was passed. The Act allowed local authorities the right to license venues for the showing of films. However, under the cloak of public safety, the authorities began to interfere and some local authorities began to insist on film-makers submitting their material to the Chief Constable for vetting before it could be shown. In 1910 the London County Council (LCC) banned a film of the world title boxing match between the legendary Jack Johnson and James L. Jeffries. Johnson became the first black man to win the title—a fact which may have had something to do with the LCC's decision to ban the film (Dewe-Mathews, 1994: 15).

Behind these interventions were the forces of 'respectability' in British society: the churches, teachers, moral rearmers of one kind or another, the police, and local magistrates. They feared the stirrings that this new form of entertainment was bringing about, as cinema established itself as the main form of recreational activity before the First World War. By 1914, annual cinema admissions stood at 364 million (Corrigan, 1983: 30) with the most regular attenders being young, urban, working class, unemployed, and including more women than men. The rapid growth of the 'movies' in the years before 1914 was likened to an 'epidemic'; according to Peter Stead (1989: 7), the cinema 'had broken through to the masses and had the power to pull in almost anybody and everybody who helped constitute the masses'. At first respectable people turned their backs on the medium, seeing it as a craze that would disappear as quickly as it had arrived. But, with the rapid growth of the cinema corresponding with political, industrial, and social upheaval in British society (see Dangerfield, 1961), there were calls for control of what could be shown in the cinema. Its growing hold over working people was seen as a threat to social order.

The new medium appealed, in particular, to the young and women. Rowntree, in his study of York in the 1930s, found that half of the film audiences were youngsters while nearly 75 per cent of adults attending were women (quoted in Jones, 1987: 10). Labelled as the most vulnerable in our society, children and women were seen as being highly susceptible to the power of the movies. Juvenile delinquency and youth crime were attributed to the early silent films, which one contemporary observer condemned as 'a direct incentive to crime, demonstrating, for instance, how a theft could be perpetuated' (Barnett, 1913; quoted in Pearson, 1983: 63). *The Times* complained in 1913 that 'before these children's greedy eyes with heartless indiscrimination horrors unimaginable . . . are presented night by night . . . terrific massacres, horrible catastrophes, motor car smashes, public hangings and lynchings.' The newspaper reported that many children 'actually begin their downward course of crime by reason of the burglary and pickpocket scenes they have witnessed' and went on to thunder that 'all who care for the moral well-being and education of the child will set their face like flint against this form of excitement' (Pearson, 1983: 63–4). For women, the cinema was the first leisure activity and recreational space, outside of the home, in which they could participate. By the 1930s, the importance of women as film goers was recognized in the exhibitors' choice of films: for example, in Liverpool in 1929–30, 45 per cent of the films shown were love stories or romances while 22 per cent were thrillers. For conservative moralists, the cinema was a threat to the sexual and social order and its appeal for children and women represented a threat to the family. The Tory Reform Committee in 1944—when cinema theatres were packed in the midst of war—summed up their view when it stated that films

suggest a false standard of life which leaves little place for children, and promote a standard of values which rates 'glamour', 'Romance' (with a capital R) and instability far above marital stability postulated by the family necessary to give children the right start in life. (quoted in Bourke, 1994: 35)

Conservative moralists were not the only people who expressed concern about the power of the picture house. The emergence of the cinema occurred at the same time as the rise of the suffragette movement and the resurgence of feminism. For some feminists, the cinema came to represent the growing assertiveness of women in playing a fuller and more active role in society. However, there were also concerns within the women's movement about the cinema's depiction of sex and violence. Social purity feminists such as Lucy Creighton made a stand against 'the idea that women exist for the pleasure and use of men'; she stated that the 'wisest and safest plan' for most people is 'to concern themselves as little as possible with the things of the body . . . the sensual desires, the flesh . . . and speak about them as little as possible' (quoted in Bland, 1985: 197). For other feminist critics of the cinema, it was not so much whether or not sex and romance should be screened, but how they should be represented. The early peep-shows contained short tableaux such as 'What the Butler Saw' and 'Love in a Hammock' and sexually explicit films—films of the 'Parisian genre' as they were named—were shown in clubs usually after midnight. As these kinds of films began to circulate more widely, there was increasing opposition to them. In 1906 the Catholic Church in France denounced such films as 'immodest' and in 1908 the Mayor of New York ordered the closure of peep-shows and 'nickel theatres' because of their threat to the city's 'moral well-being' (quoted in Christie, 1994: 76). It was the forces of conservative moralism rather than feminism that had most influence in shaping the policing of the output of the cinema by local and national authorities.

However, film censorship was not directly imposed on the industry by the government. Cinema entrepreneurs were making large profits from the new industry. To retain control over the industry, they attempted to show that they could be responsible. In the search for respectability, they decided to pre-empt the possible introduction of government regulation by setting up the British Board of Film Censors (BBFC) in 1912. Funded by the film industry, without any legal status and with the chief censor appointed by the Home Office, the BBFC was to play a decisive role in determining what could be shown in the British cinema from this time onwards. It started with only two rules—no nudity and no portrayal of Jesus Christ. However, by 1914 it had established the general principle to eliminate 'anything repulsive and objectionable to the good taste and better feelings of the English [sic] audiences' (quoted in Robertson, 1985: 7). The BBFC expanded its influence over the political and social content of films shown in the British cinema throughout the inter-war years. The 1926 BBFC report lists a range of topics that were not admissible in films, including any travesty and mockery of religious services, lampoons of the institution of the monarchy, equivocal situations between white girls and men of other races, officers in British regiments shown in a disgraceful light, girls and women in a state of intoxication, white men in a state of degradation amidst native surroundings, abortion, incidents which reflect a mistaken conception of the police in the administration of justice, and inflammatory subtitles and Bolshevist propaganda (see Robertson, 1985: 180–2). In the 1930s, the grounds for banning or cutting films were extended to include depictions of conflict between capital and labour; in the words of one censor, if a strike is 'the prominent feature of the story we would consider the subject unsuitable' (quoted in Richards, 1984: 120). In 1937, the President of the BBFC boasted: 'We may take pride in observing that there is not a single film showing in London today which deals with any of the burning questions of the day' (quoted in Street and Dickinson, 1985: 8).

Censorship and control of the film industry was justified by the arguments that the medium caused crime, promiscuity, violence, and delinquency and that there was a direct correlation between exposure to the media and actual behaviour. Early moves to clean up the cinema were accompanied by attempts to explore such common-sense views of the effect of films on their audiences. In 1917, the National Council for Public Morals, which represented all Britain's moral reform groups, from a variety of backgrounds and political persuasions, set up an inquiry into the harmful impact of the cinema on the young. The Council's hearing was one of the first in a long line of enquiries into the cinema. Held by a Commission including figures such as Lord Baden-Powell, the founder of the Boy Scout Movement, and Marie Stopes, the campaigner for contraceptive birth control, the inquiry took evidence directly from nearly fifty witnesses, including doctors, policemen, social workers, and probation officers as well as representatives of the film industry and BBFC (Dewe-Mathews, 1994: 27). It received written submissions from many others. The evidence was collated in a four-hundred-page document, comprising nearly a quarter of a million words, detailing the views of the witnesses on topics ranging from the educational value of cinema to something ominously referred to as 'the moral dangers of darkness' (Pearson, 1984: 95). Some witnesses expressed their concern about the display of the enlarged view of the face which emphasized pain, lust, hate, and grief (Pearson, 1984: 96). Others linked the rapid spread of the cinema with rising lawlessness and juvenile delinquency. Much of the evidence was anecdotal and for every chief constable who took the opinion that the cinema caused copy-cat crime, there was another who disagreed. Crucial evidence came from those who worked in deprived areas with young people. One probation officer from the East End told the inquiry that the cinema made his job easier by taking children off the street. In his view, they learned more about crime at home than they ever did by spending a few hours in the cinema. Such evidence—as well as police statements denying any link between crime and the cinema—led the Commission to reject calls for the banning of children from picture houses. The Commission concluded, on the topic of juvenile crime, that 'the problem is far too complex to be solved by laying stress on only one factor and that probably a subordinate one, among all the contributing conditions' (quoted in Dewe-Mathews, 1994: 29). It also stated that the cinema does not cause imitative behaviour but 'suggests the form of activity rather than provides the impulse to it'. However, ever since the inquiry, the finding that the cinema does not have a harmful impact on its audience has been contested. Today we are more familiar with these arguments around the effects of television, especially as the medium invaded the home and breached the ramparts of that bastion of middle-class values—the family.

Central to the debates around censorship throughout the history of the media has been a set of common-sense ideas about what the media do to people. The reader, viewer, and listener have been portrayed as passive recipients of what they read, see, or hear and there is a direct relationship between exposure to the content of the media and actual behaviour. Research into the direct impact of the media on its audience has always been far from conclusive. In relation to television violence, for every piece of research proving a link between the medium and violent and/or delinquent behaviour, there is another piece which refutes the link. Even when effects are found, they are small and usually based on laboratory experiments. Research that casts doubt on the role of the television and the cinema has a long tradition—going back in this country, as we have noted, to the 1917 inquiry. However, in the debate over the impact of the mass media, such research findings are lost in the midst of the whipping up of moral fervour and political indignation. The fear of arousing and stimulating the masses appears to overcome the attempts to uncover real evidence as to the effects of the media and encourages attempts to control what the mass media say, show, and report.

Changing Forms of Control and Censorship

Ever since Henry VIII issued an edict banning 'naughty and lewd words'—by which the Tudors meant any statement that was critical of the Crown—concerns about the moral well-being of children and the nation have hidden agendas to censor what we hear, see, and read. In the early days of print, the state exercised direct control over the medium through pre-publication censorship and the licensing of printers. The Archbishop of Canterbury for most of the sixteenth century was charged with the task of vetting the content of everything and anything that was to be printed. The printing of material was confined to officially approved printers, of which there were 22 in 1586 (Hartley *et al.*, 1985). The system proved effective for much of the Tudor period. For most of the sixteenth and seventeenth centuries, censorship of the press was enforced and there was a fairly high degree of popular compliance, particularly under the Tudors, who were accorded a high degree of legitimacy by the British people. The exceptions were the Civil War, during which there was a vast outpouring of popular political literature, and the early years of the Interregnum, during which the state allowed considerable popular discussion, which was put to an end by Oliver Cromwell's dictatorship. The Civil War was an important stage in the development of the British newspaper: it was in the period of the Civil War and the political strife that led up to it that the first newspapers or 'corantos' were born and many of the features of modern journalism developed. Cromwell's dictatorship and the restoration of the monarchy in 1660 saw the reintroduction of direct censorship, which had collapsed during the Civil War. A Surveyor of the Press was appointed to ensure that the public did not become 'too familiar with the actions and counsels of their superiors' through the control of news which he saw as giving 'them not only an itch but a kind of colourable right and licence to be meddling with the government' (quoted in Cranfield, 1978: 20). This system of direct state censorship collapsed in 1695. Its end was not the result of a conversion of those in power to the principle of the freedom of the press, but of the inability of the system to deal with the vast amount of material that was being published.

Direct state censorship was replaced in 1712 by economic controls on the press and printed material. Press taxation—or 'taxes on knowledge'—were introduced to restrict the dissemination of news to those who could pay—that is, the respectable elements of British society. Taxes were levied on advertisements, raw paper, and newspapers: between 1712 and 1815, press taxes were increased by 800 per cent (Aspinall, 1949; quoted in Curran, 1977b: 38). However, the 'taxes on knowledge' were challenged by the rise of the radical press, who refused to pay the stamp and, as one of the most famous radical newspapers, *The Poor Man's Guardian*, stated on its masthead: 'published in Defiance of the Law to try the Power of Right against Might'. Between 1830 and 1836 over 560 unstamped newspapers were published, most of them associated with the rise of the political and industrial organization of the emerging working classes. *The Poor Man's Guardian*, for example, was the official voice of the National Union of the Working Classes, the first trade union organization in this country. The aim of the radical press was to make working people aware of their exploitation by producing knowledge 'which makes them more dissatisfied and makes them worse slaves' (O'Brien, quoted in Harrison, 1974: 103). The newspapers played a role in articulating the demands and aspirations of the working classes as well as helping the development of class consciousness during the first half of the nineteenth century. The government, fearful of the threat posed to the social and political order, reacted with vigorous prosecution of the law and many radical publishers and printers were gaoled, fined, transported, or had to flee the country. The 150 vendors and shopmen who sold Richard Carlile's radical newspapers are estimated to have served over 200 years' imprisonment for disseminating 'seditious literature' (Hartley *et al.*, 1985). However, these measures failed to crush the sales of radical papers and the response of the government was to look for other means by which they could combat the radical press.

There was a debate within government circles as to the best way to combat the 'malignant influence' of radical newspapers which peddled 'doctrines injurious to the middle and upper classes'. Traditionalists, who sought more repressive measures, were overcome by those who argued that the press and printed material was a means to secure the good opinion of working people. As one reformer stated in 1851: 'readers are not rioters: readers are not rick burners' (quoted in Curran, 1977*b*: 212). From the 1830s, the middle class began to mobilize resources to capture the hearts and minds of working people. The Society for the Diffusion of Useful Knowledge (SDUK) published *The Penny Magazine* between 1832 and 1846 which, in its heyday, reached a circulation of 200,000. To assist these newspapers to compete more effectively with the radical press, the government had to free them from the shackles of press taxation. The stamp duty was reduced to one penny in 1836 and gradually all press taxes were phased out by the 1860s. The market and competition were seen as a mechanism by which the press would be placed in the hands of 'great capitalists', thereby taking ownership out of the hands of those who sought to promote unsound doctrines amongst the people of Britain (Curran, 1977*b*: 211).

The market did its job well. Within twenty years the 'commercialization of the press' led to the virtual disappearance of radical newspapers from this country. The introduction of market forces increased competition and resulted in a rise in the costs of newspaper production—when Henry Hetherington launched *The Poor Man's Guardian* in 1830, it cost him £30 while in 1896, the launch of the *Daily Mail* cost Lord Northcliffe nearly £600,000. The operating costs of newspapers rose rapidly as more pages had to be filled. The removal of press taxation allowed newspapers to expand, with the average number of pages in a daily newspaper rising. As more newspapers entered the market, the cover price of a newspaper fell, with the consequence that more copies of a title had to be sold to cover costs. Soon, most newspapers came to depend on the selling of advertisements to cover their costs and make a profit. However, advertisers were particular about where they displayed their products.

They wanted to reach people who had sufficient purchasing power. Radical newspapers had large circulations but their readers, according to one advertiser in 1856, 'were not purchasers and any money thrown upon them is so much thrown away' (quoted in Curran and Seaton, 1991: 40). Hence the new economic realities of the press worked against radical newspapers. Radical newspapers either closed down or became less political or simply ended up as specialist political journals selling to small dedicated audiences. In later years, attempts to launch radical daily newspapers failed—for example, *The Clarion* (1897) and *The Daily Citizen* (1912)—because they were undercapitalized and unable to attract sufficient advertising revenue. Subsidies from the trade union and labour movement could not maintain their viability.

The fate of *The Daily Herald* is a good example of how the changing economic structure of the newspaper industry worked against left-wing and radical newspapers in the twentieth century. Begun in 1912 as a strike newspaper, *The Daily Herald* lurched from crisis to crisis with a circulation of 250,000 until the end of the First World War (Curran, 1977*b*: 215). In 1919, under the editorship of George Lansbury, a future leader of the Labour Party, there was an infusion of capital into the newspaper. Circulation increased but, as George Lansbury stated, 'our success in circulation was our undoing. The more copies we sold, the more we lost' (quoted in Curran, 1977*b*: 221). The rise in sales did not offset the shortfall in advertising and by 1922, the newspaper was only kept going by donations from miners and railwaymen. In that year, it was taken over by the Labour Party and the TUC, becoming their official newspaper. However, the financial effort of maintaining the paper proved too much and it was eventually sold to the Odhams Group with the stipulation that, editorially, it remain supportive of the Labour Party. Odhams spent £3 million relaunching *The Herald* and its circulation increased throughout the 1930s. Many of the new readers were middle class but, in the process of attracting these readers, the newspaper had toned down the nature of its politics and increased the amount of space devoted to advertising. Despite the increase in circulation and the growth of advertising, the newspaper only obtained a fraction of the advertising revenue per copy of its main rivals, *The Daily Mail* and *The Daily Express*. The newspaper with the largest readership in the Western world at the time, *The Daily Herald*, was still trading at a loss. When the newspaper folded thirty years later, its circulation stood at over 1.25 million, a relatively healthy figure for Fleet Street at the time. However, its share of advertising revenue for the national daily press stood at only 3.5 per cent (Curran and Seaton, 1991: 108). The structure of the newspaper market had worked against *The Daily Herald*—the paper was later bought by Rupert Murdoch and renamed *The Sun* in 1969.

The market reforms of the press were accompanied by the government devoting more resources and developing new techniques to manipulate the information environment. Increasingly less able to influence the press directly, the government sought to develop ways of managing what the press reported. The laws of criminal and seditious libel and blasphemy were resorted to, at times, to muzzle the newspapers. For example, in 1925, leaders of the British Communist Party were prosecuted for remarks in their official newspaper, *The Daily Worker*, on the grounds that their 'language tended to subvert the government and the laws of the Empire' (quoted in Whitaker, 1981). While the big stick was still a part of the government's armoury in dealing with the media in the twentieth century, carrots were increasingly used to manage what was reported.

Cockerell, Hennessy, and Walker (1985) identify three pillars to the system of information control in British society laid down from the end of the nineteenth century. The first pillar consists of draconian legislation, encompassed in the Official Secrets Act and the D-Notice laws, which make disclosure about government activities very difficult. These laws were passed during the years of tension preceding the First World War; the government exploited the 'German scare' and, under the pretext of combating espionage, introduced rigid controls on the flow of official information. The second pillar was the development of a news cartel. The Lobby, which is still today the primary mechanism for the reporting of government decisions and party politics, was first established in 1884. Lobby correspondents comprise nearly all the political reporters of major media outlets based at Parliament. They operate according to a set of rules which require that they do not reveal the workings of the Lobby to the outside world. These rules also include not revealing what happens inside Parliament and who says what to them— something Cockerell, Hennessy, and Walker (1985) regard as running contrary to the professional ethics of journalism. In return, Lobby correspondents are guaranteed a regular supply of information through government and opposition briefings on the issues of the day. A large amount of government information is funnelled through the Lobby. The third pillar is the commercialization of official information. From the end of the First World War government started to establish apparatuses to 'sell' information it wanted to be released. These apparatuses consisted of press officers, official spokespersons, public relations advisers, and information officers. The first such body set up to perform this function was the News Department of the Foreign and Commonwealth Office, which was established during the War. But the key development came in 1931 when the Press Office was created at Number Ten Downing Street. George Steward, as the Prime Minister's Chief Press Officer, was to exert considerable control over the media in the 1930s, being able to prevent much critical reporting of the government's policy of appeasement and of the German government (see Cockett, 1989). These mechanisms enabled the government to exert some influence and control not over the journalist but over the information which he or she gathered.

Thus, the market and the system of information control became central to the government's strategy to manage the media in the twentieth century. This task was made more urgent with the arrival of more powerful means of mass communication—cinema and the broadcast media. These two aspects of the strategy came together during the First World War. War allows us to glimpse the 'normal practices of peacetime' in media–government relations as the veil of secrecy slips at times of crisis. The First World War witnessed the first systematic attempt to organize official information. A Ministry of Information (MOI) was established with the objectives of informing the public about the progress of the war, maintaining morale at home, and co-ordinating the propaganda efforts abroad. A Press Bureau was established to manage government relations with the press. The MOI was particularly successful in managing news about the huge casualties sustained by the British armed forces and putting the best interpretation of what was happening over to the British public (see Knightley, 1982). Two men who played a crucial role in the Ministry's efforts were Lords Beaverbrook and Northcliffe—the two leading newspaper owners of their day. Their involvement was an acknowledgement by the government that the mass media had an important role to play in the propaganda and political process. But the power of the press barons was also seen as a threat to democracy.

Part II

Media Players and Practices

Chapter Three

Press Barons and Media Moguls

So much is written and spoken about 'the power of the media' that we sometimes overlook some basic considerations. Not only can there be different opinions, but there are also different points of reference. We can, for example, think in terms of institutional power. How do we understand the way media institutions relate to say political, economic, military, and religious institutions? This conveys the possibility that different institutional sectors can be in conflict with one another, or again, they may collude and collaborate for particular purposes. The conflicts can demonstrate, at least in particular instances, that one institutional sphere dominates another. Thus, we sometimes hear that the media are dominated by the state or that the media set the political agenda and such statements indicate an understanding of the nature of media power within a web of other institutions. We can consider the ways in which power balances emerge and shift between these groupings.

The Power of Ownership: The Era of the Press Barons

One of the main characteristics of the rise of the popular press in the early years of the twentieth century was the trend to the increasing concentration of ownership and control of the industry in the hands of a smaller and smaller number of men. Between 1890 and 1920 there was a rapid acceleration of newspaper chains which changed the relationship between the owner and the newspaper. A considerable proportion of the British press fell into the hands of three brothers—the Harmsworths. Alfred Harmsworth, Lord Northcliffe, who launched *The Daily Mail* in 1896 and, within a few years, turned it into the country's first million-selling daily newspaper, had established a vast press empire by 1921. He controlled *The Times, The Daily Mail, The Weekly Dispatch,* and *The London Evening News* while his brother Vere, Lord Rothermere, owned *The Daily Mirror* and *The Sunday Pictorial* as well as *The Daily Record, Sunday Mail,* and *The Glasgow Evening News* in Scotland. Together they owned the Amalgamated Press, Britain's largest magazine group and their brother, Lester Harmsworth, controlled a chain of local newspapers in the south-west of England (Curran and Seaton, 1991: 51). The total circulation of these newspapers was just over six million. Another press lord, Lord Beaverbrook, on the other hand, owned fewer titles but his Express Group, which included *The Daily Express, Sunday Express,* and *Evening Standard,* had a combined circulation of 4.1 million by 1937 (ibid.). At the local level, the Berry brothers from South Wales, ennobled as Lords Camrose and Kemsley, bought up a considerable number of daily and Sunday newspapers in the provinces of England and Wales. The inter-war years saw the consolidation of the hold these press empires had over the British newspaper industry. The five leading companies in the industry by 1937 controlled 43 per cent of all newspaper titles in Britain (Murdock and Golding, 1978: 135). The press barons built their empires by takeovers and amalgamations which meant the closure of many newspapers—in particular, regional morning and evening newspapers, as the national Fleet Street press established itself at their expense (see Murdock and Golding, 1978: 132–4). This concentration of ownership came at a time when the circulation of newspapers was rapidly growing. Britain, in the inter-war years, became a newspaper-reading nation as total national daily newspaper circulation rose from 3.1 million in 1918 to 10.6 million by 1939. For a number of observers, the coincidence of the emergence of mass-circulation newspapers and the concentration of ownership meant that a small number of press barons had acquired a considerable amount of power, which was a direct threat to the development of democracy.

For the press barons of the inter-war years, newspaper ownership became a means by which to impress their views on politicians and political parties, as well as shape the pressing issues of the day. Northcliffe was clear that his intent was to achieve political power and influence. He wrote, in 1903, 'every extension of the franchise renders more powerful the newspaper and less powerful the politician' (quoted in Boyce, 1987: 100). Beaverbrook's declared purpose for becoming involved in the industry was to 'set up a propaganda paper' (Murdock and Golding, 1978: 142). In some ways their motives were no different from newspaper owners and editors in the nineteenth century.

Hetherington, through his radical newspapers, sought to build a pol
ical movement of the working classes while Delane and Barnes of *The
Times* sought to influence the conduct of government policy. But, where
the press barons differed was in their claim to represent the public. They
claimed to be 'representative' of their readers in the same way as politicians represented their voters. For the first time, owners of mass-
circulation newspapers could claim the right to speak for British public
opinion on an equal footing to the politicians. Northcliffe stressed that
he represented and spoke for his readers—the '1,104,000 Who Know
Daily'—or the 'mobocracy' as one contemporary labelled the readers of
The Daily Mail (quoted in Boyce, 1987: 101). It was by being 'mass'
media that the British press conferred on its owners in the inter-war
years the power to pursue their political whims.

For contemporary critics such as Norman Angell, the era of the press
barons represented 'the worst of all the menaces to modern democracy'
(Angell, 1922: 16). Rather than articulate the voice of the 'masses',
Angell, a socialist, saw the cheap, mass-circulation newspapers as
depriving them of the facts that are necessary for collective decisions in
a democracy. Like the moral reformers and intellectuals, he believed in
the power of the mass media to shape the views and opinions of their
audience. This was the basis of his concern that

what England [*sic*] thinks is largely controlled by a very few men, not by virtue of
the direct expression of any opinion of their own but by controlling the distribution of emphasis in the telling of facts: so stressing one group of them and keeping another group in the background as to make a given conclusion inevitable.
(Angell, 1922: 26)

The press barons, according to Angell, did not play a role in building an
educated democracy, but rather used their newspapers to manipulate
public opinion for their own personal crusades. But it was not only critics such as Angell that expressed their concern about the power of the
press barons. Tory Prime Minister Stanley Baldwin accused them of
exercising 'power without responsibility' and running their newspapers
as 'engines of propaganda for their constantly changing policies,
desires, personal wishes, personal likes and dislikes' (quoted in Boyce,
1987: 99). The arrogance with which the press barons attempted to
influence politics in the inter-war years brought them into direct conflict with politicians of all persuasions. These developments were witnessed by some as calling into question the whole concept of the
'freedom of the press'. Burns notes that, in the 1920s, the concept shed
its quality of absoluteness. The press lords exercised arbitrary control
over what passed for news and continually pandered to 'giving the audi-

ence what it wants'—thereby, in the view of the first head of the BBC, John Reith, making the content of newspapers silly, vulgar, false, and contemptible (Burns, 1977: 51).

If the era of the press barons highlights concerns over the growing power of the press and the threat posed to freedom of the press by the concentration of ownership, it also raises some questions about the nature of 'press power'. The political influence of the press barons was tempered by a number of factors. The heyday of the political power of the press barons was during the period of the First World War, when Northcliffe and Beaverbrook were credited with bringing down the Asquith coalition in 1916 and elevating Lloyd George to the premiership, as well as forcing the government to bring in conscription. Rothermere's *Daily Mail* was regarded as having been responsible for the Labour Party's failure in the 1923 General Election, when it published an alleged letter from Zinoviev, head of the Communist International, purporting to show Soviet influence in domestic British politics. However, many of the more high-profile interventions by the press barons in British politics ended in overt failure. Northcliffe failed to become elected as MP for Portsmouth, despite buying up local newspapers and using his press to promote his cause. Beaverbrook's attempts to push Empire Free Trade in the 1920s by supporting candidates at the election box also came to nothing. Rothermere's flirtation with the British Union of Fascists in the 1930s ended in disaster as the circulation of his papers began to fall. And even the Zinoviev letter did not actually result in its intended aim of getting people not to vote Labour—the Party's vote actually increased by a million at the 1923 election. Northcliffe also used his newspapers to no avail to try to get men to buy a new kind of hat which was a cross between a bowler hat and a Homburg. Thus, the direct influence of the press barons was limited. However, as Curran and Seaton point out, to assess the influence and power of the press barons in terms of their ability to persuade people to vote for new parties or candidates, or to buy new products, or take up new causes, is to misunderstand their influence. Rather, this lay in the ways in which their newspapers 'provided cumulative support for conservative values and reinforced opposition, particularly among the middle class, to progressive change' (Curran and Seaton, 1991: 61). In other words, the power of the press in this sense is to provide support for the *status quo* and the dominant culture, selecting certain issues for discussion while marginalizing or ignoring others and, in particular, those voices calling for progressive change.

Within the media sphere itself, the question of power comes up when we refer to different media groupings such as 'the press' or 'broadcasting'. Within each of these categories there are different segments, whose power relations are indicated by the nature of the competition between them for markets—readers, viewers, listeners. Thus, we can have price wars between the tabloids or the broadsheets. In broadcasting, there may be battles for audiences, say Radio 1 compared to Capital Radio or Radio Clyde. Many concerns about television schedules are about who can get the biggest audiences by putting on a soap, a costume drama, or a sports event at a particular time, thereby 'beating the competition'. It is here too we encounter commercial concerns. The battle for audiences and readers is, in one crucial respect, about the ways in which commercial interests can be advanced through advertising. Advertising is the linchpin upon which the survival of the press and commercial broadcasting depends. This is not so in the direct sense as far as the BBC are concerned, but there are indirect influences. The BBC has taken to advertising its own programmes, not only in the simple sense of telling us what is coming up on the schedules later that day or week, but also in taking the equivalent of a commercial break to tell us about the range and quality of what they do. There are also advertisements that are carried within a programme, as in the Cornhill cricket test matches, when the logo of the company etched into the turf is seen by the viewing millions.

All of these ways of thinking about media power relate to considerations of structure—in broad terms they are about the structure of ownership and control, the constraints that surround the media industries, as well as the ways they impinge on other parts of society. But there are, of course, categories and groups of people who are agents in the process and who play their parts in shaping what we see, hear, and read. There are the big owners such as Rupert Murdoch of News International. There are the big managers such as John Birt of the BBC. There are the editors of the national press. There are the journalists, the feature writers, the programme producers. Unless we have a very monolithic, one-dimensional view of media power, we can readily appreciate that various kinds of power struggle will take place, involving these and other groups. These people do not exist outside the media institutions and networks and the ways in which they exercise their skills and use their resources can make a difference to the outcomes. In other words, when we have recognized the importance of institutional structures, we still have to see that the processes that enable these structures to exist also contain the potentiality for change and that these are the stuff of flesh-and-blood encounters which give us the kind of media we have and not something different.

The concept of power can itself be slippery. We can think of it in terms of the capacity to make things happen and the array of resources and skills that can be deployed to achieve defined ends. We can think of it in relation to the mode in which power is exercised, ranging from brute force and coercion to persuasion and manipulation, from the visible to the opaque. And we can recognize different dimensions of power—the political, the economic, the cultural—in and through which power is pursued and manifested in organizations and social relations. As we look at particular expressions of power in action, we can see that 'media power' is a complex of very different activities with consequences that can be very far-reaching. When Rupert Murdoch proposed the setting up and financing of a Rugby League arrangement, involving teams from Australia, New Zealand, and Great Britain, with the aim of extending his pay-TV audiences, with enormous sums of money being offered to the players, the consequences for the structure and organization of the game and its spectators were potentially to destroy the culture that had brought it into being. When it is also understood that this was an aspect of his conflict with the Australian media baron Kerry Packer (who, a generation ago, formed the breakaway cricket organization for his own media purposes) over the control of Australian Rugby League, we can see, in a concrete way, the global nature of media power. We can also see the way in which two spheres of life—sport and media—become heavily entangled, such that sport becomes a commodity in a highly developed sense, rather than a leisure activity with its own intrinsic pleasures.

Let us stay with Rupert Murdoch in order to delineate some of the issues of media power. Murdoch himself makes news in more senses than one. He is the subject of much discussion, not only about his contribution to the well-being or otherwise of the media in our society and beyond, but also as to its future development. William Shawcross, in his very full biography, paints a fascinating picture of Murdoch's Scottish family origins and his Australian roots, where his own father pursued a career in journalism leading to significant proprietorial interests in the Australian press (Shawcross, 1992). Keith Murdoch, during the later part of the First World War, served as the Australian Prime Minister's unofficial 'fixer' in London and, in that capacity, met senior British politicians such as Lloyd George and, perhaps even more importantly for his future career, Lord Northcliffe. Keith Murdoch worked for *The Times* and described Northcliffe as 'the Chief of all Journalists' and freely acknowledged his influence, clearly regarding him as a role model. When Keith Murdoch returned to Australia in 1920 to take up the editorship of *The Melbourne Herald*, he sought and received advice from Northcliffe on how to improve the paper. These comments he described as his bible, which he referred to every day. He went on to move into newspaper ownership and publishing across Australia and was indeed popularly known as 'Lord Southcliffe'. Into this milieu, Rupert Murdoch was born. He certainly developed a good understanding of the processes of newspaper production and also had a spell as a sub-editor on Beaverbrook's *Daily Express* and in 1953, at the age of twenty-two, entered into his father's media inheritance. He has spent his life since then building and extending it and turning it into a multi-national conglomerate, with major interests in Australasia and the Pacific, the USA, and the UK. Let us consider one or two aspects of his power in action.

First, there is the relationship with editors. Rohan Rivett, appointed by Keith Murdoch as editor of *The Adelaide News*, was a great admirer of Aneurin Bevan, the Welsh socialist and architect of the National Health Service. When Bevan died in 1958, Rivett gave it full and sympathetic coverage. Rupert Murdoch sent Rivett a letter ordering him to leave his office immediately. That is power, the power of the autocratic owner against whom there is no redress. We should not assume there was no history to this dismissal but the arbitrary, brutal manner of it is clear in the action. Murdoch had a different agenda from Rivett. Shawcross sums it up thus:

It seemed that Murdoch had outgrown both Rivett and Adelaide. He felt he could no longer depend on his old friend. He replaced him with Ron Boland, who had been the editor of *The Sunday Mail*, and who was much more of a nuts-and-bolts journalist. Under Boland, *The News* became less of a crusading newspaper. There were more cats up trees in Adelaide and fewer uprisings in Ankara. Murdoch had had enough of advocacy journalism. He was expanding his empire and was more interested in cash than in confrontation, in profits than in political positions. He wanted editors who were safe rather than scintillating, whom he could rely upon, however far away he might be. From now on that would almost always be so. (Shawcross, 1992: 102)

In the UK, the dispute between Harold Evans, as editor of *The Times*, and Murdoch, the proprietor, which led to Evans's resignation, tells us much about power relationships. Shawcross deals with this, as does Evans himself (Evans, 1984). By the time Murdoch bid for the ownership of *The Times* and *The Sunday Times* in 1980–1, he was already in control of *The News of the World* and *The Sun* and had been through the 1970s. During this time, Murdoch had moved his own political position from left of centre to the right. Whereas in 1972 *The Sun*, under the editorship of Larry Lamb, had supported the miner's strike and opposed the Tory Prime Minister Edward Heath, by 1979 it was fully in support of Margaret Thatcher. Lamb is credited with the headline 'Winter of

Discontent' to describe the public sector strikes in the last months of the Callaghan government, a phrase which has been deployed against the Labour Party many times since then. And on election day, 1979, *The Sun's* front page editorial was headlined: 'Vote Tory This Time. It's The Only Way To Stop The Rot.' It is a matter of record that Thatcher wrote to Lamb thanking him for his help after her election victory. In 1980, he was knighted 'for his services to journalism'. (So too was John Junor, editor of *The Sunday Express*, and the proprietor of *The Express*, Victor Matthews, was given a peerage.) Commenting on the more general significance of this Shawcross writes:

Throughout the 1980s Murdoch and Thatcher had a symbiotic relationship in which the one consistently and almost constantly encouraged and reinforced the other. The Thatcherite revolution and the Murdoch revolution strode hand in hand across the decade. (Shawcross, 1992: 210)

When, therefore, the struggle for ownership of Times Newspapers took place, a great deal was at stake. Murdoch's bid not only entailed a greater concentration of ownership of the British national press, but could be expected to tilt the balance even more towards support for the Tory government in both the tabloid and broadsheet segments. And, of course, *The Times* had a very distinctive history and place as the heavyweight of British journalism. As a symbol of 'serious' and 'quality' journalism, albeit usually on the side of the Establishment—church, state, monarchy—there were concerns as to whether Murdoch, with his known tabloid record, was an appropriate owner. The proposed Murdoch purchase could have been referred to the Monopolies Commission, since it could have been construed as an erosion of a pluralist media. The fact that it was not has sometimes been accounted for in terms of the political advantage to the government, a Murdoch–Thatcher axis. At the same time, there were other considerations. Particularly, there were claims that Times Newspapers were losing money. This was disputed. Harold Evans maintained that *The Sunday Times* was certainly not to be properly described in that way. Even so, the owners, Thomson Newspapers, had put a deadline on the sale, after which the company would cease publishing, with all the attendant redundancies that entailed. To go to the Monopolies Commission was not easy in the time allowed and the unions, for their part, wanted the titles to remain publishing.

Harold Evans was, at the time, the editor of *The Sunday Times*, where he had developed a good reputation as a crusading journalist, who encouraged and developed the practice of investigative journalism, notably through his Insight team. When the titles went up for sale, the bidders included what might be called 'the usual suspects': Robert Maxwell; Lord Matthews; Lord Rothermere, owner of Associated Newspapers; Atlantic Richfield, the American oil company, which at that time owned *The Observer*; and Murdoch. But Evans himself also put together a bid on behalf of *The Sunday Times* management and in partnership with *The Guardian*. And William Rees-Mogg, then editor of *The Times*, also bid on behalf of journalists of *The Times*. Intriguingly, the unions supported Murdoch on the grounds that he had successfully built up *The Sun* newspaper and created more employment. In the light of the events at Wapping, which we discuss below, there is some piquancy to this. As the power struggle continued and began to move in Murdoch's favour, Murdoch met Evans and offered him the editorship of *The Times*. We can see, in many contexts, how power can be exercised in terms of 'sweet stuff' and 'fear stuff'. Murdoch, by the testimony of many, is an adept at both. So it was that when Evans's associates in his consortium urged him to resist publicly the Murdoch takeover, he refused to do so, a decision he was later to regret. What he did do was to provide a framework within which editorial independence could be ensured against the encroachments of the owner. Murdoch agreed that there should be an overseeing group of directors to supervise these matters, that they should approve the appointment of editors, and that the editors would have the freedom to set the political policies of the papers. Harold Evans was duly appointed editor of *The Times* and Frank Giles replaced him as editor of *The Sunday Times*.

Evans's editorship of *The Times* lasted little more than a year and proved to be a period of great turbulence. The conflict between Murdoch and Evans was, according to Murdoch, provoked by Evans's failure to carry out a consistent editorial policy. Moreover, there were internal differences: not all the directors thought Evans had been a good appointment and not all the journalists approved of what he was doing. In March 1982, just before he resigned, a group of *Times* journalists publicly called for his resignation, citing the erosion of editorial standards, frequent changes in layout and design, and bad management. For Evans, the fulcrum of the account is to be found in the foreword of his book *Good Times, Bad Times*:

Early in 1982, ten months after he had taken over *The Times* and *The Sunday Times*, Rupert Murdoch went to see the Prime Minister, Mrs Thatcher. They shared a problem: it was me. I was editor of *The Times* and Murdoch's difficulty was how to dispose of me. *The Times* was supposed to be protected from political interference, and its editor from dismissal, by a spectacular series of pledges Murdoch had given in 1981. The irony was still fresh on them: they were given to

Mrs Thatcher's government and they were her justification for sparing Murdoch an investigation by the Monopolies Commission. (Evans, 1983: 17)

What Murdoch actually did, according to Evans, was to encourage disquiet and disaffection within the paper concerning changes which he had encouraged Evans to make. Evans readily admitted that much of what they had published during 1981 had been critical of the Thatcher government, including full coverage of an opinion poll which concluded that Thatcher was the most unpopular Prime Minister since opinion polls began. Denis Thatcher, the Prime Minister's husband, had also been criticized. He had written a letter from 10 Downing Street to the Secretary of State for Wales asking him to speed up the planning appeal on a housing development in Snowdonia, for which he was the development's adviser. The Welsh Secretary had responded with alacrity.

By the end of his tenure, Evans was getting reports back that the undertakings Murdoch had given to the Secretary of State for Industry regarding editorial freedom were not worth the paper they were written on (Evans, 1983: 489–90). Evans, disillusioned, concluded that this was how it was:

Editorial guarantees are a paltry defence and they may be delusive as well. Times Newspapers enabled an air of respectability to be given to an unnecessary and hazardous extension of monopoly power . . . I found in reality that the national directors are incapable of monitoring the daily turmoil of a newspaper. This has nothing to do with their theoretical powers and increasing or entrenching them would make no difference . . . What it amounted to with Murdoch was for me symbolised on the day he placed his hand on a few paragraphs of *The Sun* and, comparing it to *The Times* coverage, exclaimed 'There! That's all you need on Poland'. Does one complain to the independent directors? Or accede to the proprietor's 'advice'? Or do battle? There is no system of external supervision which can protect an editor from proprietorship of this kind. (Evans, 1983: 490–1)

Meanwhile, over at *The Sunday Times*, Frank Giles remained editor but, immediately after the Tory election victory of 1983, was invited to retire. His place was taken by Andrew Neill, whose politics and attitudes proved to be close to Murdoch's and who remained in office for over a decade.

We turn now to another dimension of proprietor power which was exercised with all the resources of a multi-national conglomerate. This concerns the movement of Murdoch's press operations in Britain from Fleet Street (which was synonymous with the home of the national press) to Wapping—Fortress Wapping, as it was later to be called—in 1986. Whatever one's opinions as to what took place, this could fairly be called a decisive moment in the history of the British press, and from it, we learn something about what it is that leads to shifting power balances between contending groups. Frank Barlow, a newspaper executive with *The Financial Times*, summarized the significance of Wapping one year on:

Sunday, January 26, 1986 was the day on which Fleet Street, as we have known it for all our working lives, ceased to exist. That was the day on which Rupert Murdoch proved that it was possible to produce two mass circulation Sunday newspapers without a single member of his existing print workforce; without using the railways and with roughly one fifth of the numbers that he had been employing before. (in Tunstall, 1996)

What Wapping represented was an overwhelming victory against the power of the print unions, where the closed shop and the ability to stop production of a perishable product had enabled them to resist the introduction of technical changes which had the potential to undermine their craft skills and occupational control. Newspaper production was a labour-intensive industry and, in the 1970s, labour costs were running at 40–50 per cent even though the cost of newsprint had doubled between 1972 and 1975 (Seymour-Ure, 1991). Crucially, the development of computer typesetting meant that journalists and advertising staff could become their own printers. The new equipment was either bought and then not used, or if the attempt was made to implement change the printers went out on strike and, in the case of *The Times* and *The Sunday Times*, the papers were shut down for a year.

There were harbingers of Wapping. In Stockport, Lancashire, Eddie Shah had used non-union labour to use new technology for the printing and distribution of local papers. This had led to very serious confrontations between the print unions, together with support from other unions outside the industry, and the company. By this time, the new Thatcher government had put trade union legislation in place and the National Graphical Association (NGA) was fined over half a million pounds for breaking the law on picketing. This was a prelude to setting up plant in London to launch the *Today* newspaper, which Shah did in the wake of Wapping. This paper was itself later to be taken over by Murdoch (and ceased publishing at the end of 1995). The political context was a crucial element in accounting for the success of Murdoch's move to Wapping. This was, we should recall, at a time when the miner's strike had lasted for a year before being defeated by the government. At the end, the miners and their families had been practically starved into submission. In other disputes too, the government had taken a hard line. They had also encouraged macho management, exemplified by

Michael Edwardes in British Leyland and Ian MacGregor in first the steel industry and subsequently in mining.

Before the Wapping episode, Robert Maxwell, who had taken over the Mirror Group Newspapers in July 1984, had his battles with the trade unions. Already, in mid-1985, 240 members of the NGA, working for his horse racing daily, *Sporting Life*, were made redundant. *The Daily Mirror* and related titles had, at that time, some 6,500 in its workforce. After a heavy period of negotiation in November and December 1985, approximately one-third of the employees were made redundant. This was clearly a very difficult period for people working in newspaper production, but it could at least be argued that *The Mirror* negotiations took place through agreed procedures and that, given the growing realization that new technology did carry implications for the occupational structure and practices of newspaper production, this could be worked through by collective bargaining. This was not easy from the trade union perspective, not only because of the job losses entailed, but also because the print unions—the NGA and SOGAT—were sometimes at loggerheads with one another and the union of journalists—the NUJ—was, from time to time, in conflict with them. It was not unknown for them to cross one another's picket lines. Murdoch, after some uncertainty, decided to take another route, what became known as the Big Bang move to Wapping.

The planning of the move to Wapping was very much a cloak-and-dagger story. Equipment was bought and transported in secretly. Meetings with key executives were held in different venues with a minimum of paperwork to avoid leaks. Crucially, Murdoch was able to reach a deal with the electricians' union (the EETPU) which would undermine the power of the printers' unions. On this Shawcross comments:

The electricians' union began to recruit men in Southampton on six-month contracts. They were bussed about a hundred miles every day to Wapping and were sworn to secrecy about what they saw and what they did. It was deemed especially important that they did not understand the huge power of the Atex system. Astonishingly, they never did. Even though gossip began to run through the pubs on Fleet Street as to what Murdoch might be secretly planning behind the walls and wire of Wapping, no one really understood. (Shawcross, 1992: 343)

The power of the proprietor in this case cannot be seen in purely individual terms, even though Murdoch was clearly a crucial actor. Resources have to be mobilized, involving many people. Even though Murdoch himself adopted a hands-on approach at Wapping as the papers went into print, taking personal charge of the process, there were wider considerations of strategy and tactics, which could be affected by the way other groups handled the situation. What the print workers and the journalists would do when the full significance of the move to Wapping could no longer be concealed was not something that could be calculated with certainty. If Murdoch had been forced to dismiss the workforce he no longer wanted, this would have cost him some £40 million in redundancy pay. Although the unions knew this, they chose to strike. Murdoch had anticipated this and registered his new operations as separate companies. In consequence, the strikers could be dismissed without redundancy payment for breach of contract and they could be penalized under the government's new laws on secondary picketing. In consequence, the print unions experienced fines and seizure of assets. The question of what the journalists would do was critical to the outcome. Here again, it was 'sweet stuff' and 'fear stuff'. There were financial inducements and the offer of private health insurance. But if they chose not to go they would be instantly dismissed. The dislike many of them had for Murdoch was set against negative attitudes to the printers. The union chapels met; there were discussions with editors. In the end, 90 per cent of them went to Wapping. Among those who did not go was Claire Tomalin, literary editor of *The Sunday Times*. In a letter to her editor, Andrew Neill, she wrote: 'You have become the mouthpiece for a ruthless and bullying management which regards all employees as cattle' (cited in Shawcross, 1992: 347). Another journalist who left *The Sunday Times* under Neill's editorship was Hugo Young. His argument was that the paper 'no longer stood up for the citizen and gave little space to discussions of poverty, inequality, injustice or other moral issues' and accepted an agenda that had been 'laid down by the government' (cited in *Scotland on Sunday*, 25 June 1995). The extent to which Neill was prepared to go (despite the fact that he and Murdoch were often portrayed as anti-Establishment) was plain to see when his paper attacked Thames Television for its current affairs programme *Death on the Rock*. This programme had critically examined and contradicted the government's case in relation to the shooting of three IRA active servicepeople, who were shot in the street in Gibraltar by the SAS. Neill attacked the journalists working on the programme in such a way that the Wapping branch of the National Union of Journalists passed a motion of no confidence in him. Such an attack not only lined up with the British government but also could be seen as an attack on a television company which was viewed as a competitor to Murdoch in the field of satellite television, and in which Neill himself had a direct interest. It was Neill who was asked, by Murdoch, to launch Sky TV.

The strike, the picketing, and the demonstrations against the move to Wapping were long, bitter, and at times violent. There were mounted police charges against pickets and riot police were deployed. A year later, 12,000 people demonstrated at Wapping on the anniversary of the move. Wapping was aptly called Fortress Wapping. There was the razor-sharp wire around the perimeter, security men patrolling constantly, surveillance cameras and armoured buses to bring the workers in. This, then, was proprietorial power in practice. It takes an imaginative leap to juxtapose pictures of Fortress Wapping with the concept of press freedom. It is proprietorial freedom, bought at a price. Part of the price of that freedom has been an economy with the truth. Thus, at the time of the last general election in 1992, *The Sunday Times* ran tendentious material on the then leader of the British Labour Party under the title 'Kinnock and the Kremlin Connection' and in 1994, Murdoch was sued for libel by another former leader of the Labour Party, Michael Foot, when *The Sunday Times* ran a piece from a former member of the KGB implying that Foot was improperly linked with the KGB. Foot won the action.

In July 1995 Tony Blair, the current leader of the British Labour Party, went, at Murdoch's invitation and expense, to speak to the senior executives of News International at Hayman Island, off Queensland, Australia. This has been referred to as a 'charm offensive' but who is taking the offensive is not exactly clear. Murdoch is said to have commented that if it was a love affair it was love between porcupines. Here we see a politician with obvious interests in getting less flak, if not commitment, from the Murdoch press in the run-up to the next election and a media mogul, in a post-Thatcher period, unimpressed with John Major, with concerns about cross-media ownership in Britain.

We may here refer back to Harold Evans who, in 1994, brought out a new edition of *Good Times, Bad Times*. Evans himself went on to become Chief Executive of Random House book publishers and is based in New York. Although more than ready to recognize his own mistakes in his own battle with Murdoch back in the 1980s, in an interview with Rob Brown in *Scotland on Sunday*, 26 June 1994, he regarded Murdoch as a 'cold-eyed manipulator who has shown a contempt for democracy and debate' and argued that he used his newspapers to promote his satellite interests and right-wing propaganda. And what about his relationships with politicians? Thatcher not only enabled him to buy heavily into British newspaper ownership in return for strong editorial support, but also to beam the pan-European Sky television into Britain from Luxembourg. The taking over of the British-based rival, BSB, was almost incidental in the process. More generally, Evans commented:

The secret of Murdoch's power over politicians, of course, is that he is prepared to use his newspapers to reward them for favours given and destroy them for favours denied. His machinations are almost Jacobean in their strategic cunning.

It is not simply former editors of Murdoch who express such concerns. The former Conservative National Heritage Secretary, David Mellor, argued that News International's effective control of satellite television alongside 35 per cent of the national press was 'an unfortunate development for the future of our country' and that the attempts by press barons to increase their share of TV ownership should be thwarted: 'No-one in their right mind would want any more organs of opinion owned by News International.' That things had got to the present state, he argued, was 'one of the great self-inflicted wounds of Britain in the 1980s' (*Guardian*, 30 August 1994).

Martin Linton has pointed out that whether we are thinking of Murdoch, or of other media moguls such as Silvio Berlusconi, who used his media empire and interests to promote his politics and become Prime Minister of Italy, the question this prompts is, what limits are there to their power? (Linton, 1995) We can note at once that Berlusconi is no longer Prime Minister in the wake of corruption charges and that, therefore, we are not talking about absolute power. This was an unusual example of a media kingmaker becoming king. Perhaps the nearest example to that in recent British history was when Cecil King, then manager of the Mirror Group, tried to promote the concept of a 'government of talents', an all-party coalition which would have ousted Harold Wilson's Labour government of the time, with Lord Mountbatten as the presiding figure. This failed. The Murdoch–Blair connection registers in a different way. Murdoch has already stated in an interview in the German paper *Der Spiegel* that he could imagine his papers supporting Labour in the next British election. Linton concludes:

The two men are achieving several objectives just by meeting. Murdoch is not like the other newspaper proprietors who are die-hard Conservatives and could not plausibly threaten to support Labour. He is motivated 99 per cent by commercial considerations and, while his executives are in no doubt he would prefer a Tory victory, he is enough of a gambler to know the benefits of backing the winner. And a flirtation with Labour could entice both parties into a Dutch auction to soften their stance on cross-media rules in exchange for *Sun* support. (Linton, 1995: 15)

In this context, we should recall that the Conservative government produced, in 1995, a Green Paper on media ownership. The ground rules, as formulated at present, include the prescription that newspaper groups with less than 20 per cent of the market share, measured by circulation, can own two ITV licences. But those above this threshold, which currently include News International and Mirror Group Newspapers, will be limited to 20 per cent of one ITV company or Channel 5 licence and 5 per cent in any subsequent ITV holdings. The long-term objectives include having single-media markets in which no one operator has more than 10 per cent control and that no one company should have more than 20 per cent control in any single sector. This is very different from the Thatcher years of Conservative government and not to Murdoch's liking. In May 1995, it was estimated that he owned 36 per cent of the newspaper market and a 40 per cent share in the satellite channel BSkyB. Under these new rules, he would not be able to expand in Britain.

If we foreground the commercial dimension, we can see that a media mogul can increase his power by crossing into different media markets—press, television, and the information superhighway. This might be associated with takeovers and mergers. It can also involve trying to shut other competitors down. Thus, in 1993, Murdoch experimented with price reductions with his press titles in Britain. The price of *The Times* was reduced to 30p. By mid-1994, sales figures for the paper went to over 500,000, an increase of 42 per cent on the previous year. At the same time, sales of *The Daily Telegraph* had dipped below the million mark by May 1994 for the first time since 1993. Conrad Black, the Canadian proprietor of the Telegraph group, thereupon reduced the price of his paper from 50p to 40p, which put its sales back to over a million again. Murdoch retaliated by further reducing the price of *The Times* to 20p. This was the same price at which *The Sun* was then selling. This also put *The Independent* in difficulties. Although it reduced its price for a day from 50p to 20p, it was clearly under pressure from the other two titles. The then editor, Andreas Whittam-Smith, was clear about what was going on:

Two right-wing ideologues . . . have set about destroying the quality newspaper market. Men like Murdoch and Black want control. They care nothing for plurality of opinion, nothing for liberal values. (*Independent*, 22 June 1994)

The Independent has not gone out of business, but the price of its survival has been that it is now within the control of the Mirror Group, MGN. Both the Telegraph group and News International were running their papers at a loss by their price cutting but were able to cross-subsidize from the profitable parts of their media interests elsewhere in the world.

At the end of his biography on Murdoch, Shawcross observed:

Whatever happens to Murdoch, he has an importance far beyond himself. The information age offers fabulous opportunities, but there is no guarantee that they will be seized. What matters are the choices of those barons who control the fantastic new holdings in the global village. Companies like News International, Sony, Bertelsmann, Time-Warner, are now in a position to set the agenda for the millennium. No one has elected them to such responsibility. Technology, the market and, in Murdoch's case, invincible energy and ambition have given it to them. (Shawcross, 1992: 554)

Some three years on, the process, untrammelled by democratic concerns, moves on. In May 1995, MCI, the second largest long-distance telephone company in the USA, announced that it would be investing $2 billion in Murdoch's News International over the next two years. MCI is linked with British Telecom. MCI is energetically pursuing the development of on-line services and launched its own Internet service in March 1993. So both the distribution and content facets of communications come together. In such ways, the very concept of a media company changes and the possibility of global agreements between different kinds of companies becomes realized. The money being injected into the Murdoch corporation could also make possible bids for buying out competitors. The Italian media empire of Silvio Berlusconi became of direct interest to Murdoch in the wake of the MCI deal, with Murdoch making an offer of around $2 billion, which, as we have seen, is exactly the figure MCI were investing into News International.

We have focused on Rupert Murdoch and News International because our concern is with British society, but the processes described have a more general character. In 1995, the Disney corporation, famed for its film studios and theme parks, took over ABC, one of the big three television networks in the USA. CBS, another of the big three, has been subjected to a takeover bid from Westinghouse, a conglomerate with interests outside of the media. And Time-Warner, with interests in film production, *Time* magazine, and *Life* magazine, made a takeover bid for the Turner broadcasting company, which became famous for its 24-hour-a-day news programme CNN. The general thrust behind these developments is not only to reduce the total number of players in the media mogul game, but to develop the ties of vertical integration. That is to say, the perceived need of the moguls is to have control of the media content side—books, music, films, information networks—and the means of media distribution—through television networks, cable systems, and so on. Thus Disney, like Murdoch, is interested in moving from being primarily a content provider to the development of its own distribution network. What is pushed off the agenda is any concern for democratic pluralism. It is difficult to see the exercise of this power within the context of democratic accountability. It is a challenge to the political will and culture of any society that claims to be or seeks to be democratic, not least since the channels of communication are crucial to the health of the democratic process.

Chapter Four

The BBC: The Struggle for Public Service Broadcasting

The BBC, since its inception, has been a very special case. It represents a form of broadcasting informed by the concept of public service. Here is a public corporation dependent on government funding but claiming a high degree of autonomy from the state. In world terms it was a pioneer in broadcasting. For many years it was a public monopoly, but today it exists in a competitive world where its future is more often evaluated in a global context. In this chapter we will consider some of the continuities and discontinuities over the seventy-odd years of its existence and the present threats to its status as a public service entity. According to Graham Murdock, the years before the First World War saw the growth of the view throughout British society that the 'organisation of public communications along purely commercial lines would not provide the cultural resources for universal and substantive citizenship' (Murdock, 1992: 25). This view was indeed to play an important part in the debate around how to organize the new mass medium that was born in the 1920s, sound broadcasting. The decision to set up broadcasting as a public service monopoly in the hands of the BBC was a clear rejection of the market as the means for organizing this new medium. The central consideration was that the audience would be treated as citizens rather than consumers and educated to play a full part in the democratic and cultural life of the nation.

The British Broadcasting Company was founded in 1922 and was to become the British Broadcasting Corporation in 1926. John Reith was General Manager of the first and moved over to become Director-General of the BBC, where he remained until 1938. The influence of Reith was undoubted and far-reaching. Here was someone with a great deal of energy and commitment, in at the beginning of a new medium of communication. There were just a handful of people involved at first and Reith was directly involved in a whole range of activities from engineering and technical concerns to management and administration as well as the broadcasting of news and special announcements. Here was a new sphere of activity for communications, with new technology and considerable, if unknown, implications for the wider society. Debates about the significance and effects of broadcasting were there from the beginning. Reith was at the centre of all this, including external contacts with government and committees of inquiry, and was involved with other groups and institutions that were to become very significant for broadcasting, notably education, music, and religion.

Who is broadcasting for? What should it do? How should it be organized? To whom should it be accountable? In one of his earliest discussions Reith wrote:

Broadcasting brings relaxation and interest to many homes where such things are at a premium. It does far more: it carries direct information on hundreds of subjects to innumerable people who thereby will be enabled not only to take more interest in events which formerly were outside their ken, but who will after a short time be able to make up their own minds on many matters of vital moment, matters which formerly they had to receive according to the dictated and partial versions and opinions of others, or to ignore altogether. A new and mighty weight of public opinion is being formed, and an intelligent concern on many subjects will be manifest in quarters now overlooked. I have heard it argued that, insofar as broadcasting is awakening interest in these hitherto more or less sheltered or inaccessible regions, it is fraught with danger to the community and to the country generally. In other words, I gather that it is urged that a state of ignorance is to be preferred to one of enlightenment . . . To disregard the spread of knowledge, with the consequent enlargement of opinion, and to be unable to supplement it with reasoned arguments, or to supply satisfactory answers to legitimate and intelligent questions, is not only dangerous, it is stupid. (Reith, 1924)

The famous trilogy, that broadcasting exists to educate, entertain, and inform, encapsulates the essence of this. It is a position that Matthew Arnold, the great nineteenth-century critic, would have understood. In 1925, Reith wrote: 'He who prides himself on giving what he thinks the public wants is often creating a fictitious demand for lower standards, which he himself will then satisfy' (cited in Scannell and Cardiff, 1991: 7). As Scannell and Cardiff pointed out, Reith presented 'a cogent advocacy of public service as a cultural, moral and educative force for the improvement of knowledge, taste and manners, and this has become one of the main ways in which the concept is understood' (Scannell and Cardiff, 1991: 7). Significantly, however, there was a 'one nation' motif in all of this. Reith, a strong Scottish Presbyterian, was a Unionist in his own political position. So, for him, broadcasting co-ordinated within one national institution, reaching out to the whole nation, could help to promote social consensus and political unity. Not everyone in Scotland, Wales, or Northern Ireland saw themselves as one nation, of course, and conflicts existed in the BBC between London and 'the regions'. But, for Reith, developing an enlightened public opinion was seen in the context of a broadcasting system which could bind British citizens together and in this way contribute to the public good and the national interest. And the national interest, from this perspective, involved a particular form of political stability.

This consideration surely goes some way toward explaining why, when political crises occurred, an early notable example being the General Strike of 1926, Reith could be relied upon, as he admitted, to side with the government. Here we may briefly recall that an argument developed in the Cabinet about the use of broadcasting. Winston Churchill thought it was monstrous that the government should not use broadcasting to its best possible advantage. But the Cabinet, Reith noted,

want to be able to say that they did not commandeer us, but they know that they can trust us not to be really impartial . . . I wanted the inconsistencies in our acts so far squared up setting us right with the other side. Davidson [the Deputy Chief Civil Commissioner, who was the link between the Cabinet and the BBC during the strike], however, thought the Cabinet would only agree to a statement that we could do nothing to help the Strike since it had been declared illegal. This does not seem to me straight. (Stuart, 1975)

The BBC, Reith sensed, was in a very difficult position. He was clear that to turn the BBC into a direct propaganda arm of the government would have destroyed its credibility, even more so if it had been commandeered. His sense of loyalty to the Prime Minister cut across his uneasiness that impartiality was a cloak concealing the government's position. The debate about impartiality, seen as a crucial element in public service broadcasting, has been with us ever since. It is a contested and problematic concept. However, this should not prevent us from the underlying concern which is identified, namely that broadcasting should be independent of state control and that the interests of the state and the interests of the civil society are not necessarily identical. While we can readily see that Reith's BBC represented a particular kind of paternalism, wherein the concept of impartiality could be used to favour one class against another, it is still possible to argue that the idea of public service broadcasting carries the seeds of pluralism, insofar as broadcasting is recognized as part of the civil society attentive and responsive to its publics. The principle this embodies is intrinsically antithetical to state control.

From the beginning, Reith had to steer the newly formed broadcasting company through a host of problems—establishing its position with the government and the Post Office in relation to the licence, coming to terms with the wireless manufacturers, dealing with the issues of advertising and sponsorship, handling questions of censorship and the broadcasting of controversial views, contributing to discussions about the BBC's Charter and Constitution, including the crucial relationship between the Director-General and the Board of Governors.

At the heart of his position was a view of public service broadcasting that, while financed by public funds so that it would not be in bondage to advertising revenue, would have its own independence from government through its standing as a public corporation. The resistance to advertising, although it has resurfaced strongly in recent years, was much more successful than the attempt to sustain political independence. From the time of the General Strike, the worm was in the apple. Scannell and Cardiff show clearly how the broadcasting of political matters came to be controlled by the political parties, which excluded dissenting opinion even from within their own ranks. Hence they conclude:

The early broadcasters thought of themselves as bridging the gulf between state and citizenry and saw no fundamental clash of interest between themselves, the world of politics and the everyday world of work, home and family inhabited by listeners. Painfully they came to understand not only the power of governments, parties and state departments to impose their definitions of political realities, but their own complicity in that process. For over thirty years, throughout the era of the BBC's monopoly, political broadcasting was structured in deference to the state. The struggle to make politicians answerable and accountable to the electorate through broadcasting was not joined until the establishment of commercial television and the new forms of broadcast journalism inaugurated by Independent Television News in the late fifties. (Scannell and Cardiff, 1991: 101–2)

But politics was only a small part of the output of BBC radio. A survey of the output of BBC radio for a three-year period published in 1935 by the Corporation found that 70 per cent of the material broadcast was music (Scannell and Cardiff, 1976: 21). Entertainment comprised the bulk of the content of the new medium but what Reith saw as entertainment was not in keeping with popular attitudes of the period. The BBC maintained its mission to educate people in the area of music and drama as well as talks and commentaries. The BBC's music policy was to develop the public taste for classical music. Popular music, such as that of the dance bands, was dismissed as music that 'doesn't wear' while classical music 'lasts, mellows and gains fresh beauties at every hearing' (quoted in Lewis and Booth, 1989: 62). Thus 'light music' was defined by the BBC as Gilbert and Sullivan, operetta, and light symphony music. The same was apparent in drama, where the task was to teach people who had never been to the theatre that 'drama can be satisfying and rewarding entertainment' (Frith, 1983: 109). In entertainment—as in other aspects of output—the BBC under Reith sought to provide a form of enlightenment which was middle class, middle brow, and middle of the road.

The BBC embarked on the policy of giving the public what it thought was good for them with a high degree of confidence. As Reith stated in 1924:

It is occasionally represented to us that we are apparently setting out to give the public what we think they need, and not what they want, but few know what they want, and very few what they need. There is often no difference . . . better to overestimate the mentality of the public than to underestimate it. (quoted in Scannell and Cardiff, 1976: 18)

However, throughout the 1930s the BBC had to pay greater attention to its audience, as more people, in particular members of the working classes, came to purchase wireless sets. When the novelty of listening wore off, listeners began to make their preferences and tastes heard and increasingly expressed dissatisfaction at the material provided by the BBC.

Take the example of the BBC music policy. Listeners in their thousands began to tune into continental radio stations to satisfy their cravings for popular music. Radio Normandie and Radio Luxembourg began to attract a large audience in Britain, especially on Sundays. The Reithian Sunday was a sombre occasion with religious services, serious talks, and heavy classical music dominating the output. By 1938 it was estimated that Radio Luxembourg frequently had higher listening figures than the BBC, with the continental stations doing especially well on Sundays, when two-thirds of the audience was found to tune into them on Sunday mornings (see Browne, 1985). Listeners, especially working-class people, were reacting to what they regarded as the 'lofty condescension' of the Corporation. The drift of the audience to the continental stations forced the BBC to rethink its programme schedules. Reith had resolutely resisted the introduction of audience research but in 1936, the year before his departure from the BBC, he relented and the Listener Research Department was established. Not surprisingly the surveys conducted by this department found that people wanted more variety and more popular music and entertainment on the radio. The BBC responded by increasing the provision of jazz, dance, and cinema organ music as well as comedy and serials. There were also attempts to represent working-class life in documentaries and drama. These changes—although limited—were greeted with disapproval by many: for one member of the Talks Department the invention of 'the hellish department which is called Listener Research' was the beginning of the 'real degradation of the BBC' (quoted in Pegg, 1983: 110).

There was no general provision of entertainment programming for the working class before the Second World War but pressures for particular kinds of programmes led the BBC to temper its educational approach. It still steadfastly refused to create a separate service for popular music and tastes—it was only with the upheavals of the Second World War that the BBC changed its mind and launched what was to become the BBC Light Programme. The aim of cultural unity was abandoned after the war when the BBC announced the establishment of the Home, Light, and Third services, which would cater for the different tastes amongst the public. However the then Director-General maintained the BBC's commitment to raising cultural tastes by stating in 1948 that the new system 'rests on the conception of the community as a broadly based cultural pyramid, slowly aspiring upwards' (quoted in Curran and Seaton, 1991: 186). The BBC's experience of the inter-war years shows that the mass media have to follow as well as lead its public.

The history of the BBC, and later, commercial broadcasting in Britain, is pock-marked with reports—Sykes (1923), Crawford (1925), Ullswater (1936), Beveridge (1951), Pilkington (1960), Annan (1977), Peacock (1986)—as well as a plethora of government proposals and White Papers. Sykes, from the outset, raised the question of who should control such a potential power over public opinion and concluded that a national, universally available service, subject to public authority within the state, and not an unrestricted commercial monopoly, was appropriate. Crawford's recommendation that a public corporation, licensed by the Post-Master General, invested with the fullest freedom which Parliament was prepared to concede, provided the institutional grounds and rationale for the new BBC. By the time of Beveridge, the BBC was called upon to make a vigorous defence of its monopoly. This was supported with some reservations. But the question of competition was treated in terms of competition for service and not for listeners. This was drafted in accordance with the value assumption that the highest purpose of broadcasting is education.

By the time of the Pilkington Report, in which the guiding hand of Richard Hoggart was widely noted, commercial television was off the ground. Concern was expressed with the programme output of the new channel, the tendency to trivialization and the lack of a public service ethic:

it seems to us that 'to give the public what it wants' is a misleading phrase, misleading because as commonly used it has the appearance of an appeal to a good democratic principle, but the appearance is deception. It is in fact patronising and arrogant, in that it claims to know what the public is, but defines it as no more than the mass audience; and in that it claims to know what it wants, but limits its choice to the average of experience. In this sense, we reject it utterly. If there is a sense in which it should be used it is this: what the public wants and what it has a right to get is the freedom to choose from the widest possible range of programme matter. Anything less than that is deprivation . . . (Broadcasting Committee, 1960: para. 49)

Thus the third TV channel went to the BBC and the TV Act of 1963 was passed to bring commercial TV within a public service framework.

Behind all this is a sense of public service broadcasting which must aim to stretch the capacities of the audience—the education of desire which can impinge on drama, comedy, music, documentaries, indeed the whole range of programming, well beyond those formally labelled education, such as the schools and, in due course, Open University slots. It is precisely the sense of range that gives meaning to the 'broad' in broadcasting. Moreover, it is the sense of access and universality that underpins the concept of public service, as opposed to private subscription arrangements. It is worth reflecting that Hugh Carelton Greene, Director-General of the BBC during the 1960s, though different from Reith in so many ways, saw this public service as a model for other broadcasting organizations. Asa Briggs, in volume 5 of his redoubtable history of the BBC, refers to this succinctly:

it was generally recognised that they both brought the world—and not just Britain—into the reckoning when they proclaimed their messages. Greene maintained as resolutely as Reith had done that in an 'age of communications', the BBC stood for a public service approach to broadcasting which had international as well as national ramifications. (Briggs, 1995: 318)

The BBC, as we all know, developed into a bureaucratic organization with its own ethos. Thus, in 1933, Reith was the Director-General at the top of the pyramid. Immediately under him were the Controller of Output and the Controller of Administration, thus establishing the principle of separation of administration from production. This was to present problems insofar as the administrators came to see themselves as policing the system. Tom Burns blames Reith for the internal stresses this created within the BBC, although he admits that the outward signs—the public face—were that the BBC was a success. The system was perpetuated, no doubt in more complex forms, as time passed. The values of consensus and public service were intertwined and, alongside this, the importance of loyalty to the organization. Administrative control over employees could be fierce, especially in times of high unemployment. Burns perceptively identifies the double-edged character of the BBC—a bureaucracy that looks like a mixture of complacency and anxiety:

The BBC . . . sees itself as perpetually beleaguered, under pressure, being lobbied, or being compelled to lobby. The outsider tends to read this as caginess, defensiveness—or complacency. (Burns, 1977: 32)

When the Annan Committee commented on the BBC as an organization it said something rather similar: 'We have come to the view that the lack of self-confidence in the BBC and confusion about its objectives and priorities spring in part from its internal organization' (Broadcasting Committee, 1977, para. 9.1). This was attributed in some measure to the swift expansion of its radio and television services, followed by a stagnation and decline of its real income. Between 1962 and 1972, for example, staff employment changed from 17,000 to over 25,000. Ironically, communication within the organization was seen as a problem, particularly between management and staff, and reference is made in Annan to the bureaucratic fog enveloping the upper slopes of the BBC. Interestingly, a good deal of attention was given to Tom Burns's evidence. He argued that the grading system in BBC occupations created a great amount of resentment because of the obsession with minute distinctions within the grades based on job evaluation. What Burns emphasized as the biggest organizational change in the BBC between the 1960s and 1970s was not so much stricter financial control or the increased power of Controllers at the expense of Department Heads, but 'the breakdown between everyone engaged in programme production of normal conventions governing working relationships'. These conventions referred to an approach to getting things done in a collaborative committed way, task networks that did not emphasize occupational distinctions but concentrated on the project itself. The grading structure became the basis for disgruntlement, invidious rivalries, and disputes about wage differentials, all of which could hamper the way work was done in the studios.

But, alongside this, Annan does refer to the post-1969 reforms, which brought a harsher financial reality to the studio floor which was not there previously and moved broadcasting a little further from a 'cultural' activity to a 'business' activity. Even so, it was recognized that the pressure for profit was not so evident as it was in the ITV companies. But both Burns and Annan point to the erosion of the public service ideal, especially among programme staff who were more likely to think in terms of a professional career. 'Dedication to providing a public service has now dwindled to a rather vague non-specific "sense of responsibility", and to attention to audience figures and to ratings. It is a form of self-censorship, but weak self-censorship' (Broadcasting Committee, 1977, para. 9.28). These producers, nonetheless, felt their professional activities were being impeded by 'the presence of a mysterious omnipresent bureaucracy brooding over them and judging their projects and programmes by some imperfectly perceived standard which is not intrinsic to the medium' (Broadcasting Committee, 1977, para. 9.40).

The playwright Dennis Potter recalls in the 1960s, when talking with his friends:

> the evident iniquities of the BBC management, the tapeworm-length persistence of BBC cowardice, and the insufferable perversities of the BBC's threat to the very existence of the single play. You can imagine how much greater our indignation would have been had we known at the time that we were sitting slap in the middle of what later observers were to call the Golden Age of television drama. Back in those good old days, there was a bureaucrat in every cupboard and smugness waiting with a practised simper on the far side of every door . . . (Potter, 1994: 36)

In 1968, the BBC called in the management consultants, McKinsey and Co. The results of their activities were never made public, nor indeed were they made available to any government department, even though it was seen in part as a public relations exercise. To bring in the consultants was to show to the world that a response was being made to the political criticisms that the BBC was a fat cat and extravagant in its financial practice, a view which might have affected the next licence award. The reorganization involved setting up 'product divisions'—TV, Radio, and External Services. Financial responsibility for operating and for capital expenditure was placed into the product divisions. Thus financial responsibility and accountability were delegated downwards to the point of production. Some of this is surely a precursor of changes that we have seen in the last few years. That is one reason why Burns's conclusion to his study of the BBC is so interesting. He recognized that, while the BBC sometimes conveys an image of impregnability and orderly growth in British society, the reality has been a variety of political pressures from right and left and a series of inquiries where its future shape and even continued existence has been in question. The issue of public service broadcasting is pummelled about in the process:

> The BBC is even now, I believe, comparatively immature and unformed. Misguided and intolerant though he may have been, Reith's conception of broadcasting as a public service, of a BBC imbued with a sense of mission, of the people who worked in it as a community dedicated to the public good was, I believe, wholly appropriate. It is also the only conception which makes political and economic sense, perhaps especially in the present situation of this country.

It is also the only conception which has a hope of superseding the miscellany of values and purposes compounded of individual commitments to professionalism, to careers to managerial efficiency, to saving money or making money, which are the prevailing currency. Potentially the BBC still represents an enormously effective agency of political, cultural and social enlightenment. (Burns, 1977: 296)

This view also helped to shape Annan's conclusion that there was external resentment and mistrust towards the BBC coupled with internal anxiety, frustration, and a sense of bureaucratic restrictions. They seriously wondered about chopping the organization up but in the end, though some members of the inquiry advocated it, they did not recommend this.

It was only two years after the Annan Report that the Thatcher years of government began. We have already observed that government–BBC relations have always had elements of tension and conflict about them. The Wilson government of 1974 remembered their days in opposition when, in June 1971, the documentary *Yesterday's Men* was shown. The intention was to show what it is like to lose high political office unexpectedly and how ex-Cabinet Ministers felt about it. The very title, *Yesterday's Men*, was twisting the knife, since that was how the Labour government had labelled the Tory opposition before the 1970 general election. This had caused great offence in the Labour Party and reinforced Wilson's view that there was an anti-left bias in the BBC. Yet there was a defence that as part of 'the fourth estate', there was a role for disrespect and irreverence in relation to those who lead us. But the row was a furious and bitter one, of epic proportions, and Harold Wilson, the Labour leader, was at the centre of it. When he returned to government he set up the Annan Committee on the future of broadcasting. Indeed, post-Annan, the Labour government was contemplating the introduction of an extra layer of authority between the BBC Governors and management—three service-management boards for TV, Radio, and External Services, respectively, appointed by the Home Office and taking over the Governor's role in the direct supervision of the BBC. The BBC, reflecting on this in its 1980 Annual Report, thought that these changes would have been 'profound and to our minds perilous'. The Report continued:

We did not believe those threats arose from ill-will so much as from an insufficient understanding of the Corporation's governing and managerial mechanisms, even among its friends and admirers. Nevertheless, the apprehensions they aroused were not assuaged until after the end of the year under review. The financial problems remained. (cited in Leapman, 1986)

If the arrival of Margaret Thatcher into office stopped the Labour Party from implementing its proposals for change, to the BBC's evident relief, she brought other hostilities and a politic of conviction to the BBC—and, more generally, to the public sector.

Thatcher's general views on the BBC ought to have been well enough known before she became Prime Minister. It was in her opinion left-wing, over-bureaucratized, badly managed, overstaffed, and not properly exposed to the winds of competition and market forces. Moreover, it was morally suspect, with a bad record for the treatment of sex and violence on television. The moral, political, and economic were intertwined in her New Right convictions. Some of the subsequent examples of hostility emerge in the form of anecdotes—her anger with Brian Redhead and the *Today* Radio 4 programme after he called her Press Secretary, Bernard Ingham, 'a conspiracy' for the way he organized selective press leaks; her anger with Sue Lawley, after the 1983 election phone-in when the Prime Minister was on the receiving end of a mauling from Diana Gould concerning the sinking of the *General Belgrano* during the Falklands conflict; her role in the sacking of Alisdair Milne, then Director-General of the BBC, after the appointment of Marmaduke Hussey as Chairman of the Board of Governors. There are a number of documented episodes in the history of the BBC during the Thatcher years that reflected an abrasive approach and a negative attitude. These include the attack on the BBC, but not ITN, for its coverage of the Falklands conflict; the Tebbit Report, from the Conservative Central Office, on the BBC coverage of the American bombing of Libya (where again ITN was praised); the *Real Lives at the Edge of the Union* documentary on Northern Ireland, when the Board of Governors willingly acceded to a request from the Home Secretary that the film should not be shown, against the view of the management from Milne downwards; and the police raid on the offices of BBC Glasgow in relation to the *Secret Society* series of documentaries by Duncan Campbell. It is difficult to see these attacks as other than politically motivated and they did, of course, raise questions of political censorship and civil liberties.

Was there an alternative to the licence fee method of funding for the BBC? This was the central question posed for the Peacock Committee, which Thatcher set up in 1986. The answer, when it came, was 'not yet'. It looked towards the possibility that the fee might gradually be replaced by a subscription system and it looked for a market system based on consumer sovereignty. Despite Thatcher's hopes, it did not support the view that broadcasting should be supported by advertising. But these were turbulent days and nothing could be taken for granted. It was the Murdoch-owned *Times* that in 1985 had recommended the break-up of the BBC into a series of commercial companies. The argument was that the new channels thus created would not only be financed by advertising but perhaps supplemented by a share of the licence fee. The fact that the advertising route was not taken (although the BBC has done some powerful advertising on behalf of itself) was a victory at least for those who saw this as a crucial element in debates about public service broadcasting. This was a position long taken by Raymond Williams and, more recently, clearly stated by Nicholas Garnham:

> in my view advertising finance is, and will remain, incompatible with the ideal of public service. . . . The aim of advertising is not to encourage the rational exchange of information and opinions in search of agreement as to the public good, but on the contrary, to exploit the irrational in the admitted pursuit of private interest. Thus, for me, the fact that the BBC is not financed by advertising, unlike many other broadcasters in Europe, is crucial and, given the level of broadcasting advertising in Britain, a remarkable social achievement. Thus, for instance, the current weakening of the BBC's stance towards sponsorship is not a peripheral housekeeping matter, but absolutely central. (Garnham, 1989: 31)

Even so, deregulation was in the airwaves and it was signalled with a flourish in the government's plan for broadcasting legislation in the 1990s (HMSO, 1988). Its chapter on the BBC built upon Peacock and emphasized the need for greater efficiency and accountability and looked for a process whereby the management would tighten up its own structure and learn to shift resources into programme improvements by making savings elsewhere. It put the licence fee question on hold and raised again the possibility of subscription arrangements for future funding. Within the BBC itself, Milne had been fired in the early Thatcher years; Michael Checkland, with an accountancy background, had taken his place. He in his turn was replaced by John Birt. Birt had been made Deputy Director-General in 1987 and was Director-General-designate while Checkland served his last year, and took over as Director-General in January 1993.

It is the Checkland and Birt administrations, with the interventionist Chairman Hussey, that have been at the centre of the 'fear and loathing' syndrome. These have been the years of task forces into BBC management operations, the document from the BBC, *Extending Choice*, and the doctrine of producer choice, with the developments of internal markets in the organization, turning programme makers into business units. What has been extraordinary is the volume of criticism from a range of different people with interests in broadcasting. Thus, David Attenborough, a distinguished programme maker and former head of BBC2, used his public platform at the British Association Science Festival in August 1992 to complain that accountants had taken over at the BBC and that the morale of the BBC's staff was being 'gravely eroded' and that 'the very things that gave the BBC its unique stature and strength are being destroyed' (cited in Horrie and Clarke, 1994: 223).

The Edinburgh Festival Television Conference in recent years has been the scene of a number of set-piece dissident statements. Michael Grade, speaking from a wealth of experience from within the BBC and later as Chief Executive of Channel 4, in 1992 criticized the Governors of the BBC for a policy of political appeasement and spoke of the 'massive revolution' taking place with 'brutal zeal' by an army of accountants. He referred to the management-speak of 'downsizing', 'delayering', and 'outsourcing' which stood, he said, in fact for closure, redundancies, and dark studios. He said that the BBC should be treated as a centre of excellence and not as a business and argued that with Thatcher gone, the BBC was still bringing in consultants and looking towards privatizing its own activities just when big question marks were being placed on the appropriateness of the whole activity. Dennis Potter, in his criticism of the BBC at the 1993 Edinburgh Festival, made a central structural point:

The Corporation has already been driven on to the back foot by the ideology-driven malice of the ruling politicians and its response has been to take several steps backwards, with hands thrown up, and to whimper an alleged defence of all it has stood for in the very language and concepts of its opponents. This palpable ambivalence and doubt, where you pretend to be the commercial business that you cannot be, has led to the present, near-fatal crisis where it seems to be thought that the wounds (often self-inflicted) can only be staunched by shuffling about word-processed words about a new 'management culture' (Potter, 1994: 47).

He spoke of the bitterness, demoralization, and hatred that he had observed while he was making *Midnight Movie*, and described seeing a middle-aged man cry after receiving a phone call from some manager at the Centre.

This was not just a personal experience of the idiosyncratic Potter. The results of a staff survey released in June 1993 revealed that employees were fearful of speaking out, felt insecure in their jobs, and had little confidence in senior management. This supported the views that Mark Tully, the BBC's veteran Asian correspondent, gave vent to when he spoke of 'a real sense of fear among the staff which prevents them from speaking their minds'. One senior correspondent was told by a line manager: 'One thing we will not take is hissing from the wings.' Tully went on to speak of his own experience and then commented on the new bureaucracy of Birtism:

The new management believes it is nonsense to suggest that the programmes would look after themselves. Now an iron structure has been set in place in news and current affairs to make sure that producers do not have freedom, that they conform to what has become known as Birtism. It's editorial centralisation, but then every revolution leads to the concentration of power or to chaos (cited in *Guardian*, 14 July 1993).

Tully was predictably dismissed by a management leak as a 'dinosaur'. Yet, as late as 4 September 1994, the *Observer*'s television critic was noting that Birt had transformed the BBC's organizational culture:

And where the old BBC was highly bureaucratic and, broadly speaking, tolerant, the new BBC is still highly bureaucratic (though with different jargon, job titles, and a consultancy habit more expensive than cocaine) and noticeably more intolerant. I am told, for example, that the expression FIFO (fit in or fuck off) has become a kind of mantra in News and Current Affairs, the flagship of the Birtian revolution. And speaking out of turn about BBC matters has become a sackable offence.

The government's White Paper, *The Future of the BBC: Serving the Nation, Competing World-Wide* (British Broadcasting Corporation, 1994), has been presented as a victory for Birt's BBC revolution, since the Charter is to be renewed for ten years from 1997 and the licence fee is to remain in place at least until 2001. But where does this leave our understanding of public institutions? Has this eroded our sense of what cultural organizations can accomplish in and for a democratic society? Is there not a more general set of considerations about public service institutions in Britain? These institutions, for all their imperfections, were set up for the common good, the common wealth in the spheres of culture, education, and health. It is the concept of the public institution itself that has been attacked to the detriment of their employees and those they exist to serve and enable. Whether in the language of 'choice', 'privatization', or 'deregulation', employees have become more insecure. The vocabulary has become filled with the concepts of goals, aims, objectives, mission statements, and performance indicators. In such linguistic ways has the public sector been taken over and captured by the private sector. And yet 'market forces', the invisible regulator, are manifestly not free-market forces. They represent varying forms of oligopoly and in some cases are close to private monopolies. 'Choice' is derivative upon these structures; it does not effectively determine them. Thus, we might say in the case of the media that between the rhetoric and the reality of choice is the Murdoch. In December 1995, for example, Granada Television went into partnership with Murdoch's BSkyB company to launch eight new satellite channels in 1996. This will give Murdoch an effective monopoly of the pay-TV market in Britain. The policy question should not be overlooked. Is this what we want for a democratic society in the mid-1990s or should we recognize that a healthy democracy has political debates about the kind of media it wants or does not want?

The BBC has stood, and still stands, as a witness to the fact that broadcasting can play an important public service role and thereby strengthen the civic society against the state. It has in its history sometimes yielded to pressures from the state, but not always. It would certainly buck the trend that one recognizes in Europe and beyond if the institutional autonomy and public service ethic of the BBC were to be sustained against the forces of privatization and commercialization. At a time when the government is cutting the budget, against a previous agreement, for the World Service of the BBC and when the word is out that the BBC is to sell its transmitters, there is no reason to feel sanguine about its future. Perhaps we need to remember that we are not, in the end, talking about economic or technological imperatives, but about a cultural struggle that will be mediated through political activity and decision making. These are matters which we hope will stay on the public agenda way beyond the tenancy of the present Director-General. Between the economics of the market place and the politics of propaganda and public relations, there is a culture of democracy. It is a contested space and always will be. If we did not know it before then, as John Reith might have said, 'Ye ken now.'

Chapter Five

Moral Panics, Media Scares, and Real Problems

'Don't panic!' Corporal Jones shouted regularly whenever the world seemed to be collapsing around the Home Guard platoon in *Dad's Army* and things looked out of control. In the study of press and broadcasting the concept of panic surfaces again and again and the most typical reference is to 'moral panic', which is applied to many different issues. What is this term? How did it emerge? What is it attempting to explain and does it have any continuing value?

The term was invented and developed by Stan Cohen for his study *Folk Devils and Moral Panics* (1987). It is a good example of the sociological imagination in action and served to trigger other work. Even where criticisms can be made, as will be done here (see also Miller and Reilly, 1995), this also serves as a tribute to the fruitfulness of conceptual innovation. Cohen introduced the concept at the outset of the study:

Societies appear to be subject, every now and then, to periods of moral panic. A condition, episode, person or group of persons emerges to become defined as a threat to societal values and interests; its nature is presented in a stylised and stereotypical fashion by the mass media; the moral barricades are manned by editors, bishops, politicians and other right-thinking people; socially accredited experts pronounce their diagnoses and solutions; ways of coping are evolved or (more often) resorted to; the condition then disappears, submerges or deteriorates and becomes less visible. Sometimes the object of the panic is quite novel and at other times it is something which has been in existence long enough, but suddenly appears in the limelight. Sometimes the panic passes over and is forgotten, except in folklore and collective memory; at other times it has more serious and long-lasting repercussions and might produce such changes as those in legal and social policy or even in the way the society conceives itself. (Cohen, 1987: 9)

Cohen was particularly interested in the emergence of youth culture after the Second World War and the way in which various groups and activities came to be defined as deviant, delinquent, and associated with forms of violence. Teddy Boys, Mods and Rockers, Hell's Angels, Skinheads, and Hippies were standard examples. Alongside this were public reactions to issues such as drug abuse, political demonstrations, student militancy, football hooliganism, vandalism, and various other activities defined as violent. It was argued long ago, by the sociologist W. I. Thomas, that if a situation is defined as real it will have real consequences. Cohen was interested in the way in which definitions of social reality came into play and the role of the mass media in defining and interpreting the nature and significance of social deviance. He proceeded to make a detailed study of the ways in which Mods and Rockers were treated as a threat to society and social order in the 1960s. Here were two groups who were seen as a law and order problem. The mass media were portrayed as presenting and representing messages that came from what Cohen called the 'control culture'. The media dramatize or even sensationalize 'the problem' and call for action and punishment against those who are defined as causing the trouble. In the process and, as part of the dramatic element, scapegoats and folk devils are located and are woven into the narrative.

Cohen argues that, as a result of the interaction between the control culture and the media, a process of amplification takes place such that the issue and definition of what the problem is comes to be treated in national, not simply local, terms. The public can be appealed to so that they may endorse ready-made opinions as to what should be done. What is sometimes termed 'the silent majority' is both defined and mobilized by the media. Thereafter, key figures in the control culture can legitimate their actions by appealing to the media and the 'public opinion' that has been constructed.

In the case of Mods and Rockers, Cohen suggests that the scene of the first recorded conflict, Clacton on Easter Sunday 1964, set the pattern for other seaside resorts such as Brighton, Margate, and Bournemouth. There were scuffles between the two groups, identified by different clothing; bikes and scooters roared up and down the streets; some beach huts were wrecked; stones were thrown and windows broken. Ninety-seven people were arrested. The following Monday every national newspaper reported it with such headlines as 'Day of Terror by Scooter Groups' (*Daily Telegraph*) and 'Wild Ones Invade Seaside—97 Arrests' (*Daily Mirror*). There was extensive coverage in the overseas press. Interestingly, the Belgian press captioned their pictures 'West Side Story on English Coast', associating it with the Bernstein musical on New York gangs.

Cohen wishes to establish the point that, although the event had a factual basis, it was subject to 'overreporting', that is to exaggerating and distorting what took place, in terms, for example, of the numbers involved and the effects of any damage or violence. 'The regular use of phrases such as "riot", "orgy of destruction", "battle", "attack", "siege", "beat up the town", and "screaming mob" left an image of a besieged town from which innocent holidaymakers were fleeing to escape a marauding mob' (Cohen, 1987: 31). Yet, as he points out, those who were on the spot knew that the weather was cold and wet and that there was scarcely anyone on the beach. Or again, one boy told the magistrate that he would pay the £75 fine with a cheque:

This story was true enough; what few papers bothered to publish and what they all knew was that the boy's offer was a pathetic gesture of bravado. He admitted three days later that not only did he not have the £75 but did not even have a bank account and had never signed a cheque in his life. As long as four years after this, though, the story was still being repeated as was quoted to me at a magistrates' conference in 1968 to illustrate the image of Mods and Rockers as affluent hordes whom 'fines couldn't touch'. (Cohen, 1987: 33)

Not only do these initial accounts and the behaviour of the immediate control agents, the police and the courts, set the frame within which and through which later events are interpreted, but a process takes place whereby roles are self-consciously played out, posing for photos, making warlike gestures, wearing the appropriate dress, and so on. But:

The young people on the beaches knew very well that they had been type cast as folk devils and they saw themselves as targets for abuse. When the audiences, TV cameras and police started lining themselves up, the metaphor of role playing becomes no more a metaphor but the real thing. (Cohen, 1987: 164)

The intervention of the media in the process as a whole can be seen to have some cumulative influence on what takes place. But it is on the control culture itself that Cohen seeks to direct our attention, rather than the 'deviance'. The moral panic that was generated had to do with a more general problem of youth culture, which is why it could be focused on other groups, when the anxiety about Mods and Rockers diminished after a few years. Yet, in Cohen's view, the control culture did not 'solve' the problem. This he puts down to their intellectual poverty and lack of imagination. He concludes, therefore, on a pessimistic note:

More moral panics will be generated and other, as yet nameless, folk devils will be created. This is not because such developments have an inexorable inner logic, but because our society as present structured will continue to generate problems for some of its members—like working class adolescents—and then condemn whatever solution these groups find. (Cohen, 1987: 204)

If that could be written at a time of relatively full employment for young people, indeed when their so-called 'affluence' was a point of criticism, resentment, and 'explanation', what is to be said at the present time, when youth unemployment remains high and job insecurity endemic? When the subcultures of drugs and raves are indicted by the control culture are we not focusing on the bruise rather than the fist?

There is an intriguing coda to the Mods and Rockers story. Under the headline 'Resort Recalls Weekend that Shook the Nation', *The Guardian* on 21 May 1994 looked back on the events of thirty years ago. One young person who was nineteen years old at the time in Brighton recalled:

My remembrance of it wasn't so much of violence as hordes of young people running around and looking for the excitement that others were committing. We were like a huge mobile audience though in fact we were the main act.

Two years later John Alton joined the police and found a different attitude:

For them it was quite frightening. There was an assumption that every youth was a dyed-in-the-wool villain out to attack society. But really you had a hectic hard core who smashed windows and there was a huge group of youngsters who had been attracted to watch. It was *the* event.

Thirty years later, Alton was Assistant Chief Constable of Devon and Cornwall.

As far as the issue of drug taking is concerned this was taken up with reference to moral panics by Jock Young, notably in his essay, 'The Myth of the Drug Taker in the Mass Media' (Young 1981). What comes out clearly is the assumption of what Young terms a 'consensualist society'. This claims that the vast majority of people in our society share common definitions of reality and ideas as to what is acceptable and what is not. Things outside the consensus should be condemned as wrong or irrational. This model is shared by the mass media. In this respect Young sees the function of the mass media as reinforcing popular consciousness. What flows from this, in his view, is a sophisticated form of propaganda which plays on widespread discontent and insecurities rather than straightforward manipulation. On this view, rather than manipulating in the sense of trying to get people to change their views or politics, by reinforcing what is already present in society it gives the public what it wants. By dealing with matters such as drugs it can titillate, then interpret, then condemn. Young's conclusion is close to Cohen's position:

The myth of the drug user is rooted in moral indignation; it bulwarks the hypothetical world of the normal citizen, it blinkers its audience to deviant realities outside the consensus, it spells out justice for the righteous and punishment for the wicked. Although much of its world view is fantasy, its effects are real enough. For by fanning up moral panics over drug use, it contributes enormously to public hostility to the drug taker and precludes any rational approach to the problem. It also provides a bevy of convenient scapegoats on to which real material and moral discontent can be directed and significant structural changes averted. (Young, 1982: 334)

The role of the media in creating moral panics was taken up with rather more theoretical baggage by the Birmingham Centre for Contemporary Cultural Studies (Hall and Jefferson, 1976; Hall, Critcher, et al., 1978). The concept of the control culture is related back to the state. And much is made of the control culture as the primary definer of media messages:

Once the media have spoken in their voice, on behalf of the inaudible public, the primary definers can then use the media statements and claims as legitimations (magically, without any visible connection for their actions and statements) by claiming press—and via the press—public support. In turn the ever attentive media reproduce the Control Culture statements, thus completing the magic circle, with such effect that it is no longer possible to tell who began the process: each legitimates the other in turn. (Hall & Jefferson, 1976:76)

What we have here is a picture of a closed circle in which the secondary definers of media messages, editors and journalists, because they stand in a position of subordination to the primary definers, develop their own definitions of what news is and how it is to be interpreted within the limits set by the primary definers. Thus, by way of example, the topic of mugging is taken up. Mugging as a form of robbery with violence, or assault, on the street comes into the public vocabulary imported from the USA. The term is deployed by primary definers and becomes a public issue. This is amplified through the media in mutually reinforcing ways. An illustration of what they have in mind is provided in a story in *The Daily Mail* on 29 March 1973: 'Mugger Jailed for Three Years. "And I Was Lenient,' Says the Judge'. The judge added: 'everybody in this country thinks that offences of this kind—mugging offences—are on the increase and the public have a right to be protected. This is a frightful case.' The amplification spiral is seen at work here with mutually reinforcing effects. Nevertheless, argue Hall and his colleagues, this should not deflect us from understanding the starting point of the process,

the point where it began and from which it is continually renewed—the role of the primary and privileged definers, who, in classifying out the world of crime for media and public, establish the principal categories across which the news media . . . run their secondary themes and variations. (Hall, Critcher, et al., 1978: 76)

What is explicitly referred to here is the interrelationship between the control culture and the 'signification culture' (that is, the media). So close is this, it is suggested, that the one merges into the other, such that the media become part of the ideological state-apparatus (a term drawn from the work of the French Marxist-structuralist Louis Althusser).

As stated, this version of the role of the media and the explanation of moral panics is very functionalist in form: the media are subsumed within the state, both serving and sustaining it. We would suggest that the circle is too closed. This is a view which Cohen also seems to share. In reflecting on the work of the Birmingham group he points out that it is strongly influenced by Gramsci's concept of hegemony. Cohen is particularly drawing attention to a theory about the ruling class which suggests its potential for shaping consent from the ruled, framing alternatives and setting agendas (political and moral) in ways which appear to be natural. This is held to account for the development of 'reactionary common sense'. But in expressing reservations Cohen comments:

At too many points, it seems to me, the Centre's determination to find ideological closure leads them to a premature theoretical closure. The actual material selected as proof of the slide into crisis (newspaper editorials, statements by MPs and police chiefs) does not always add up to something of such monumental proportions . . . And the assumption of a monolithic drift into repression gives little room for understanding why some objects are repressed more than others. (Cohen, 1987: xxiv–xxv)

The reference to the monolithic drift into repression is important. It underlines what the Birmingham project was about: namely an attempt to identify why the social democratic consensus, at that time with a Labour government, was coming apart. In order to prevent such anarchy, of which groups as different as 'muggers', strikers, and football hooligans were seen by the state as examples, a sense of crisis had to be engineered in order to re-establish social control. The danger was, as the Birmingham group saw it, that British society would become in the process an authoritarian state. What remained a difficulty was that while it was explicitly denied that this was a conspiracy theory, the notion of engineering a crisis in order to re-establish control does look like one. It was a state response to incipient disorder. The media, wittingly or unwittingly, reproduce the definitions of the powerful. But, at the same time, it remains unclear who the agents are who are operating in such an anticipatory way. As Barker points out, in a critical review of the study, the emphasis on structures tends to give a feeling of agentless acts. The problem of agency, he contends, constantly retreats from view. For example, when we are told that the police and the judiciary are crucial actors in the drama of the moral panic but are acting out a script they did not write, it is reasonable to ask who did write it (Barker, 1992).

If we are to understand the relationship between what is termed the control culture, the media, and the public we really need to know more, for example, about the relationship between journalists and their sources, about the variations that exist within the world of journalism, about news values and their salience, and about how the public receive and respond to media messages (Miller and Reilly, 1994). We need an approach that can take account of struggles for definitions and interpretations that take place between contending groups. This is much more untidy, although it should be emphasized that it still tries to take into the reckoning questions of power and control. We will illustrate this with some more recent examples.

Take first media representations about AIDS (see Miller and Kitzinger, 1996). As early as 1988, Kaye Wellings reported on the coverage of the topic in the national press for the period 1983–5. In her view, AIDS gained a large amount of media attention for two reasons. There was first the seriousness of the disease itself, for which there was no known cure. Secondly, 'in the popular imagination it has been associated with forms of sexual behaviour which have provided opportunities for sensationalist and voyeuristic reporting' (Wellings, 1988: 83). She also noted that there was resistance to evidence critical of the view that AIDS was an exclusively gay disease. We might say that there was a clear case for the development of a moral panic. Indeed, Wellings noted that the term 'gay plague' was used in the tabloids and also in the quality press. Thus *The Observer* on 26 June 1983 ran a piece titled 'Gay Plague Sets Off Panic'. Moreover, the language of blame and retribution could figure. John Junor, *The Sunday Express* columnist, wrote on 10 February 1985: 'If AIDS is not an Act of God with consequences just as frightful as fire and brimstone, then just what the hell is it?' And Peregrine Worsthorne wrote in *The Sunday Telegraph* in similar vein:

Is it not time that the bishops brought God into the act, since one suspects that religious fanatics—condemned by homosexuals as ignorant bigots—who talk about the wrath of God may know more about the cause of the disease, and its cure, than at present do all the scientists working together? (10 February 1985)

From this it would already appear that the bishops were not playing their role as laid down in Cohen's original formulation.

In work conducted by the Glasgow Media Group on media representations of AIDS after the Wellings study it was still possible to find statements that used the language of threat and panic (Glasgow University

Media Group, forthcoming). On World AIDS Day, 2 December 1988, *The Daily Star*, in its editorial, proposed 'leper-like' colonies:

Surely, if the human race is under threat, it is entirely REASONABLE to segregate AIDS victims otherwise the whole of mankind could be engulfed. Some experts have even suggested that off-shore islands should be used for colonies. Pro-homosexual groups like the Terence Higgins Trust will scream that it is unfair. But they would . . .

A moral panic thesis would expect that this kind of comment had originated from primary definers, from political and moral sources, which would in turn provide the basis for repressive action from the control culture. But the opposite was the case. The political campaign for 'safer sex' was directed at the heterosexual and homosexual population. And the media split on the issue, some contesting the validity of the campaign and others endorsing it.

A position antagonistic to the government's campaign was taken up by *The Sun*. Under the heading 'AIDS—THE FACTS NOT THE FICTION', it made the following editorial comment:

At last the truth can be told. The killer disease AIDS can only be caught by homosexuals, bisexuals, junkies or anyone who has received a tainted blood transfusion. FORGET the television adverts, FORGET the poster campaigns, forget the endless boring TV documentaries and forget the idea that ordinary heterosexual people can catch AIDS. They can't. The risk of catching AIDS if you are heterosexual is 'statistically invisible', in other words, impossible. So now we know—anything else is just homosexual propaganda. And should be treated accordingly. (17 November 1989)

The above editorial, and its associated treatment of Lord Kilbracken's claim that official figures showed the government's health education message to be unjustified, was subject to an adjudication by the Press Council. The report was described as misleading in its interpretation and the headline a gross distortion of the statistical information supplied by the minister. The editorial, said the Press Council, compounded the distortion. At the same time, *The Sun* and *The Daily Star* ran stories that contradicted their own editorial line. On 20 July 1991, for example, there was a feature beginning: 'SEX-SPREE HOLIDAY BRITS IN AIDS PERIL . . . British girls are ignoring the terrifying risk of AIDS to go on sex orgies in the sun. And many admit they do not make holiday lovers wear a condom. *Sun* reporter Antonella went to the Greek holiday island of Rhodes to investigate . . .' In similar manner, *The Daily Star* reported on sex tourism in Thailand, where the bar girls were depicted as Angels of Death (7 September 1995).

But other tabloid newspapers supported the government's health education campaign, notably *The Mirror* and *Today. The Mirror*'s news, features, and editorials were routinely supportive. At the time when *The Star* was calling for AIDS colonies, *The Mirror* feature for World AIDS Day commented:

And what we must never forget is that there is still no cure or vaccine for AIDS. So the way to stop its spread is through information, education and changes in human behaviour. Only then will there be any hope of curing this deadly scourge. (1 December 1988)

Nearly three years later, under the title 'AIDS PERIL WE STILL IGNORE', *Today* drew attention to its own commissioned research showing evidence that 'millions of people are continuing to ignore the safe sex messages' and commented:

the sad truth is that everyone, irrespective of their sexuality, who is sexually active but not in a monogamous relationship, runs a risk of contracting the HIV virus. Radio and television adverts using real people have made the point powerfully and it is impossible to believe that those at risk do not understand their message. Yet, as their response to our survey shows, the campaign must continue. (5 August 1991)

What we observe then are real differences within the media, sometimes within the same newspaper. Moreover, we see a Conservative government mounting a campaign that did not fit the beliefs of the moral right. We can see a vocabulary that includes 'threat', 'scourge', 'peril', and 'plague', yet the 'primary definers' did not endorse the problem in terms of moral panic. Of course, insofar as there was outright opposition from some quarters of the press, they were not primary definers at all (further discussion is to be found in Beharrell, 1993).

The significance of this point can be further underlined. In their discussion of the ways in which HIV/AIDS information is negotiated, Miller and Williams show that the process of media production is an arena of contest and negotiation, in which official sources cannot always take it for granted that they will be able to set the agenda (Miller and Williams, 1993). Even when a government campaign strategy is in place it is not a straightforward matter to get it into media outlets. The ability to do so in this case was affected by health educators' distrust of the media, the educators' own relationship with the Department of Health, and the low status of health educators in the eyes of the media. The government had to win support rather than take it for granted. Its success with the press was, as we have seen, variable. From television and radio it received support and commitment to the campaign. Moreover, it proved possible for the Terence Higgins Trust, a campaign group, to establish itself as a credible source alongside 'official' sources. It is the element of negotiation between journalists and their sources which is worth stressing here. Whereas journalists may want to stress their investigative role in relation to their own news values, drawing attention to cover-ups or incompetence, lobby groups need to establish their own credibility and to develop a proactive role in order to bring to the attention of the press things they want to be made public.

Let us take a further example from the study of media representations of child sexual abuse. Kitzinger and Skidmore undertook a study of the production, content, and reception of press and television coverage of sexual violence against children. This included a content analysis of all press and TV coverage of the topic in 1991 (Kitzinger and Skidmore, 1995a,b). They pointed out the lack of attention given to either the causes or the prevention of child abuse. But the stories do have their folk devils, part of the original vocabulary for describing moral panics. This turned out to be so in a double sense: the treatment of social workers as a category and the actual topic of ritual abuse and satanic practices. Within the context of child sexual abuse cases a number of public agencies come routinely into the reckoning: social workers, the police, the medical profession, and the legal profession. In the 1991 sample, 81 per cent of reports about sexual abuse prevention focused on social workers and 19 per cent on the other three. The image portrayed is largely a negative one.

The Sun, under the headline 'Tyrants Stopped Dying Dad Seeing Kids', described the investigation of a case of alleged abuse as being part of 'the growing catalogue of incidents of jackboot behaviour' and their columnist, Richard Littlejohn, wrote that the children in the case had been 'interrogated by social workers—their narrow minds no doubt filled with the latest theories about satanic sex and hobgoblins' (24 January 1991). It is almost as though we have moved from the metaphor to the reality of folk devils. Under the heading 'Sack the Lot and Start Again', David Marsland wrote in *The Mail*:

the fact remains that social workers have moved from amateurs with common sense and not too much power, to 'experts' with unbridled powers and heads filled with zealous ideology so for the sake of all the broken-hearted families, we must get rid of the social workers and think again. (5 April 1991)

Occasionally, another voice could be heard, as in *The Daily Express* on 12 April 1991:

An expert in child psychiatry claimed yesterday that social workers and the childrens' hearing system in the Orkney ritual abuse affair had been made 'scapegoats' by society. Professor Fred Stone warned that the sheriff's dismissal of the case last week had already produced a dangerous backlash which could mean genuine cases of child abuse being ignored.

What is interesting in terms of the news reports is the way social workers are singled out. While arguments can be advanced quite properly as to the appropriateness of particular kinds of intervention, no attempt was made to consider the reasons behind the actions. The police, for example, who are closely involved in such interventions as part of their criminal investigations, do not get referenced in this way. This kind of scapegoating displaces discussions about causes and prevention of child sexual abuse. That is why the Head of Press at the Royal Scottish Society for the Protection of Children said in interview with the researchers:

I say that the minute you give the journalist or the media the opportunity to sensationalize the issue, it moves into the realms, further into the realms of disbelief or incredulity for the public . . . so that creates a climate whereby people find it very hard to believe and that makes the whole issue of informing the debate very difficult. It certainly makes the whole issue of protecting children or leading prosecutions much more difficult.

Yet although the scapegoating of social workers was clear enough in the media, the relationship of the media to the 'control culture' has almost been the obverse of moral panic. The public controversy, generated by the media, concerning the contention that in some cases children subject to sexual abuse had also been subject to bizarre rites, variously referred to as witchcraft, satanism, or devil worship, led the government to commission a report. This was undertaken by the social anthropologist, Professor Jean La Fontaine. She examined all the case material available and came to the conclusion that there was no evidence of satanic abuse and only three cases where ritual abuse had occurred. She concluded that 'concern with satanic abuse draws attention away from the very serious state of this minority of damaged children. An excitingly dramatic but unicausal explanation replaces careful assessment of the many causes of their disturbing behaviour' (La Fontaine, 1994: 31). Her conclusion is significant in that it argues that myth-making of this kind can distract attention from what is actually happening and, therefore, what can or should be done.

A belief in evil cults is convincing because it draws on powerful cultural axioms. People are reluctant to accept that parents, even those classed as social failures, will harm their own children, and even invite others to do so, but involvement with the devil explains it. The notion that unknown, powerful leaders control the cult revives an old myth of dangerous strangers. Demonizing the marginal poor and linking them to unknown satanists turns intractable cases of abuse into manifestations of evil (La Fontaine, 1994: 31).

But whether we like it or not the term 'moral panic' has now entered into the public domain and is no longer just the property of sociologists. We have seen the term used in relation to the police treatment of New Age travellers, to questions of pornography, to single-parent families, to the violence of young children, to controversies about satanic and ritual abuse, and indeed to the welfare state itself. These are certainly topics which surface in the mass media in Britain. Moral panic actually becomes a topic for discussion in the press rather than the press simply being a site for amplification. A good example of this concerns single-parent families. In 1993, for example, *The Guardian* ran an editorial titled 'The Moral Panic and the Facts'. This was a comment on the Conservative Party conference:

what many feared was going to be a 'cost panic' conference over welfare expenditure turned instead into a 'moral panic' over unmarried mothers. Mr. Howard [the Home Secretary], along with several of his Cabinet colleagues, made much of the myths of single parenthood, the suggestion that higher benefits encourage single women to 'marry the state' and have children; direct causal links between lone parent families and juvenile crime; and the single teenagers who become pregnant to jump housing queues. We now know that each of these myths had already been knocked flat in a special Cabinet briefing paper . . . (9 November 1993)

It is the invention and creation of myths that remains important. These are things that are untrue in the generality even if particular instances may be identified of a confirming nature. In this case the myth provides the justification for proposing punitive measures such as the withdrawal of benefits entitlements and new restrictions on access to housing. Why bother to commission the Cabinet report in the first place in which the myths had been destroyed? *The Guardian* drew the conclusion that 'they have clearly abandoned rational policy-making in favour of undiluted political prejudice' (9 November 1993).

Here, clearly, is an attempt both to examine and to criticize the government's position. But the editorial is explicitly refusing to concur with what standard moral panic theory would hold to be the primary definers. And on the same topic, when the BBC's *Panorama* ran a programme entitled 'Babies on Benefit', its conclusion, based on the study of part of a Welsh housing estate which suggested that young women were having babies to jump the housing queue, as already argued by the then Minister of State for Wales, John Redwood, was strongly challenged on empirical grounds. It became the subject of a successful complaint to the Broadcasting Complaints Commission. In this respect, therefore, issues which are talked about in terms of moral panic do not get a free, uninterrupted run on well-oiled ideological media tracks.

Nowadays, the concept of moral panic is both used and criticized by journalists. A recent example, which connects with the single-parent issue, is to be found in Will Hutton's feature article 'A State of Decay' (Hutton, 1995). He argues that the cross-party consensus about the role of the welfare state in Britain has been split asunder:

The shared post-war belief that social insurance should provide for life's inevitable hazards and taxes should pay for collective goods like education and health is no more. In the face of a lethal cocktail of moral panic, tendentious claims about affordability and the Conservative crusade for more individualism, the forces holding the welfare state together are crumbling; we look set to abandon one of our great 20th century achievements for no good reason.

The moral panic he refers to is precisely about single parents, which he does see as being engineered by the government. There is a much more central cause for concern, he argues. Despite the fact that study after study about unemployed men shows that they are very much wanting to work, there are still 1.6 million unemployed men and two million men of working age (excluding students) are economically inactive. Essentially, we are running an economy with a reserve army of unemployed, which is one of the prices we pay for low inflation. The trade unions have been weakened, companies are pressurized to achieve impossibly high financial returns, and the competitive international context has had a desperate effect on people struggling with poverty and unemployment. Yet, Hutton maintains, this has had little impact on public debate and media interviewers questioning politicians about tax cuts are silent. Yet to redefine the issue would be an important agenda-setting shift:

Besides the tens of billions spent on men—a return to male full employment would save the Treasury £36 billion in social security spending and foregone taxes—the £5.5 billion spent on single parents and £8 billion spent on child benefit is comparatively small. The ideas for cutting the spending—taxing child benefit and restricting allowances for more than one child—are flea-bites. They would raise trifling sums and do little to arrest the growth of a social security budget driven by demographics and the advance of poverty.

What is interesting about this analysis is that it challenges the attempt to create a moral panic. Moreover, it does so on the grounds that the issue of single parents both in diagnosis and solution is a dangerous digression from a realistic appraisal about the economic and political situation we are in. The real issue for him is social cohesion. If we approach such issues in terms of the illusions created by moral panic we may, as a society, contribute to our own destruction.

Chapter Six

Photo-Journalism: Every Picture Tells a Story

The development of the practice of photography in nineteenth-century Britain is associated with names such as Thomas Annan (1829–87), Julia Cameron (1815–79), Roger Fenton (1819–69), David Octavius Hill (1802–70), Robert Adamson (1821–48), Paul Martin (1864–1944), Frank Sutcliffe (1853–1941), and William Fox Talbot (1800–77). Annan produced a series of photographs on the old closes and streets of Glasgow. If we look at those pictures and again if we look at Paul Martin's photograph of street urchins in London taken in 1898, we can see in Oscar Marzaroli's Glasgow photographs (Marzaroli, 1984) and Bert Hardy's pictures of slum life in London's Elephant and Castle and Glasgow's Gorbals a continuity with those pioneers. As social documents such photographs are invaluable, no doubt containing details which the photographer did not see or think about at the time. Outside Britain there are photographs to be found of the American Civil War, the Crimean War, and the dead Paris Communards of 1871.

Photo-journalism was to find its outlets in the twentieth-century press and notably in weeklies such as *Life* magazine in the United States and *Picture Post* in Britain, both of which were begun in the 1930s. *Picture Post* was explicitly aware of the history of photography. In 1939 it ran a series titled 'The History of a Hundred Years in Photography'. The Indian Mutiny of 1857 was the subject on 3 June 1939. These included scenes of destroyed buildings, of bones on a Delhi battlefield, of public hangings. One picture was taken by Octavius Hill of two Gordon Highlanders standing by a cannon at Lucknow. Similarly, the Crimean War was treated on 20 May 1939. This included a picture by Roger Fenton of British infantry piling arms, described as one of the first war photographs ever taken. Another of his, entitled 'When War

Becomes Boring', shows three soldiers wearily waiting to be relieved, while a fourth kept watch.

Primarily, of course, *Picture Post* existed to cover the news of the day in a popular, extensively illustrated way, alongside feature articles. The 20 May number, for example, carried pictorial features which included 'Newmarket Prepares for the Derby', 'Toscanini Conducts', 'Bond Street', 'Against the Nazis', 'Children's Museum', 'A Week-End with the Crazy Gang', 'Some Flowers and Some Faces', 'The Importance of Knees', and 'The West Indian Cricketers'. The mixture is of sport, fashion, celebrities, human interest, and politics. We should note that 'Against the Nazis' dealt with the ways in which anti-Nazis in Germany produced and distributed their propaganda material at risk of their lives. Even so, the 3 June 1939 number could still manage a pictorial feature on 'Berlin on a Sunny Day'. There we see the pictures of the open-air café, the shoppers and the soldiers and, under the title 'A Berlin Girl Goes Home', we read: 'Tall, well-dressed, attractive typical product of Western civilisation. What does civilisation hold in store for her?'

Among the photo-journalists at *Picture Post* from 1941 to 1957 (when it ceased publication) was Bert Hardy. His photographs included those which highlighted social conditions in Britain, as already noted, but he published memorable photographs of London in the Blitz and later went to Normandy soon after D-Day, was present at the liberation of Paris, and was among the first party of reporters to enter Belsen in April 1944. He was much sought after by journalists of the calibre of James Cameron, Kenneth Allsop, Ann Scott James, and Sydney Jacobson. It was with James Cameron that Hardy went to Korea. The UN had intervened in the war between North and South Korea (1950–3). There they witnessed, wrote about, and photographed the brutal treatment meted out to North Korean prisoners. These activities took place close to the UN headquarters in Seoul. The editor of *Picture Post*, Tom Hopkinson, was prepared to publish but he was overruled by the proprietor, Edward Hulton. Hopkinson was sacked. James Cameron reported that the magazine *Public Opinion* commented:

The despatches from Korea which *Picture Post* had published up to now have been distinguished by two things, their obvious integrity and their technical brilliance. That this valuable combination should be snuffed out by a peremptory managerial decision is more than a matter for regret: it is a denial of a genuine but highly inconvenient comment on a situation that involves several thousand British troops and at least ten million British tax payers . . . Many years ago the men of goodwill could not be so summarily deprived of their posts as public commentators at the whim of irresponsible persons who employed them, and who had profited from their talents and integrity. That these things should occur now is a surly comment on our society. (in Cameron, 1985: 147–8)

The issue of proprietorial power has already been discussed, but this was a legendary instance. Cameron concluded that by the time *Picture Post* went out of business it had lost its cutting edge and distinctive character. More generally it disappeared at the time when television was moving centre stage, bringing moving pictures and news bulletins into people's homes night after night.

Another English pioneer of photo-journalism was George Rodger, whose career paralleled Bert Hardy's. He worked with the American magazine *Life* during the Second World War. His stated intention was to influence his American readership. He wanted his photographs of the Blitz to show how much Britain needed American help in the war. His experience of taking photographs in Belsen was for him horrific and decisive. He determined never to photograph war again or to make profit from other people's misery:

I lived with the horrors of war for a very long time. It's one of those sorts of things that does eventually fade with the seasons because the memory's like a herbaceous border. But I couldn't look at the Belsen pictures for a good 45 years. They lay in a box and did nothing. I think, at last, they no longer have the power to affect me. (quoted in *The Observer*, 4 June 1995)

He became a founder member of the photographic agency Magnum, which included some of the greatest names in photo-journalism, including Robert Capa, Henri-Cartier Bresson, Maria Eisner, and David Seymour (see Rodger, 1995).

It is images of war that have taken up so much of the efforts of photo-journalists and we must reflect further on the power and problems of these images. We can get an important clue about the emergence of this kind of photography when Robert Hughes comments upon the way the First World War was covered in the European press:

After the catastrophes of Verdun and the Somme, this generation—or, at least, those of it who had done time in the trenches—knew it had been lied to. Its generals, bunglers like Haig, and cattle herders like Joffre, had lied about the nature and length of the war. Its politicians had lied about its causes, and a compliant and self-censoring press had seen to it that very little of the realities of war, not even a photo of a corpse, found its way into any French, German or British newspaper. Never had there been a wider gap between official language and perceived reality. (Hughes, 1980: 59)

Hughes also argued that war photography rendered the war artist negligible. For him, Picasso's famous painting, *Guernica*, a response to the German bombing of the capital city of the Basque Republic during the Spanish Civil War, was 'the last modern painting of major importance that took its subject from politics with the intention of changing the way large numbers of people thought and felt about power' (Hughes, 1980: 110). Through the mass media, the commentary which contextualized its presence in the Spanish pavilion at the Paris World Exhibition in 1937, its political message was amplified and endorsed. But this was against the current in that war photography was seen as being more credible and presumably, therefore, more effective.

With this in mind, consider Robert Capa's photograph, which was to make him world famous, of a soldier in the Spanish Civil War. It appeared in various places but most notably in *Life* magazine (12 July 1937) with the caption: 'Robert Capa's camera catches a Spanish soldier the instant he is dropped by a bullet through the head in front of Cordoba.' Capa himself used to say that 'the truth is the best picture, the best propaganda' (cited by Ritchin in Manchester, 1989), but the status of this widely acclaimed picture remains a matter of controversy. Philip Knightley (1982: 194) points out that the picture is essentially an ambiguous image. Capa himself never left an account of the circumstances in which it was taken. Where was the photograph taken? Could it have been a behind-the-lines staged manoeuvre for the benefit of the photographer? Was Capa the photographer? All these questions have been raised. But war correspondents Martha Gelhorn and John Hersey believed it was authentic. Hersey referred to a conversation he had with Capa, which convinced him that it was indeed a picture of a man at the moment of death. Knightley is not so sure since the story as told rested on a million-to-one chance of a camera framing the soldier at precisely the moment he was hit. The soldier still has his cap on and there is no sign of a wound, let alone explosion of the skull. Knightley concludes that like so many other things in time of war the photograph cannot be taken as the simple fact the caption would have us assume. The external evidence of authentication is not decisive. None of this stopped it from having immense symbolic value at the time as an anti-fascist statement and, as a result of its widespread circulation over the years, as a representation of the fight for freedom against right-wing dictators.

It is, then, the notion of the neutral photograph (as opposed to the committed art) which cannot be sustained. Fred Ritchin (1989) suggests that the best photographers know that despite the many visible details, the photograph can conceal and that even what it shows can be ambiguous:

Those photographers working in the mass media are also aware that distant editors, exercising other points of view and having the overriding stylistic or editorial interests of their own publication in mind, can markedly change the intended meaning of the photographers' images. This can be accomplished with captions and titles that redirect, or even contradict, the photographer's original intent, taking advantage of the image's ambiguity . . . It is also possible when cropping and sequencing photographs in a particular layout to transform and sometimes corrupt their intended meaning by creating different visual contexts: placing a car advertisement next to an image of famine victims might trivialise their desperate circumstance . . . (Ritchin, 1989: 417–18)

The mechanical fidelity of the photograph, which was seen to give it 'objectivity' over and against the 'subjectivity' of the artist, is now routinely questioned. It does not reveal truth in an unmediated way. It is a medium whose products have to be understood in the context of conflicting values, competing interests, and all the selectivity and, at times, propaganda that go with it. Yet photo-journalism remains very much with us in the press and, not least, in the colour supplements of the weekend press. And, just as *Picture Post* could look back into the history of photography, so now contemporary newspapers will give us retrospectives on the likes of Cartier-Bresson and Rodger. Thus *The Independent on Sunday* on 2 July 1995 gives the front page of its Review Supplement to a picture of Cartier-Bresson, with pictures recently rediscovered in the Paris Magnum Agency on London in the 1950s. These are, we are told, examples of Cartier-Bresson's work which have captured 'decisive moments' about the essence of the human condition the world over. Reference is also made to the aesthetic qualities of the photographs, which brings us back full circle to art. And it is Cartier-Bresson who makes a conscious link. When the photo-journalist Don McCullin showed an exhibition of his work in Paris, in 1994, it was Cartier-Bresson who said to him: 'I have one word to say to you—Goya' (in McCullin, 1995: 15).

Every Picture Tells a Story

We might better say, every picture tells more than one story. Here we look at some examples and instances of visual material which are in the public domain. There are pictures, photographs, cartoons, films, and videos that are intended for a wide audience—people who are not likely to be connected in any way with one another as a totality, but share in common exposure to the images. The purposes of these pictures may be manifold—education and instruction, entertainment and pleasure, persuasion and propaganda, advertising and publicity—and, as anyone who has seen advertisements can attest, different purposes can co-exist.

Figure 6.1 A French shop in London pre-empts anti-French protests (*Guardian*, 9 September 1995)

Rather than give some developed theoretical statement here, for example about encoding and decoding, let us work with some instances.

Figure 6.1 appeared in *The Guardian* newspaper on 9 September 1995. Consider first that you are reading a book which is reproducing a picture from a newspaper which in turn has taken a picture from another newspaper, the French newspaper, *Libération*. With each change we can say that the picture is being recontextualized. *Libération*, for example, is only part of the *Guardian* picture, and we are now reproducing it in the context of additional comment. We can see that it is a front page picture in both newspapers, which, conventionally, gives it high news value from the editorial perspective. How do we make sense of the picture? We are given verbal clues, which is usually the case in press photographs. Indeed, *The Guardian* provides a headline for the *Libération* picture, in which the word 'French' occurs twice, and a text underneath which allows us to identify the man in the picture as the French President, Jacques Chirac. We can see that the face of the President is disfigured. Why should this be? Although the *Libération* text can scarcely be read, we can see, in bold red print, 'Mururoa son amour'. In case we do not know what all this refers to, most unlikely given the television and press coverage, we are referred to page 2 for a 'full report'. The reference is indeed to the French government's decision to undertake nuclear tests in the South Pacific at Mururoa. There we learn from two Paris-based correspondents that the ruling party had taken out full-page advertisements in the national press to counteract opposition from other political parties and from Greenpeace. This was described as a public relations battle. As a result of this and other available information, for example about the boycotting of French products, we can fill out our own understanding about the significance of the picture. As for the child in the picture (who might be male or female) we can see the contrast between the man and the child. In our culture we might read particular things into it—the innocence of the child versus the guilt of the President, or the significance of nuclear tests for future generations. None of this means that we all read the picture in exactly the same way, despite all the verbal assistance (not everyone will read the full report anyway). Those who agree with the French President could see the protests as misconceived and the picture of the disfigured President as dishonouring his office and his nation, and therefore harbour hostile thoughts about *Libération* and *The Guardian*. Yet, at the time the picture was taken, there are enough clues and references within the picture and in terms of other available information, widely disseminated in the media, to make sense of it and to appreciate its political connotations. It does not stand isolated and unsupported.

The second instance is also from *The Guardian* (18 September 1995). It is a front page photograph which is evidently contrived. The subject is the Liberal Democrat leader Paddy Ashdown who was in Glasgow to attend his party's annual conference. He is framed against the background of a bridge which gives the appearance of angel wings sprouting from his shoulders. The caption reads: 'Wings and a prayer'. Here there is a simple connection made between a visual trick and a verbal pun—'wings and a prayer'. The phrase itself goes back to the RAF in the Second World War when pilots sometimes brought their damaged planes back to base with a mixture of skill and luck. Here the comment can be applied to the party leader or to his party. With more information or political knowledge we could 'read' more into the picture. Where is the Liberal Democrat Party going given the changes in the leadership and direction of the Labour Party? Does not the party remain marginal to British political life as it has done for the last seventy years? The picture itself remains at the surface of political life, with a humorous allusion. Yet it can set off a range of connotations and judgements derived from other sources and previous knowledge.

More generally, we may notice that pictures (including film, of course) of politicians, which may have been contrived or staged at a particular time for particular purposes, can be recycled in ways which are intended to give new or different meanings. A picture of Mrs Thatcher, then Prime Minister, surveying a scene of urban dereliction in the North-East of England, was originally used to depict her stated intention to 'do something' about urban blight and industrial decline. It was a 'photo opportunity' for the press. The same picture could be used and applied by her political opponents several years later to suggest that she signally failed to deliver. The same site, still derelict, could be used in similar fashion to signify failure rather than success.

In the summer of 1995, a picture of Prime Minister John Major, Tony Blair, leader of the Labour Party, and Paddy Ashdown was widely circulated. They were all smiling at one another in a non-adversarial way. This prompted the question: what were they talking about? The truth (if such it be) was eventually leaked by Ashdown that it had to do with the state of health of the Prime Minister's goldfish during a period of drought and what he was doing about it. Thus, whether or not to our satisfaction, the ambiguity of the photograph of the three smiling men is resolved. In *Another Way of Telling*, the writer John Berger and the photographer Jean Mohr explore the issue of ambiguity. They suggest that

a photograph is a meeting place where the interests of the photographer, the photographed, the viewer and those who are using the photograph are often contradictory. These contradictions both hide and increase the natural ambiguity of the photographic image. (Berger and Mohr, 1982: 7)

Mohr went on to illustrate this in a simple way by showing a series of photographs which he had taken to a number of people, asking them to say what they were about. Without any verbal clues or additional information their responses varied considerably. What the photographer had done and what he had intended to convey was by no means generally grasped. It was not possible to tell, for example, that a young person, seated amidst tree blossoms, was a young man attending a demonstration against the Vietnam War, staged in Washington in 1971. He had climbed the tree to see better and take his own photographs. When we know this, we can bring our own interpretations to bear upon the photograph in relation to the event, but we need to know this if we are to connect with the photographer's intentions.

According to the cliché, the camera cannot lie. If we recognize the force of Berger's concerns with the power of the image, how it is used and for what purposes, we can scarcely let such a cliché remain undisturbed. According to Berger,

We are surrounded by photographic images which constitute a global system of misinformation: the system known as publicity, proliferating consumerist lies. The role of photography in this system is revealing. The lie is constructed before the camera. A 'tableau' of objects and figures is assembled. This 'tableau' uses a language of symbols (often inherited . . . from the iconography of oil painting), an implied narrative and, frequently, some kind of performance by models with a sexual content. This 'tableau' is then photographed. It is photographed precisely because the camera can bestow authenticity upon any set of appearances, however false. The camera does not lie even when it is used to quote a lie. And so, this makes the lie *appear* more truthful. (Berger and Mohr, 1982: 96–7)

Already then we can notice two distinctions that need to be taken into account. There is the photographer's intention (and interpretation) and there is the viewer's. Alongside this there is the difference between appearance and 'reality'. Yet this suggests to us that there are two quite different kinds of processes. One is to clarify, to disclose and reveal what otherwise might not be known or at least be doubted. The other is to deceive by deliberate contrivance, to suggest that things are other than they are. Thus, there are photographs and film of concentration camps which become part of the historical record. The images testify to that reality and become part of it. But the public relations advertisement for a product or a political party can become part of the mechanism and technique of deception, notwithstanding the requirement that advertisements are supposed to be honest.

With this in mind, let us take another example. The fashion house

Comme des Garçons produced a clothes show on the theme of sleep in Paris, in January 1995. The photograph in *The Independent on Sunday* (5 February 1995) was of an instance of clothing that was strongly criticized by the World Jewish Congress among others. Not only did the clothing give the appearance of the uniforms of Auschwitz victims (coinciding with the 50th anniversary of the relief of Auschwitz), but two male models appeared with shaved heads modelling striped pyjamas with numbers on them. While the head of the fashion house, Adrian Joffe, said that the connection was totally unintentional and referred to the date of these two events as a 'terrible coincidence', the designer of the clothes, Rei Kawakubo, was quoted as saying 'the meaning is there is no meaning.' Such a flip phrase is difficult to take seriously since fashion is about ways of constructing identity through clothes and accessories. It is an important aspect of the management of appearance. More generally iconography from the Nazi period, including jackboots, uniforms, and insignia, have been used in fashion contexts. We can scarcely make sense of it without reference back to its origins, even if the wearers or designers wish to insist that the meanings are ironical or playful. Indeed, they can be neither of those things if the original context of their display is not known. Symbols are never without meaning. Clothes, fashion, images, photographs are iconic. Compare the statement that 'the meaning is there is no meaning' with Susan Sontag's reflective comment on photography:

One's first encounter with the photographic inventory of ultimate horror is a kind of revelation: a negative epiphany. For me, it was the photographs of Bergen-Belsen and Dachau which I came across by chance in a book store in Santa Monica in July 1945. Nothing I have seen—in photographs or real life—ever cut me as sharply, deeply, instantaneously. Indeed, it seems plausible to me to divide my life into two parts, before I saw those photographs (I was twelve at the time) and after, although it was several years before I understood fully what they were about. (cited in Berger, 1980: 57)

But it is the case that with the passage of time and in changed circumstances we can look at past images in a different way from those for whom they were originally intended. The next example is a picture of Hitler in the Reichstag in September 1939. It was reproduced in *The Guardian* (22 April 1995) as part of a series of articles on the VE Day anniversary. The verbal message helps to transform our reading of the picture: 'Theatre of complicity . . . Adolf Hitler receives a standing ovation from his acolytes when addressing the Reichstag in September 1939 to announce the declaration of war against Poland.' We can be sure that that was not how it was originally signalled. Within the one picture there is a panoply of reinforcing symbols: the German Eagle, the Nazi swastika, the Führer in the centre receiving the Nazi salute. But the caption now used recontextualizes the message, as does the knowledge of what came after. What was once a propaganda photograph is now part of a record which helps us to understand propaganda rather than be seduced by it. It is salutary to compare this photograph with the first example of the current Liberal Democratic leader, Paddy Ashdown, which registers so differently upon us, not least for its playfulness and intended humour.

The framing and contextualising of the picture by a language commentary becomes an important routine tool for the communication of meaning. Consider the way the next picture operates (Figure 6.2). Here we have a young man kneeling. There are logo-type symbols designating the Church of England and the Nine O'Clock Service. With that information, we can see more faintly in the background the image of a crucified person. This appeared in *The Observer* on 27 August 1995. The reason for it was the disclosure by the Church of England that Chris Brain, an Anglican priest and leader of a worshipping community in Sheffield, had confessed to practising sexual abuse on members of his congregation. It is Chris Brain in the picture and we are now invited to

Figure 6.2 A cult, From Genesis to Revelations (*Observer*, 27 August 1995)

reconsider what the photograph represents. There is the headline with the biblical resonance: 'A Cult, from Genesis to Revelations'. There is a quote by the side of the picture from an essay written by Brain from a book associated with the Archbishop of Canterbury, where the theme of abuse is emphasized. And there is a feature article by the journalists Peter Beaumont and Martin Wroe. They describe what took place in Sheffield as an experiment in Anglican evangelical worship for the young generation. Brain had called it 'the Planetary Mass of the Nine O'Clock Service' and used elements from the club scene—banks of video screens, a dance floor without chairs, and 'chill out' ambient music. A multi-media activity no less. How, they ask, did the activity turn into a cult? 'Pictures of the priest provide a clue. Behind the dark, softly primped Pre-Raphaelite curls and the pouting lips lies a suggestion of vanity. In one photograph Brain's hair is framed by a projected circular logo: the appearance of a halo is perhaps not entirely accidental.' By these linguistic interpolations, we are invited to see the photograph in ways which may not have been originally intended. We can say that our reading of the photograph and its significance is no longer innocent.

Chapter Seven

The Royal Family and the Media

Today it is common to refer to the relationship between royalty and the media in terms of a soap opera. The royal family is the subject of endless storytelling, speculation, and gossip. The press is never far away, from the tabloids, with their royal watchers, gossip columnists, and paparazzi photographers, to the broadsheets with their reflections on the monarchy and its future. Bookshops like Smith's, Menzies, and Waterstone's will carry biographies of members of the royal family, periodicals like *Hello!* will carry stories about younger members of the royal family. At the same time satirical magazines like *Private Eye* will offer sceptical comment and cartoons. Thus the Queen recently featured on the cover of *Private Eye* looking through the sights of a machine gun with the caption 'I don't think a divorce will be necessary'. In similar vein, the royal family featured regularly in the long-running puppet series *Spitting Image*. Let us consider some recent happenings that have been interpreted in the soap opera vein.

In 1995, members of the British royal family continued to be a pervasive presence in the media. The Princess of Wales, variously known in the media as HRH Princess Diana, Diana, and Di, gave her interview to BBC's *Panorama*, which became the subject of intensive and extensive comment and speculation in all parts of the media. She had already been the subject of a biography, and she confirmed in the interview that friends of hers had supplied the author with information and opinions. The Prince of Wales, in 1994, had already participated in a documentary on his life and future with the journalist Jonathan Dimbleby, who also wrote a book alongside the television programme. In their interviews, both the Prince and Princess admitted to extramarital affairs. One of the Princess's lovers wrote a book about it and was branded a 'cad' for doing so. The media also reported on the friendship between the Princess and the England Rugby Union captain, Will Carling, and the subsequent break-up of his marriage. There was, from time to time, speculation about whether the Duke and Duchess of York would mend their broken marriage and a flurry of interest when jewellery belonging to the Duchess, a gift from the Queen, was stolen at a New York airport and later recovered. 'Who Grabbed Fergie's Baubles?' asked the *Sun* headline (6 December 1995). The romance of Prince Edward with Sophie Rhys-Jones was reported on, together with speculation as to marriage plans. 'Public relations girl Sophie, 30, will now concentrate on preparing for her future career as a Princess' (*Sun*, 30 November 1995).

The Queen Mother, now in her nineties, had a hip replacement operation. The comings and goings around this were observed. The Queen Mother does not give interviews or comment directly to the press, although on her birthday she meets well-wishers outside her home at Kensington Palace. But, as usual, when well enough, she has appeared in various ceremonial occasions with other members of the royal family. Over the years these have included events such as the Trooping of the Colour, the memorial gatherings at the Cenotaph, Ascot Races and the Derby, the Edinburgh Tattoo, Royal Command Variety Shows at the Palladium. In 1995, there were special national events to celebrate victory, fifty years after VE Day and VJ Day. Since the Queen Mother was, during the war, King George VI's Queen, there were cultural resonances consciously evoked on those occasions. Other cultural resonances sounded when a Channel 4 documentary in the *Secret Lives* series and media comment around it drew attention to Edward VIII's sympathies towards Nazi Germany. This story had a much harder edge than the perennial media stories about his abdication in 1936 and celebrity-style stories about the Duke and Duchess of Windsor which, in times past, were a staple part of royal news, albeit of somewhat disgraced royalty. Little was heard of Princess Margaret, the Queen's sister, with one important exception. When Group Captain Peter Townsend died, obituaries recalled his relationship with Princess Margaret many years before. The Archbishop of Canterbury advised her against marrying this divorced man, who had been an equerry to George VI. She publicly announced that on his advice she had decided to put duty before love. Her life thereafter was regularly reported in the media, including her marriage and divorce to Lord Snowdon, the photographer, and her holidays in the Caribbean, where the activities of friends and celebrities were the subject of gossip.

The Queen herself was duly recorded at ceremonies which required her presence such as the Queen's Speech at the State Opening of Parliament, which is now a televised event. She visited New Zealand, where she apologized to the Maori population for injustices over land appropriation perpetrated by the early colonists with British government support. While in the Antipodes, she was present at the Commonwealth Conference. She gave her annual televised Christmas message to Britain and the Commonwealth. Two years ago, she referred to the year that had passed as her *annus horribilis*. In 1995, the speech came in the immediate wake of her letters to the Prince and Princess of Wales, which the *Sun*, under the banner of a World Exclusive, headlined 'Queen Orders Divorce' (21 December 1995):

the Queen and Prince Philip were said to be 'in despair' after the Princess's *Panorama* interview in which she confessed to an affair with calvary officer, James Hewitt. They feared unprecedented damage was being done to the monarchy.

For the Queen, it was beginning to look like one *annus horribilis* after another.

In all of this the media are inextricably involved. We can recall some of the history that has led to this state of affairs and the ways in which this impinges on concepts of monarchy in Britain and what this might signify. In 1953 the Coronation of Queen Elizabeth II took place, amid much contemporary comment about a new Elizabethan age. The Coronation ceremony took place at Westminster, where she was crowned by the Archbishop of Canterbury. This event is associated with the development of the television audience as we now know it. The commentators, notably Richard Dimbleby, provided the voice for the occasion, with a distinctive mix of the professional and the reverential, and their present but non-intrusive hushed tones. The occasion gave rise to a paper by Edward Shils and Michael Young on 'The Meaning of the Coronation' (Shils and Young, 1953). The Coronation was seen in Durkheimian terms as a collective representation, embodying a sense of nation, community, and values, through which people come to interpret what it is to be a British subject. The relation between state and church represented the conjunction of the political, constitutional monarchy and the mystical, sacred, inherited charisma of the office. The reference to the Coronation, together with the colourful pageantry of events on the great state occasions, represented the fact that we lived in a society with a high degree of moral consensus. This, we should recall, was a Britain whose government in the early post-war years had nationalized key industries, set up the welfare state and the National Health Service, only to be replaced by the Conservatives under Winston Churchill. The debates about the nature and structure of British society were fundamental ones, reflected in these political divisions.

Shils and Young were concerned with an important topic, the problem of moral order in modern and modernizing societies. The monarchy, trimmed of its absolute power, could be seen as harmless and we, the people, could enjoy the colourful charades of the state events, pleasurable cultural relics, yet its inherent conservatism could now be seen as so plastic that it contained a vital sense of permanent contemporaneity.

Thus, it seemed, was the paradox of change and continuity in British society resolved. The Shils–Young view was explicitly challenged by Norman Birnbaum in his essay 'Monarchs and Sociologists' (Birnbaum, 1971). For him, the analysis skated over real differences, especially class differences, by its emphasis on common values. The Coronation was a diversion from the realities of everyday life, the bread and circuses routine that could be traced to Roman times, and a ritual that allowed for fantasies and adulation not so very different from that given to film stars. Here the word 'glamour' touches both our understanding of royalty and film 'stars'. Tom Nairn (1988) reminds us that 'glamour' is an old Scottish word for magical enchantment, for spells cast upon humans by witches or fairies, and he notes the role of spectacle in all of this. For him, the relationship between the monarchy and modernity is intrinsically problematical, despite the attempt to claim a positive link. Nairn offers us a longer-term picture of the role of monarchy in Britain (or Ukania, as he mockingly calls it):

The glamour of this backwardness is its legitimation through icons of continuity and reassurance: the human presence of Royalty with its concrete, familial guarantee of all being well in the longer run. British history since around 1800 is a slow and staged counter-revolution which for long retained the appearance of liberalism because so much of the political world was worse. As decline and failure have corroded this antique liberality the appearance has been shed, but in the same period the Monarchical glass of national identity has constantly brightened and extended its radiant appeal. Originally . . . the myth of Monarchy was employed to build up national-popular identity, in the time of George III—a safely anti-Republican nationalism which would keep the spirit of democracy at bay even when democratic forms of government had become inescapable. Now the myth is amplified and diffused in order to rally this same identity, to preserve a traditional self-image (and the old power-reality it serves) against the greater tensions of a polity in disintegration. (Nairn, 1988: 215)

To amplify and sustain this myth necessarily requires a good deal of ideological labour. This has long been so. Nairn reminds us of the occasions when the House of Hanover (later named the House of Windsor with the advent of the First World War) was most unpopular. Both George IV and William IV were extremely unpopular and this was reflected in the press, including *The Times*. For long parts of Victoria's reign, at the beginning and later during a long period of mourning for her husband (who, as Prince Consort, had played a modernizing role in relation to the monarchy) when she chose to live in seclusion, she was unpopular. Posters appeared outside Buckingham Palace with the words 'These commanding premises to be let in consequence of the late occupant's declining business' (in Nairn, 1988: 331). Nairn traces the ways in which anti-republican feelings were mobilized by politicians, notably Gladstone, by creating a concept of a modern monarchy which could engender class harmony. It was he who pushed for the National Thanksgiving Ceremony at St Paul's to give thanks for the recovery of the Prince of Wales from serious illness, in 1872. Mother and son later appeared on the balcony of Buckingham Palace to acknowledge the crowd outside—a much-repeated feature of later royal occasions. These spectacles were to be precursors of the Jubilee celebrations of 1887 and 1897, great media events in their time. Out of the Thanksgiving Ceremony, what we would now describe as a public relations triumph in which the Queen had to be persuaded to participate, came the resurgence of the connection between monarchy and nationhood. Thus Walter Bagehot, then editor of *The Economist*, wrote after the Thanksgiving Ceremony that the monarchy was 'the most national thing in the nation . . . the standard to which the eyes of the people perpetually turn to keep them all together' (in Nairn, 1988: 334).

There are elements of political orchestration about the invention and sustenance of this myth. Lloyd George schooled Edward in a few Welsh words for use at his Investiture as Prince of Wales. In time of war, politicians have realized the value of monarchy as a symbol of unity and a representation of the concept of the family. The royal family, present in London at the time of the Blitz in the Second World War, was a strong and effective image. At the time of the Falklands conflict, the Queen's son Prince Andrew served as a pilot and the concepts of family, patriotism, and national purpose were deployed in support of the war effort (Glasgow University Media Group, 1985; Aulich, 1992).

All of this can and has been massaged by the mass media. During the Falklands conflict, the royal family was presented as a symbol of national unity and solidarity and the viewer could be offered some kind of personal identification. 'For the royal family it's a *personal* anxiety: Prince Andrew is a helicopter pilot with the Task Force' (ITN, 21.15, 26 May 1982). Messages from royalty could be used to frame stories about other families, as if to set the appropriate tone. And amid the crisis 'normal' life must go on. 'Despite what's happening abroad in the South Atlantic the yearly pattern of life here seems to be unchanged . . . The royal family are traditional visitors to the Chelsea Flower Show' (BBC2, 18.50, 23 May 1982). And the ceremonies, too, continue. Thus, with the royal-military spectacle of the Trooping of the Colour, 'Things weren't totally normal . . . everyone conscious of the situation in the South Atlantic' (ITN, 21.00, 12 June 1982). There is the mystique, together with the illusion of access to the royal family. And there is a use of backward-looking glamour, as in the description of President Reagan's visit to Windsor Castle:

She [the Queen] led him through the Waterloo Chamber, pointing out the delights created by her ancestor George IV to commemorate Napoleon's defeat . . . Their cheerful steps led them to St George's Hall, a great chamber built by Edward III . . . Especially for the occasion, Queen Victoria's dining table had been installed. (ITN, 22.00, 8 June 1982)

The royal family, depicted in certain ways in a potted history that could reference Napoleon's retreat from Moscow, Waterloo, the Dunkirk spirit and the White Cliffs of Dover, led the journalist Jonathan Dimbleby to write:

The broadcasting authorities have felt as though they're on a desert island, which the sea is gradually eating away, and have moved more to the centre of the island . . . At precisely the time when conflicts in our society demand a greater degree of courage to interpret the realities of what is going on—it's easy to get caught in the web of the Establishment's perception—I find it happening to me. (*Stills* magazine, November 1982)

At the same time, the monarchy and members of the royal family have sought to develop relations with the media on their own terms, hence the existence of a press office at the Palace, through which news is filtered. In 1932 the King, George V, was persuaded to do a Christmas broadcast to the Empire by the BBC's Director-General, John Reith. The text itself was prepared by Rudyard Kipling. Reith reflected in his diary that by allowing people to hear the King's voice it 'had brought the solicitude of fatherhood in where before was the aloof dignity of the throne' (in Nairn, 1988: 64). The problem was what kind of communication was appropriate without losing something of the mystery of monarchy. Would familiarity breed contempt? The issue has remained. With the advent of television new possibilities and problems emerged. In 1969, following the experience of television coverage of the Investiture of Charles as Prince of Wales in 1968, the BBC television documentary *Royal Family* was made, obviously with the Queen's consent. Richard Cawston's documentary was the controlled answer to the question: what are they really like? Alongside activities that go with the job, such as meeting foreign dignitaries, audiences with the Prime Minister, official overseas visits, we could get glimpses of the royal family at leisure, having a barbecue by a Scottish loch, watching television together, even laughing at the comedy programmes. Who could have guessed it? They are like us and yet, of course, they are also different. The difficult question from the Establishment perspective, in an age of mass media, is how to cultivate this while sustaining an overall commitment to the legitimacy of the monarchy in a democratic society. The presentation of a controlled documentary or illustrated Queen's Christmas address is one thing; the participation of younger members of the royal family in the television programme *It's a Knock Out*, where they took on a celebrity team in various contrived games and stunts, is quite another.

The more general question is, when does it start to get out of control and with what consequences for the future of the monarchy? Tom Nairn suggests that the royal watching activity can tolerate some difficulties and snags without monarchy itself losing credibility:

The general logic which sustains the circular logic must (naturally) be that They are Nice. However, this can also be fed by salty rumours (and even the occasional fact) indicating lapses from Niceness. A dose of naughtiness, tantrums, fainting fits and familial squabbles feeds the appearance of intimacy without really threatening the faith. To be so like normal mortals in this way, makes it even more wonderful that They are who They are, do what They do, and so on. (Nairn, 1988: 45)

Here is a context in which to consider the more recent separate media activities of the Prince and Princess of Wales. The contrast between the choreographed 'fairy tale' wedding in May 1981, a media event with world coverage, and their present estrangement could not be greater. But what we have come to understand is that their relationship to the media is much more complex. Both of them use it and are used by it. The publication of tapes of telephone calls made by the Prince and the Princess to various friends, intended to embarrass them, reminds us that the media are not only a means of communication but also a means of surveillance. How is the information obtained? Who is listening? Who sells it? Who buys it? This takes on the character of a 'dirty tricks' campaign, especially if, subsequently, some of the material is shown to be false. Martin Bashir was chosen by the Princess for the *Panorama* interview in part because he was known to have compiled a dossier about the alleged involvement of MI5 in leaks and tip-offs in a campaign against her. More prosaically, the differences of opinion as to the rights and wrongs of their marital dispute are reflected in the success with which each of them recruited press support for their case. When journalist Andrew Morton's book, *Diana: Her True Story*, was published in 1992, and serialized in *The Sunday Times*, all the evidence was there to suggest that she had colluded in its publication. She even organized a public visit to her friend Caroline Bartholomew, known to be one of Morton's chief sources, in the wake of the publication of the book, thus giving it her seal of approval. In a comment on the more general implications of this activity, Melanie Phillips and Georgina Henry wrote in *The Guardian*:

> The Princess of Wales is certainly not the first member of the Royal Family to have manipulated the press and won't be the last. For the wider hypocrisy is, of course, that the press is used as a matter of routine by one vested interest or another and is more than happy to be so used. (Phillips and Henry, 1993)

In anticipating the *Panorama* interview of 19 November 1995, *The Observer* described her as 'one of the most adept of media manipulators' and then specifically commented: 'She will damn Charles with her niceness.' This was an interview that was initiated by the Princess, behind the back of her Press Secretary (who resigned in consequence) against all the protocols and without the knowledge of Buckingham Palace. *The Observer* article, by Euan Ferguson, 'Goodbye to All That', argued that 'the uneasy dance of royalty and media comes to an end with Diana's BBC interview' and asked: can the Palace ever hold the floor again? The interview itself was watched by some 23 million people, far larger than the normal viewing figures for this long-established cur-

Figure 7.1 Cartoon by Martin Rowson on Princess Diana's *Panorama* interview (*Guardian*, 20 November 1995)

rent affairs programme presided over for so long by that most august of royal broadcasters, Richard Dimbleby. Behind the personal rancour and bitterness of the two adversaries now lurks the constitutional question. Republicanism can now reappear on the media agenda without immediately leading to knee-jerk reactionary cries of treachery and treason. But we can learn from history that we have been there before and we can have no certainty as to the future. Behind the soap and the glamour real struggles will take place with real consequences for the nature of our democracy.

Chapter Eight

Advertising: A Word From Our Sponsors

Advertisements are now so numerous that they are very negligently perused, and it has therefore become necessary to gain attention by magnificence of promises and by eloquence sometimes sublime and sometimes pathetic. Promise, large promise, is the soul of an advertisement. I remember a washball that had a quality truly wonderful—it gave *an exquisite edge to the razor!* The trade of advertising is now so near to perfection that it is not easy to propose any improvement.

(Dr Samuel Johnson, in Williams, 1980*a*)

The Observer newspaper was first published on 4 December 1791. In its Address to the Public, essentially its first-ever editorial, the conclusion reads as follows:

From the certainty of a systematic and unerring regulation, the Merchant, Manufacturer, Tradesman, Broker, Artist, and, in short, all classes, whose interest occasionally depends upon public information, may rely upon having their several Advertisements dispersed to the remotest parts of the three kingdoms—Servants also, as *The Observer* cannot fail of becoming a favourite family Paper, will find it in their peculiar interest to give it their decided preference. Thus, then to every rank and order will *The Observer*, have its separate recommendation; to the widest and most exalted, as the vehicle of rational amusement; in the middling lines containing safe and grounded information, and rendering, even to the very lowest, the most essential services; whilst it breathes, invariably, towards all, the spirit of enlightened Freedom, decent Toleration, and universal Benevolence.

Here we see, over 200 years ago, the founding issue of a newspaper which is advertising itself to a potential readership, placarding, as it were, its own values. At the same time, it is identifying itself as a conduit for advertisements. The readers were also a potential market. We can see how deep-rooted and long-standing this reciprocal relationship between the press and advertisers is. The front page of the paper consisted entirely of advertisements. There were books and magazines offered for sale, including *The Witticisms, Jests and Sayings of Dr. Johnson*. The Royal Lottery Bank offered tickets and shares 'at the lowest rates'. 'Infallible' German Corn Plasters, 'a certain cure for corns'—'this is the celebrated Plaster that gained so much reputation in Germany; and has been sold in London upward of fifty years with the greatest reputation.' There was also a Patent Laundress or Washing Machine, which is advertised in terms still recognizable:

This ingenious Invention, made wholly of wood, is highly esteemed by men of science, and persons of every description . . . The act of Wringing, so destructive to linen, is changed for Pressure, which cannot injure, is made to fit the Machine or Rinser, a most valuable appendage, which makes it the completest Machine now known for the purpose of Washing.

On the back page there are advertisements for soaps. There is a Violet Soap to counteract chapped skin—'a White Hand having at all times been considered as a very peculiar ornament in either sex'—and which 'to prevent the deceptions which might be practised in the sale of this article . . . is confined solely to houses of known respectability and credit'. It gives, we are told, 'a pleasing softness and delicate whiteness to the reddest or coarsest hand'. What looks like the same soap, selling from the same shops, although the seller is concerned to establish product differentiation, is advertised separately under the heading 'Interesting to Ladies'—'a refined, a delicate soap calculated more immediately for feminine use' which 'will be found to possess all the powers of thoroughly cleansing the pores of the skin, and at the same time giving to it an animated firmness, and delicacy of tint, equal to the finest natural complexion'. Medicines are also advertised, with letters published from satisfied customers. Thus Dr. Howell's Celebrated Powders offered 'the only effectual Remedy ever yet discovered for curing all kinds of Fits, particularly EPILEPTIC or FALLING FITS' and is advertised 'By His Majesty's Royal Authority'.

We can see the growth of advertising as it accompanies the growth in trade, commerce, and industry. In these early examples there are claims and testimonials to the value or efficacy of a product. And the newspaper advertises itself both in terms of its values to readers and a conduit by which producers may be put in touch with potential consumers. When we look at the kind of advertisements produced in Victorian and Edwardian times, in both newspapers and, importantly even to the

Figure 8.1 Beecham's Pills advertisement, 1908

present time, on billboards and hoardings, we see plenty of evidence of medical and toilet products. These included well-known examples such as Pears' Soap and Beecham's Pills (Figure 8.1). Pears had an advertisement showing a black child being scrubbed white under the rubric 'for improving and preserving the complexion'. Such an advertisement, with its racist connotations, was obviously thought to be unexceptional in Victorian society. It was the same company that, under the title 'The Formula of British Conquest', purported to show a group of Sudanese. Underneath it gave the following quote from Phil Robinson, War Correspondent of the *Daily Telegraph* in 1884:

Even if our invasion of the Sudan has done nothing else it has at any rate left the Arab something to puzzle his fuzzy head over, for the legend PEARS' SOAP IS THE BEST inscribed in large white characters on the rock which marks the farthest point of our advance towards Berber, will tax all the wits of the Dervishes of the Desert to translate.

Robinson would have had little difficulty writing for *The Sun* a century later, with its racist, ethnocentric treatment of the Argentines in the Falklands War—'STICK THIS UP YOUR JUNTA! A *Sun* missile for Galtieri's gauchos' (1982).

But we also see evidence in this period of the large food and drink companies advertising their wares (Figures 8.2–8.4). Some of these names are with us still: Frys, Nestlé, Hovis, Kelloggs, Bovril, Oxo, Schweppes, Rowntrees, Cadburys. 'Drink Cadbury's Cocoa' advised one advertisement, showing a railway carriage with Queen Victoria and a companion with cups and saucers before them. The royal seal of approval 'By Appointment to Her Majesty' was much sought after.

Raymond Williams (1980*a*) argued that the lineaments of modern advertising really appear in the late nineteenth century with advertising on a large scale for an increasing range of products. He viewed it as part of an attempt to control markets at a time when early capitalism was being overtaken by monopoly or corporate capitalism, with large firms and international markets becoming more in evidence. Thus, in 1901, a British tobacco advertiser tried to buy the total space of *The Star* newspaper (they eventually obtained half of it). We can compare this to Bill Gates, who in 1995 made it possible for *The Times* to give their paper away for one day, as a way of advertising Word for Windows 95. But it is, Williams argues, at the beginning of the twentieth century that we see advertising emerge in more sophisticated ways and, significantly, it is not only products that are offered for sale to individual consumers but the techniques of persuasion are applied to selling war. Kitchener's now famous poster, during the First World War—'Your Country

Figure 8.2 Nestlé's Milk advertisement, 1901

Figure 8.3 Hovis advertisement, 1907

Figure 8.4 Bovril advertisement, 1902

Needs You'—was a direct appeal to patriotism. The poster of the child asking his father 'What did YOU do in the Great War Daddy?' touched directly upon personal relationships and anxieties. The techniques of persuasion, once invented, can be variously applied. We can see at once the intimate connection between advertising as a practice and public relations as an activity. The latter is about selling persons or policies in a particular kind of culture. Williams pointed to the way in which conventional borders can be broken down:

the borderline between the item or photograph picked up in the ordinary course of journalism and broadcasting, and the similar item or photograph that has been arranged and paid for, either directly or through special hospitality by a publicity agent, is obviously difficult to draw. Enough stories get through, and are even boasted about to indicate that the paid practice is extensive, though payment, except to the agent, is usually in hospitality (if that word can be used) or in kind. Certainly readers of newspapers should be aware that the 'personality' items, presented as ordinary news stories or gossip, will often have been paid for, in one way or another, in a system that makes straightforward advertising, by comparison, look respectable. Nor is this confined to what is called 'show business'; it has certainly entered literature, and it has probably entered politics. The extension is natural in a society where selling, by any effective means, has become the primary ethic. (Williams, 1980: 184)

Today, the blurring of lines is a much more developed phenomenon. We should notice, in particular, the role that public relations agencies play in the preparation of video news releases. These are pre-packaged news stories prepared on behalf of business or other interest groups which are then sent to newsrooms or transmitted by satellite to TV stations throughout the world. These can come in two versions. The fully developed video is an already edited story, including voice-overs, and can even include a script indicating where the local newsreader should read the appropriate lines. The second version is raw footage, from which the edited version comes. This can then be edited locally and interspersed with other material. These 'story segments' can be shown on news programmes without attribution, and to that extent can be described as a hidden form of manipulation (Stauber and Rampton, 1995).

So it is that advertising, public relations, and propaganda are interrelated in contemporary social practice. Why does Williams call it a magic system? It is because we are encouraged to think that when we buy a product we do not just buy the object but other goods such as social respect, health, beauty, success, power, and the ability to control our own environment and we can be seen by others to show good taste. This is not necessarily simply a fantasy. A society that works with and through these signs may validate these meanings. Yet it remains a fantasy in the sense that social needs are not addressed by this selling ethic and may be obstructed by it. To consider the range of social needs in terms of hospitals, schools, roads, and public services is at the same time to raise questions about the ideals of consumerism. The organized fantasy that is modern advertising can obscure these real needs and even block their development because they challenge the economics of market forces and the priorities that they embody. In such ways the production decisions of major corporations are projected through the charms of the magic system as 'our' choice and the 'consumer's' selection of priorities. Actors are hired

to mime the only available choices, to display satisfaction and the achievement of their expectations, or to pretend to a linkage of values between quite mundane products and the now generally unattached values of love, respect, significance or fulfilment. [It] . . . is now a system of mimed celebration of other people's decisions. As such, of course, advertising is very closely related to the whole system of styles in official politics. Indeed, some of its adepts have a direct hand, in propaganda, in the competition of the parties and the formation of public opinion. (Williams, 1980a: 193)

We will return to the political dimensions of this. Williams's critique of the role of advertising in modern society does not stop with comments about its unreliability, intrusiveness, or superficiality. He argued that it is no longer a manageable support system which can help to develop freedom of communications, as in our opening examples from *The Observer* of 1791. It has moved into a position that has made many other services dependent upon its temporary needs. It is in the end not a detached, free-floating set of sign systems but is connected with corporate competition and its 'needs'. These, he concludes,

increasingly demand not a sector but a world, not a reservation but a whole society, not a break or column, but whole newspapers and broadcasting services in which to operate. Unless they are driven back now, there will be no second chance. (Williams, 1980a: 195)

If Williams's central theme is about the centrality of selling in late capitalist society and the implications this has for our culture, our way of life, we can recognize that this touches on power as manipulation. Yet there can be sales resistance and advertising agencies can face credibility problems and even go out of business, so it is not all one-way traffic. If it were not so we would be identifying a mass society, in which opinions are manipulated by the few over the many, not so far from the cultural pessimism of the Frankfurt School, who after all had reason to know about the ways in which Nazi political propaganda could penetrate German society. But even that power was not total. Wright Mills reflected on the ways in which views had fluctuated in American society about the power to manipulate through propaganda and public relations. On the one hand, there was the view that words can win wars and sell soap, they can move people and they can restrain them, that in principle public opinion can be moved in any direction on any topic. This view of the omnipotence of mass persuasion is conditioned by the assumption that the public trust the mass media. That is not necessarily so, especially if evidence of deception comes to light. But those who seek to persuade us can become more sophisticated and try to tailor their messages to more specific groups. Mills refers to such groups as primary publics and observes:

Anyone who has seen the inside of an advertising agency or public relations office knows that the primary public is still the great unsolved problem of opinion makers. Negatively, their recognition of the influence of social context upon opinions and public activity implies that the articulate public resists and refracts the communications of the mass media. Positively, this recognition implies that the public is not composed of isolated individuals, but rather of persons who not only have prior opinions that must be reckoned with, but who continually influence each other in complex and intimate, in direct and continual ways. (Mills, 1956: 316)

Social scientists can track the ways in which instruments and techniques of persuasion are deployed and also indicate some of the ways in which resistance is mobilized and practised. The point of that is to make manipulative forms of persuasion and power less opaque, so that we may better evaluate the purposes of the powerful. In modern societies such as ours, as Berger (1972) points out, we are surrounded by publicity images. They are extensive and intensive. There are the billboards, the messages on buses, in railway stations, on the back of tube tickets, in newspapers, in the flashing advertisements and neon signs of Piccadilly Circus, in cinemas, on television, and so on. The images are so pervasive that they are easily taken for granted, although some may arrest our attention for a moment, especially if they address a personal interest. The images may exhibit continuities from earlier ones, but they need to be replenished and renewed; they are constantly being worked on by those who produce them. This must represent an incredible amount of ideological and semiotic labour, which can involve language, art and visual representations, and music. In Berger's view, such images often speak of the past and always speak of the future.

We can, of course, see contemporary examples, as in the use of old films, sometimes juxtaposed with new products, or traditional jazz standards to advertise the joys of travelling by train, or cobbled streets of a northern town and brass band music to sell Hovis bread. There are now agencies which have a bank of photographs, film, and other archive material which can be bought by advertisers for use in their productions. This can be deployed and edited in ways which can make, say, Humphrey Bogart or Marilyn Monroe appear to be actively involved in selling the product even though they were dead before the object existed. There are clever techniques which can show us different generations of Manchester United footballers apparently playing in the same team. Berger goes so far as to argue that publicity is in essence nostalgic, in that it has to sell the past to the future, and that it constitutes the culture of the consumer society. What we are given is a visual language with historical dimensions, which in practice makes history mythical. This culture trades on anxiety, it commonly uses representations of sexuality to sell its products, it nourishes envy and manufactures glamour. Indeed, for Berger, 'glamour cannot exist without personal social envy becoming a common and widespread emotion' (Berger, 1972: 148).

Berger emphasized the continuity between oil paintings and the colour photographs of modern advertising. Nowadays we can see examples of tableaux of actors mimicking a well-known painting, say by Manet, and then actors move in or out of frame and we are, as it were, amused to discover what the product being sold is. Or again, reference may be drawn to real historical or contemporary political figures, say Castro or Mao, to advertise cigars, vodka, cigarettes, or whatever. This decontextualizes the real situations connected with such people and depoliticizes the political sphere. More generally Berger argues that

publicity turns consumption into a substitute for democracy. The choice of what one eats (or wears or drives) takes the place of significant political choice. Publicity helps to mask and to compensate for all that is undemocratic within society. And it also masks what is happening in the rest of the world. (Berger, 1972: 149)

To illustrate this, he draws attention to the way in which a colour supplement of *The Sunday Times* (seen as representative of the genre) could show, in close juxtaposition, photographs of suffering in a third world country alongside the fantasy world of advertisements. It is, he suggests, the mark of a cynical culture that it can do such a thing. Yet as our attention is drawn to the contrast between the fantasy world of the dreams of happiness bought by the consumer and the real suffering of poor people, we can reflect on the significance of that contrast, and reconsider our own relationships to these two worlds. However, the cynicism is there and in recent years we have seen controversial pictures of that world of suffering and pain incorporated into the very advertisements themselves, as in the case of Benneton's use of pictures from war-torn Bosnia.

A more recent study which acknowledges its debt to Berger's work is Robert Goldman's *Reading Ads Socially* (Goldman, 1992). Goldman sees modern advertising as emerging out of the transition from competitive to corporate capitalism. He argues that we are living with the consequences of the attempt to transform the sphere of culture and desire, via corporate advertising, into a sphere of the capitalist economy. Clearly, advertisements are intended to connect with potential buyers. Typically this entails a process of framing; we, as audience or reader, have to recognize that it is an advertisement we are looking at. There will be differentiating factors, which is why so much attention is given to the logo. We can easily recognize the logos for Coca-Cola, Levis, and other internationally marketed consumer products. The messages are encoded in ways which we can interpret and by now advertisers can assume that we have a general understanding of the advertising codes, as distinct from other messages (excluding attempts at subliminal advertising, which seeks to bypass the conscious mind). They do require work to decode them and the advertiser, in trying to organize the reader's perceptions, has to review continually how far the intended meanings and connotations are received as such and, moreover, approved.

We know that when an advertiser is confident that the advert is recognized and significantly approved as reflected in market sales, then a long-running campaign, sometimes over years, can be established. We can see this in the history of Guinness adverts in Britain. The first slogan, 'Guinness is Good for You', begun in 1928 with distinctively styled posters, became so established that the slogan could eventually be assumed to be known by the reader, to the extent that it could be playfully left out. Other slogans, 'My Goodness, My Guinness', and 'Pure Genius', have entered into the vocabulary of our culture. Recently, Guiness has shifted its underlying macho image and in one advertisement has featured a gay couple. There are market researchers who consider advertising strategies and there are advertising analysts who offer comment on such innovations. Virginia Valentine of Semiotic Solutions is one such:

The question you have to answer is this: is Guinness exploiting its own code of eccentricity or is it breaking beer codes, trying to place Guinness outside beer culture? The gay couple is right on line with Guinness codes of playfulness. (*Guardian*, 22 June 1995)

It is no accident that advertising analyst companies with names like 'Semiotic Solutions' exist. We need to recognize that those involved in such practices are very likely to have read the likes of Barthes, Eco, and Baudrillard and to speak confidently about signs, codes, signifiers, and symbols. They may indeed have degrees in media studies, cultural studies, or public relations and see themselves and their practices as part of a postmodern world. This helps to explain why publicity can now become very self-conscious and reflexive about the activity of advertising. Goldman's work is full of examples of how this happens. A kind of 'knowingness' enters into the process—the advertisement can break existing frames by which we traditionally understand what advertisements are since they have recognizable ways of giving definite clues to their meaning and purpose. Goldman gives the example of the 1988 advert for Honda motor scooters, which dispenses with familiar techniques of voice-over and recognizable musical forms. Instead we have grainy photography and a cacophony of noisy sound effects with a series of crudely written, apparently disconnected questions rapidly posed: Who am I? What is a quadratic equation? Is there truth? Is there any pizza left? and so on. Only at the end do we see the shiny red Honda scooter with a male voice-over stating: 'The new Honda Elite 50. If it's not the answer, at least it's not another question.' Goldman argues that such an advertisement seems intent on subverting cultural codes that put questions in a hierarchy of importance. He comments:

As the ad propels along, the speed of the questions accelerates until it is impossible to recognise all the questions without slowing the tape of the ad. Of all the questions the anxiety laden 'What if I'm captured?' and 'Are they laughing at me?' are the most fleeting and the most viscerally disturbing. The fragments of consciousness which dribble out at the end seem an apt metaphor for media implosion. (Goldman 1992: 165)

The reference to anxiety, for all the newness of style and disassociation with older conventions, does link back to the critiques and concerns of Williams and Berger which we have already noted.

The reflexivity of the advertiser addresses the reflexivity and scepticism of the consumer—we know that you know we are trying to sell you something and know how to resist these things. We also know that you can identify the bogus world of adland, its models and actors, and its media distortions of reality and want to see some connection with 'reality'—life as it is, with evidence of real people (far removed we may note from those real people in detergent ads who have learned to say why they prefer one cleaner to another, even when tempted with the alternative). As Goldman points out, the advertising that emerges can have something of the 'knowing wink' about it. Levi jeans, for example, in the 1980s were losing out to other producers. Their advertising campaign was based on the idea of reducing the diversity of its product lines and reverting to the basic blue jeans. In terms of reflexivity, the campaign sought to falsify claims of individuality for mass-produced consumables. In doing so, it was reflecting popular critiques of consumer conformism. Then by use of various techniques, especially the use of 'street-wise' real people, it offered the message that Levi jeans, although common to all wearers, really did shape the body of the individual wearer. So the critique is acknowledged and then rejected in relation to this particular product. Commodity fetishism stops here, although, of course, it applies elsewhere, including, by implication, the competition. The art-form that emerges in these examples includes real people in real streets where we might see graffiti on the walls. Various forms of activity may be seen, miming, dancing, street music. Goldman terms this commodity bricolage, in which commodity culture and youth culture confront one another in mutually knowing ways. The corporate commodity strategy is an attempt first of all to acknowledge critiques of consumer culture and then to celebrate particular forms of defiance and resistance by bringing them into the advertisements. But, however this mutual reflexivity goes, the corporate capitalist is well aware that success will be measured in sales and profitability.

What is still usually bracketed out from all this knowingness, sophisticated referencing systems, and the ability to deploy cultural quotations through music, art, and photography is any understanding of the division of labour and organization of production which makes these commodities available at all. Hence questions of low wages, unemployment, poor working conditions, long hours of work, non-recognition or derecognition of unions are, we might say, out of frame. The urban young people who feature in Levis advertisements are not dissimilar from those who work for low wages in fast-food establishments, for example. Or the clothes and shoes we buy may come from low-wage economies, which may even use child labour. Those who make garments for the fashion industry, that produce the highly visible products for fashion advertisements, often work on very low wages and in uncongenial conditions without union protection. This we do not see. Goldman does well to remind us of it. And he does so by commenting on the way postmodernism has failed as an approach to social theory:

As postmodernism makes its way into mass culture, it becomes little more than a fetishised fascination with the image, the edit, the jump cut. Cynical fascination replaces critique and self-reflexive consciousness materialises as a new form of consumer fetishism. Postmodernism fails not because of its readings of social texts but because of its inability to go beyond the text into the world of production. Even in the stylised shopping malls identified as sites of 'postmodern hyperspace' the society of the spectacle is subsidised by paying sub-standard wages to an urban service proletariat. Postmodern theorists so intently foreground the simulations that they miss the exploitation and inequality which makes possible a public space devoted to glorifying, and reproducing, sign values. (Goldman, 1992: 231)

Is it not possible, however, to recognize the existence of such inequalities and exploitation and seek to use the means of communication and techniques of persuasion in the service of values which oppose this? This, after all, is the rationale of pressure groups relating to ecological and peace issues and those who have an interest in addressing the widening gap between North and South. The case of Nestlé represents an instructive example of the possibilities and problems. In the 1970s, concern was expressed by non-governmental organizations (NGOs), aid organizations, and publications such as the *New Internationalist* about the sale of artificial baby food in third world countries. One serious problem had to do with the difficulty of guaranteeing the safety of water supplies with which to mix the powder. Babies can thereby contract diarrhoea, a killer disease in such countries. UNICEF argued that one and a half million children die each year because they are not breast-fed. Nestlé's products were faced with an international boycott in 1975 as a result of these concerns. The boycott was called off in 1984 given Nestlé's expressed willingness to comply with their critics' requirements and, in particular, to comply with the 1981 World Health Organization International Code of Marketing on Breastmilk Substitutes. The boycott was restarted in 1988. Critics have pointed to repeated breaches of the Code (see, for example, *The New Internationalist*, January 1995, 23–4).

In the light of their experience of hostile criticism, Nestlé revised their public relations strategy. Thus the company's public relations director saw the struggle as a political one and commented:

I feel it is essential that multi-national firms under attack create a united group of talented and experienced professionals and, when needed, occasional consultants, who, isolated from the everyday public relations of the firm, can concentrate their efforts on the political issues encountered by the multinationals. In the search for a receptive public and the elimination of a critical attitude, multinationals have an invaluable weapon at their disposal: marketing and management personnel in the field. (cited in Mattelart, 1991: 181–2)

In consequence Nestlé joined with other agro-food companies to form the International Council of Infant Food Industries (ICIFI) with its own code of conduct. It set up its own newsletter, *Nestlé News*, and in doing so was prepared to learn publicity lessons from its critic, *IBFAN News*, and show more awareness of the relevance of grassroots organizations. In its Annual Report of 1993, Nestlé referred to the company symbol of the mother bird feeding babies in the nest, which, it said, personifies the business:

The symbol, which is universally understood, simultaneously evokes security, maternity and affection, nature and nourishment, family and tradition. Today it is the central element in Nestlé corporate identity.

The question that remains is how far the symbol relates to the practice. What we see from this example is that the media are a site of struggle in which competing definitions of reality are offered. This is not to conclude that the multi-nationals always win or that pressure groups have no effect but that the struggle itself is continuous and calls for resources of time, talent, and energy from those who wish to challenge the working assumptions of the global economy.

Chapter Nine

Public Relations and Propaganda Wars

In the previous chapter we commented on the ways in which advertising, public relations, and propaganda are interlinked. Here we will concentrate on the political dimension and draw attention to some of the elements involved in what Franklin has called 'packaging politics' (Franklin, 1994). He argued that, while there are variations in different societies, there is a central tendency:

> The process of packaging politics signals politicians' growing enthusiasm and facility for managed political communications. Skilled and highly paid marketing and communications professionals create favourable media images for politicians and their policies, which are presented to the public via the mass media. The attractiveness of the marketed image of politicians and policies has become at least as influential in winning public support as an understanding of the policy itself. Media no longer simply offer public information about political affairs, but are increasingly being managed by politicians in ways that allow them undue and improper influences over voters' choices. Such tendencies pose a potential threat to democracy. (Franklin, 1994: 13)

Before the advent of broadcasting, politicians fighting elections would go out to the hustings, to such places as the town hall, the market place, the street corner, and state their case. They could be subject to robust heckling from opponents and encouraged by cheers from their supporters. It was a very direct way of communication. Radio offered a new medium. President Franklin Roosevelt became an exponent of 'fireside chats' to the American people. Television offered new kinds of opportunity for impression management. As early as 1954, there is an account by Jack Gould of *The New York Times* of the way in which one of President Eisenhower's 'information talks' was constructed, which touches on many of the features that have been repeated many times since:

Figure 9.1 The spin doctor swung into action (*The Ecologist*, September/October 1995)

The President and his television consultant, Robert Montgomery, apparently found a 'format' that enabled General Eisenhower to achieve relaxation and immeasurably greater freedom of movement. The result was the attainment of television's most desired quality—naturalness . . . As the programme began the President was shown sitting on the edge of a desk, his arms folded and a quiet smile on his lips. To his right—and to the viewer's left—was seen the flag. Then casually and conversationally he began speaking. The same mood and tone were sustained for the next half hour . . . In past appearances when he used prompters, the President's eyes never quite hit the camera, he was always looking just a hair to the left or to the right. But last night his eyes were dead on the lens and the viewer had a sense of being spoken to directly . . . As he neared the end of his talk and wanted to employ added emphasis, the General alternately knotted his hands or tapped the fingers of one on the palm of the other. Because they were intuitive his actions had the stamp of reality . . . The contents of General Eisenhower's talk admittedly were not too earth shaking. (cited in Mills, 1956)

Note in that passage the references to format, naturalness, stamp of reality—and, of course, the figure of the television consultant is close at hand. Attention is given to style, symbols, surroundings, and technique. And all of this over forty years ago. But persuasive though it was as a performance Gould was not overwhelmed by the content and that, too, is worth remembering.

In the British context the adoption of these explicit kinds of public relations techniques came to be associated with Margaret Thatcher and the Conservative Party from the 1979 election and on into the 1980s (Cockerell *et al.*, 1985). Much of the razzmatazz associated with American electioneering was imported. There were the photo opportunities of Harvey Thomas, once associated with publicity for Billy Graham's evangelistic campaigns, a well-known public adviser to the Conservative Party until 1991, who was credited with the view that a good picture can say more than a thousand words. Thus, Mrs Thatcher holding a two-day-old calf in a field was filmed for its image value: obviously it tells us nothing about agricultural policy. Great care was taken on the stage setting, colour, design and use of music and the parading of celebrities for Mrs Thatcher's keynote addresses. The teleprompter, which is scarcely visible to the television audience, with its two screens either side of the speaker, allows the speaker to look directly at the audience in the hall, and has, as a result, been nicknamed the 'sincerity machine'. One of Thatcher's close advisers was Gordon Reece, who had a say in the choice of her speech-writers and, on the basis of market research, set out to change her image, with attention to voice, dress, and hair style. Reece was later deployed by the National Coal Board to advise on public relations during the miners' strike of 1984–5. Another key adviser was Christopher Lawson, who at the beginning of 1982 became the Conservative Party's first-ever Director of Marketing. He had already studied President Reagan's techniques of marketing political persuasion and had a business career behind him that involved the selling of Mars bars. How different was it, he was asked, between selling such a product and selling a political party to the electorate?

I think there is a slight difference . . . I mean we had a saying in the old days that marketing involves everything from conception to consumption. I think it does in product terms. I think the big difference in marketing party political policies is that of course one has much less to say about what goes into the product than one did then but apart from that I think it's more or less the same. It's communication. It's getting the message across. (cited in Cockerell *et al.*, 1985: 198)

Essentially party leaders and policies are seen as products which have to be sold to the voter. The success of the Conservative Party at the polls in 1979 and 1983 was widely attributed to its public relations strategy. Peter Mandelson, the media adviser for the Labour Party, also urged the adoption of professional communication techniques. However, public relations are not everything. The Labour Party under Neil Kinnock did pay much attention to its image presentation, including a soft-focus, lyrical film focusing on Neil and Glenys Kinnock in Wales. It was made by Hugh Hudson, director of *Chariots of Fire*. Yet Labour still lost. The success of public relations activity is not easily assessed, although the consultants and advisers of the party that wins the election will stake their claim for credit. But in Mrs Thatcher's last election victory, it was well known that there was dissatisfaction with the management of their public relations by Saatchi and Saatchi, the company which had invented the well-known poster 'Labour Isn't Working' in 1979, which showed a long queue of people outside an unemployment office. This was a comment on Labour's unemployment record at a time when the figure was still under a million. We think of public relations management in terms of the politicians trying to set agendas, offering sound bites, and using 'spin doctors' to encourage the media to present news about their party in a favourable light. In doing so they may try to control or restrict access to information. However, their control is not absolute and their relationship with their respective parties can be precarious. Moreover, journalists (from whose ranks spin doctors are usually recruited) can show an awareness of what is going on, so that the public relations attempts to manage news can sometimes be exposed or discussed. The existence of a BBC programme series, *Spin*, presented by *The Observer* journalist, Jon Sweeney, is an important example of such possibilities.

Apart from election time, the parties also make widespread use of public relations and advertising. In 1987, an article in *The Financial Times* pointed out that the Thatcher government had emerged as the largest single advertiser in the UK:

When Mrs Thatcher came to power in 1979, the Government spent a mere £31 million on advertising, on things like road safety campaigns. But a decade which has seen record unemployment levels, the selling off of State assets, and the emergence of diseases such as AIDS, has pushed the Government into the forefront of the advertising world . . . it was perhaps hardly surprising that her government should try to use the techniques of persuasion to convince the public that her policies were right. Advertising expenditure by the government has risen steadily since 1979 to a total of £81 million [in 1986] . . . this year will push the figure up to at least an estimated £125 million . . . (cited in Mattelart, 1991: 192)

Philo has commented in more detail on the ways in which the government went on a propaganda campaign to 'sell the eighties' (Philo, 1995). When the government-owned British Telecom was privatized, the campaign leading up to it entailed the two advertising agencies involved spending £7.6 million in little more than three months, which is as much as even the biggest advertisers in the UK would have disposed of in a year. The selling of British Petroleum was very instructive. Both BBC and ITN ran news reports that mirrored the government's own political advertising. In other words, the publicity campaign became a news item in its own right, so, in effect, making television news a space for free advertising. Indeed, a media event was organized involving Royal Marines climbing down the side of the BP building to reveal the price of shares posted there. All this news coverage took place alongside interviews with government ministers, oil experts, and City analysts. Thus the ITN item concluded: 'The issue is not likely to fail—today's razzmatazz was just to make sure of success' (15 October 1987). But, as Philo points out,

some no doubt wish they had been better informed. Nemesis awaited this share issue four days later in the form of the great stock market crash of 'Black Monday', on 19 October 1987. The price of BP shares on the open market was driven down to well below the £3.30 at which the government was offering its own stake for sale. The razzmatazz ended in something close to debacle. (Philo, 1995: 212)

We should not be surprised that governments want to communicate good news. They will want to tell stories and interpret events in ways which redound to their advantage. Public relations and propaganda are built into this process. Attempts to control this flow also mean that what may be regarded as the bad news from the government's point of view is censored, ignored, or downplayed. Since British governments have a civil service at their disposal, who are expected within our concept of democracy to be neutral in providing information, it can become a sensitive matter if their impartiality is called into question. The annual conference of Professional Civil Servants in 1988 called for a code of ethics to protect their members who, they claimed, were sometimes required to expound half-truths on behalf of the government. An information officer claimed that colleagues were required to write articles of a party political nature for insertion into the press on such matters as the poll tax, social security measures, privatization, and the Action for Jobs campaign (Philo, 1995). This should make us very sceptical about the concept of an information society when we know that at the heart of governmental processes, 'information' can be a cloak for propaganda and that there can be disinformation and misinformation as well as the suppression of unwelcome information.

The case of Northern Ireland is an important example of these processes at work. The treatment of Northern Ireland in the media has been the subject of various studies (e.g. Elliot, 1977; Schlesinger *et al.*, 1983; Curtis, 1984; Schlesinger, 1987; Miller, 1993, 1994, and 1995). Miller draws attention to the role of the Northern Ireland Information Service (NIIS), which is the public relations division of the Northern Ireland Office (NIO). This service in 1989–90 spent £7.238 million on press and public relations activities. Miller argues that the overall strategy of the NIIS was to work through two main themes:

the wickedness of terrorism and a community on the move. Thus there was a concern to get across 'good news' about Northern Ireland. This could be done through official publications from the NIIS which could include pictures of laughing policeman wearing red noses for Comic Relief and of industrial developments as evidence of the government's success in attracting overseas investment. There is no space in such publications for images of poverty and underdevelopment. The Industrial Development Board had its own publicity strategy as well and in 1990 paid the public relations firm Shandwick £3 million for the first year of their contract, to supply the world's media with good news stories. Given that news values in relation to Northern Ireland gave prominence to stories about violence during the period of the troubles, this was not always easy. Stories from the NIIS have been placed in the world's media when the sources have not always been clearly specified. Staff are employed to write and distribute stories without charge and free of copyright restrictions. It was not clearly stated that Northern Ireland News Features was produced by the British government, when packages were sent out saying 'the enclosed articles highlight some of the many positive aspects of life in Northern Ireland.' (Miller, 1994: 125)

Miller also drew attention to the London Radio Service (LRS), which is a semi-covert British government organization. It provides verbatim transcripts of ministerial speeches and conferences, news reports, features, and interviews. These are 'placed' in radio programmes across the world with no charge. But as a Central Office of Information commentator pointed out,

The distinguishing feature of Central Office of Information Radio (i.e. LRS) as compared with other services is that material . . . is then broadcast by a station as if it were its own. (in Miller, 1994: 127)

This activity, of course, applies to the range of British government concerns and not just Northern Ireland. The media coverage of Northern Ireland is also full of examples and instances of censorship and attempted censorship. The most well-known and explicit in recent times was the legally imposed ban which prohibited the broadcasting of direct statements by representatives or supporters of eleven Irish political and military organizations. This was introduced in October 1988 and lifted in September 1994 in the aftermath of the peace process. The ban was not welcome to the broadcasting organizations. There were also arguments about how such news should be reported. Thus we had examples of the use of reported speech, subtitles, and later actor voice-overs, with the speakers' lips out of synch with the voice. The practical significance of this was pointed out by John Conway, then Editor of News and Current Affairs in BBC Northern Ireland:

The perception has grown up that we can still interview Sinn Fein about the state of the roads, blocked drains, or other innocuous local issues. Not so. Every broadcast interview with a member of the party has to go through a much finer filter and that's what's so time consuming for editors and their journalists. . .To ensure that an interview with [a] councillor could be broadcast, the news editor at [Radio] Foyle had to check with me in Belfast and I, in turn, had to consult with senior colleagues in London about potential legal and policy implications before the green light to broadcast was given. All that for the everyday voice of grassroots politics which local radio is there to articulate. (cited in Miller, 1995: 53)

Of course, problems do not go away through attempts at media control or manipulation, whether we are contemplating the intimidation tactics of law and censorship or the 'sweet stuff' of public relations. In the case of Northern Ireland, while the NIIS might wish to present the British government as neutral and above the fray, the fact remains that it is a party to the problem. As Miller observes,

However successful the Information Service is in managing the media, in the end the political problem of the legitimacy of the state remains. It is precisely this problem which the information management of the NIO attempts to obscure. (Miller, 1993: 98)

Public relations is about what you want people to know but also about what you do not want them to know. That is why censorship or other means of information control can be seen as the flip side of public relations. There are journalists who recognize the significance of this for our democracy. Cockerell, Hennessy, and Walker (1985), with case studies drawn from routine practices and crises, such as the Falklands conflict, concluded that the official managers of political news are too often allowed to dictate the agenda so that the machinery of government news management operates with the active collaboration of the press and broadcasters. They argued that, with important exceptions, there was too much complacency in the media instead of a passion for disclosure that could match Whitehall's passion for confidentiality:

Very few journalists have had the incentive to dig deeper, to mine the bedrock of power rather than merely scour its topsoil; too many have remained under the illusion that Parliament disposes, when power has so obviously passed to the Prime Minister and executive departments. Our colleagues will say: this is a counsel of perfection. Cliche haunted news-desks, unenterprising editors, cautious proprietors, conservative readers—all these explain why newspaper coverage of political news is as it is. But journalists have a wider obligation. We have failed to build an adequate information base for the voter. Until we do, the British political process will remain a pastiche of democracy. (Cockerell *et al.*, 1985: 11)

This is no less than a reminder that the press and now broadcasting are to be seen as a fourth estate, telling us what the powerful are doing in our name, uncovering secrets that elected representatives try to keep from the public, and by effective investigative journalism making the activities of our rulers and those in positions of authority in our society less opaque.

It is important to remember that both in press and broadcasting there remain significant examples of critical journalism, in terms of interviewing practice, television documentaries, and investigative journalism. When Jeremy Paxman says that his interviewing of politicians is based upon the question 'Why is this bastard lying to me?', he is exemplifying the irreverence of authority that is a healthy element in the democratic process. The fact that he and other journalists such as John Humphrys and the late Brian Redhead have been castigated by politicians is worth noting, as are the attempts by senior politicians to avoid being interviewed by people who they fear might give them a hard time. More generally, John Simpson, the BBC's Foreign Affairs Editor, has argued that when the government starts attacking the media it is an infallible sign that it is getting rattled (Simpson, 1993). He refers to the situation in Northern Ireland and in Bosnia, and to the attack from Norman Tebbitt, when Chairman of the Conservative Party, of the

BBC's coverage of the American bombing of Libya in 1986, when aircraft based in Britain were deployed.

It is in time of war that critical journalism can be especially difficult to practise, against a background of propaganda and government pressures (see, for example, Knightley, 1982 and Taylor, 1995). It has often been observed that the Vietnam War was the first to be covered extensively by television reporters and the relationship between the media and governments has been affected on both sides by that experience (Williams, 1993). This would include the Falklands conflict, the American invasion of Grenada, and the Gulf War. The Gulf War of 1991 came in the aftermath of the Iraqi invasion of Kuwait in August 1990, which Iraq claimed as its nineteenth province. With the backing of the United Nations, the United States, under President Bush, obtained a coalition of thirty nations, including other oil-producing states in the Middle East. The original purpose of defending other states, notably Saudi Arabia, against Iraqi aggression and developing a diplomatic offensive against Iraq by the use of economic sanctions was transformed into one of a war against Iraq, which was launched in January 1991. The propaganda for this 'war of liberation', with the promotion of the just-war concept, was intense. This was supported by black propaganda. A well-circulated example was the story that Iraqi troops in Kuwait had snatched babies from hospital incubators and thrown them to the floor, where they died. This story was false and had been manufactured by the American public relations company Hill and Knowlton, who were working for the Kuwaiti government in exile.

The Gulf War was covered worldwide on television networks and in the world's press. Some 1,500 journalists were in the region. The paraphernalia of satellites, cameras, telephones, and computers went with them. The 24-hour American news channel, CNN, was conspicuous. Their coverage included reports from Baghdad on the opening night of the Allied offensive, which attracted the largest television audience in broadcasting history (Taylor, 1995: 288). They were also in Jerusalem the next night wearing gas masks, when misleading reports about Scud missiles with chemical warheads went uncorrected for several hours. The overall impression given was that the Allies were co-ordinating a technologically sophisticated war machine. This meant that the weapons were 'smart' laser-guided missiles of great accuracy, able to do their work with surgical precision. Press conferences given by the army typically showed video film of such attacks, from cameras that had been placed on the noses of the weapons. Yet, after the war, it became known that only 7–8 per cent of the weapons used were smart bombs. Most of the bombs dropped were free-fall, coming from B-52 aircraft flying from a height of 30,000 feet, on Iraqi troops in Kuwait and southern Iraq. These planes were the same type as those used in the Vietnam War. In all the hype surrounding the weapons technology it was difficult to hear alternative questioning voices. John Pilger, who had been in Vietnam, was one who drew attention to the role of the B-52s and the practice of 'carpet bombing', but one would have had to be up very late at night to hear him. Some 30,000 Iraqi soldiers were killed in this way. The Vietnam War was also remembered for the use of napalm bombs. One photograph of a naked child running, burned by napalm, had brought the horror of it back home to America. It was a sensitive subject. The use of napalm in the Gulf was acknowledged when an American citizen, under the Freedom of Information Act, obtained the reply that the US Marines had dropped 489 napalm bombs on the trenches (Maggie O'Kane, *Guardian*, 16 December 1995).

Despite the large numbers of journalists, they were not present when the ground fighting took place. They did not witness the burying alive by tanks and tractors of up to 2,000 Iraqi troops in their trenches. At the end of the war two Iraqi columns retreated from Kuwait. Both of these were attacked by Allied planes, but only one of them was later filmed. At this stage some journalists referred to it as a 'turkey shoot', as had some of the attackers. Out of that came the recognition that it had not, after all, been such a clean war. In particular, *The Observer* published Kenneth Jaercke's photograph of the charred corpse of an Iraqi soldier in his tank. This was done to remind us of the absence of human death and suffering throughout most of the coverage. The emphasis on immediacy and on-the-spot reporting did not make for more information or under-standing despite all the accumulated technology of modern commun-ications. It was, indeed, as Taylor suggests, a significant example of the new world information disorder (Taylor, 1995). This was not easy to challenge at the time, although possibilities existed, as journalists such as Charles Wheeler, John Pilger, Philip Knightley, and Robert Fiske appreciated. It was also possible to have inquests on journalistic cover-age, as the BBC did both for the Falklands conflict and the Gulf War. Moreover, subsequently, journalistic work has been done on the plight of the Kurds, of the Marsh Arabs in South Iraq, and on the emergence of health problems among combatants in the Gulf—what is collectively termed the Gulf War Syndrome.

The war in former Yugoslavia, with all its labyrinthine twists, has been the subject of an impressive BBC series, accompanied by a book of the same title, *The Death of Yugoslavia* (Silber and Little, 1995). This is an outstanding example of what journalism—press and television—can do to interpret this period of pain and tragedy in Europe, in which the language of 'ethnic cleansing' and 'genocide' was used to describe the brutal realities taking place. A year earlier Ed Vulliamy (1994) addressed squarely the problem of objectivity in journalism:

For some reason the instinct to stand by democratic Europe's basic principles was to be considered 'pro-Muslim' in Bosnia and the principles were sunk beneath what people shrugged off as 'the realities on the ground' or some bizarre requirement that we remain 'objective' over the most appalling racialist violence. (Vulliamy, 1994: 11)

He and other journalists found that their reports of atrocities and concentration camps, although drawn to world attention, appeared to have no impact on international policy and action, especially in Europe itself. Many of them concluded that this was the most dangerous war they had ever covered. In June 1993, Maggie O'Kane observed that few journalists work alone anymore:

The Croats hate the press, accusing them of taking sides with the Bosnian Muslims. The Bosnians, who have so long clung to the hope of international military intervention, now know the cavalry is not coming and realise that winning the propaganda war no longer matters. (O'Kane, *Guardian*, 19 June 1993)

Magazines like *Time*, press agencies like Reuters were reducing their coverage:

Who cares? The Serbs, Croats and Muslims have begun the final scramble for Bosnia. The Serbs are battering the 'safe havens' of Gorazdne, Zepa and Srebrenica. In Gorazde 40,000 people are trapped while thousands of Muslims surrounded in the stinking ghetto in Mostar are waiting for the final Croat offensive. In the central valley of Vitez over 70,000 Croats are packing their bags for exile. (O'Kane, *Guardian*, 19 June 1993)

But journalists like Vulliamy, O'Kane, and Simpson were able to be present as witnesses even if they were not able to influence outcomes as they sometimes hoped. They were also able to report on the conditions under which they worked. And it was still possible to do investigative journalism, as Jon Sweeney showed. He wrote a report for *The Observer* (10 September 1995) and produced a film for BBC's *Spin* (13 September 1995) showing the United Nations cover-up about events in Srebrenica after its designated 'safe area' was overrun by Bosnian Serbs. Some 2,700 Muslim men were taken away and have never been seen since. They are widely believed to have been massacred. Dutch UN troops who were there took photographs and film of some of the violence and brutality, including evidence of murder that took place. The video material was destroyed on the orders of the Head of the Royal Netherlands Army, General Hans Couzy.

However, Sweeney obtained some other film taken by a Serb camera-man, which showed UN troops standing by while Serb troops separated Muslim men and women, with the men being led into a remote field. He also saw a memorandum written by a UN civil affairs officer which detailed some of the executions that had been witnessed by the UN troops and reported that dead civilians had also been found. He also pointed out that a disinformation campaign about the fall of the town was carried out by British MI6 intelligence officers when they briefed defence correspondents in London, even when the truth of the matter was already known to them. They operated what Sweeney called 'an anti-Muslim spin' and claimed that the Muslim troops disappeared before it fell. This led to *The Times* headlining the fall of Srebrenica on 14 July 1995: 'Muslim Troops Fail to Defend Town from Serbs'. Such a spin would make the story of the fall of this so-called safe area less hor-rific and the UN that much less culpable. It is the investigative journal-ist who, by disciplined curiosity, can tell us that things are not always as they seem. When this is done in relation to the great affairs of state, then the perks of corporate journalism are subordinated to the public inter-est. At such moments we can begin to recover the concept of a free press.

Part III

Media Audiences and Reception

Chapter Ten

Audience Reception Theory

Why does it matter who controls the media? Why do governments employ spin doctors and PR consultants? Why is anyone interested in how the media report industrial disputes, immigration, war, famine, AIDS, or sexual violence? Why does anyone care how the press and television represent different political parties, ethnic minorities, or lesbians and gay men? Concern about the control, operation, and content of the mass media is based on the assumption that the media are powerful—that they influence the beliefs and ultimately the actions of viewers, listeners, and readers. One therefore cannot look at power and the media without examining media audiences.

This final part of the book explores some of the different ways in which the relationship between the media and their audiences has been theorized. This chapter provides a brief overview of the history of audience reception theory and concludes with an introduction to Stuart Hall's analysis of audience decodings and David Morley's attempt to explore this empirically. The next chapter, Chapter 11, concentrates on a critical discussion of the 'domestic technology' approach to audience theory, examining people's use of media technologies and the process of consumption. Chapter 12 concentrates on theories about audience pleasure and Chapter 13 introduces the Glasgow Media Group's research into media influence on public understandings.

The public and political debates outlined in Chapter 2 have been paralleled by academic theorizing about the effect of the media on their audiences. Attempts to investigate systematically the role, influence, and ethics of communication pre-date the invention of televison, radio, or even the printing press. They pre-date the debates about rock and roll music in the 1950s, cinema in the 1930s, or even the music halls of the 1840s. We know that centuries earlier, political and military leaders, preachers, poets, and playwrights theorized about the effect of different types of communication. They were concerned to move their audiences to obedience or revolutionary fervour, anger or joy, critical thought or strong emotion. The ancient Greeks, for example, developed highly sophisticated theories about how to impress one's audience through the power of the spoken word. Aristotle's *Rhetoric* (fourth century BC) was concerned with theorizing about the art of speaking and examined 'the recesses and windings' of the human heart in order to discover how to 'to excite, to ruffle, to amuse, to gratify or to offend it' (Copleston, 1810; cited in Cooper, 1932).

The origin of modern media studies, however, is usually located in 1930s Germany with the work of scholars such as Adorno, Marcuse, and Horkheimer. It is these writers who coined the term 'mass culture'—a concept originally suggested by the Nazi propaganda machine but then applied to the American capitalist media. Their theories were developed in response to Germany's descent into fascism and the apparent failure of the revolutionary social change predicted by Marx. This group, collectively known as 'The Frankfurt School', theorized that the breakdown of society into a collection of atomized individuals left people vulnerable to propaganda. It promoted a 'hypodermic model' of media effects whereby media messages were directly absorbed into the hearts and minds of the people.

This thesis was challenged by work carried out by American researchers in the 1940s and 1950s, who were concerned with the role of personal influence. These writers highlight the role of social networks in mediating public responses to the media. Merton's work on mass persuasion (1946) focuses on the importance of reference groups in influencing the messages which people accept from political campaigns. Katz and Lazersfeld's research on personal influence (1955) posits a two-step model whereby media messages are mediated by 'opinion leaders' who influence how ideas are taken up by members of their communities.

The Frankfurt School was also challenged by a third theory, the Uses and Gratifications (U&G) approach. Uses and Gratifications theory is diametrically opposed to the 'hypodermic model'. In fact, it turns traditional ways of thinking about media effects on their head. It replaces the question 'what do the media do to people?' with the question 'what do people do with media?' Rather than thinking of a media message as a powerful substance injected into the public mind, Uses and Gratifications scholars explore how people actively process media materials in accordance with their own needs. These theorists argue that individuals make a conscious selection between the various items of media content—choosing what they will watch and for what purposes. The degree and kind of media 'effect' will therefore depend on the need of the audience member concerned and is more likely to reinforce rather than change beliefs.

The Uses and Gratifications approach was most prominent during the 1970s and 1980s with the work of academics such as McQuail (1972), Blumler and Katz (1974), and Rozengren *et al.* (1985). However, an early example of U&G theory is evident in Herzog's pioneering work in the 1940s on women's consumption of radio serials (the earliest form of soap opera). Her research is based on interviews with 100 women from a variety of age and income groups and provides a fascinating portrait of women's lives at that time. She demonstrates how listeners could interpret the same radio serial quite differently according to their own needs and identifies three main types of 'gratification' obtained from these programmes. First, she argues that the serials provided an outlet for 'pent-up anxieties in giving the listener a "chance to cry" '. Secondly, she states that they permitted a wishful escape from isolation and drudgery. For example, she describes the life of a 'colored maid' in 1940s America who 'listens to twenty-two stories daily. To this person of very little education, with no friends or relatives and few opportunities for a normal life, the radio stories are practically everything. "Sunday", she said, "is a very bad day for me. I don't know what to do with myself. During the week I have the stories" ' (Herzog, 1941: 69). Thirdly, Herzog argues that the radio serials provide 'recipes for adjustment'. These early soap operas

explain things by providing labels for them. Happenings in a marriage, in a family, in a community are verbalised in the programs and the listeners are made to feel that they understand better what is going on around them. Listening provides them with an ideology to be applied in the appraisal of the world which is actually confronting them. (Herzog, 1941: 69)

This perspective was explicitly articulated by her interviewees, although some people might interpret their statements as evidence of the ideological power of soap opera, rather than evidence to support Uses and Gratifications theory. For example, the woman who spoke to Herzog made comments such as: 'Listening to the stories lets me know how other girls act and listening to the way that girl argued today, I know how to tell my boy friend where he can get off' (Herzog, 1941: 90), and:

I like family stories best. If I get married I want to get an idea of how a wife should be to a husband. Some of the stories show how a wife butts into everybody's business, and the husband gets mad and they start quarrelling. The stories make you see things. (Herzog, 1941: 90)

Such empirical investigation of radio and television audiences is in striking contrast to the dominant research paradigm emerging out of film theory in Britain during the 1970s and 1980s. The most influential film theory can be found in the journal *Screen*. It is this '*Screen* theory' which marks the fourth major strand of thinking about audiences. The contributors to *Screen* rarely speak to real-life viewers. Instead they approach the audience through a detailed examination of the structure of the text and an examination of how that text positions the reader. Writers such as Stephen Heath, Laura Mulvey, and Colin MacCabe draw on French film theory and Lacanian psychoanalysis, which emphasize the 'de-centred' nature of subjectivity—its necessarily provisional and precarious status. Subjectivity, they argue, does not simply exist as a static and unified entity but is created through language and culture. They use these Lacanian insights about the nature of subjectivity in analysing films. In particular, they are interested in how the cinematic text confers subjectivity upon readers, sewing or 'suturing' them into the film's narrative through the production of subject position. A prime example of cinematic 'suture' (Heath, 1977) is the shot/reverse shot formation—where the camera presents the audience with, for example, a shot of the protagonist looking at something, followed by a shot taken from the protagonist's perspective (or vice versa). The viewer is therefore literally offered the fictional character's perspective, or placed in their shoes.

This analysis offers an effective analytical tool. It is possible, for example, to examine rape scenes to see whether they are shot from the perpetrator's or the victim's point of view and, more generally, analysis of camera angles reveals that films tend to construct masculine subject positions—the spectator is encouraged to identify with the male protagonists and objectify the female figure via the voyeuristic 'male gaze' (Mulvey, 1975).

Writers from the *Screen* theory perspective focus on the power of such traditional cinematic devices and argue that such positioning of the spectators sucks them into the film's ideology. *Screen* theorists therefore argue less for the reform of film *content* than for an abandonment of structures which smoothly absorb the viewer into the film's text. They criticize the realism of film-making Hollywood-style, which erases the constructed nature of the text, making the editing, framing, and selecting process invisible. Instead, they praise productions which foreground the machinery of representation, such as in the theatre of Brecht or the avant-garde practices of film-makers such as Jean-Luc Godard (MacCabe, 1980).

The four schools of thought outlined above represent different ways of thinking about media power. This outline is by no means comprehensive. It ignores a whole strand of mainstream psychological theorizing using stimulus–response models and laboratory experiments (e.g. to examine the impact of media violence). Nor have we covered all the more sociological analyses. It is worth reading, for example, the 'cultivation theory' developed by Gerbner (1973). However, the overview presented above does show some of the key variables in the history of thinking about media influence (whether in the form of film, television, newspapers, or radio). *Screen* theory presents the traditional Hollywood film as extremely powerful, forcing the hapless viewer to take on the identity and ideology preordained by the text. The Frankfurt School, from a different point of view, adopts a similarly pessimistic position: the masses are manipulated by the powerful forces of propaganda. A quite different perspective is presented by the researchers who highlight the importance of social networks, reference groups, and 'opinion leaders' in mediating media effect. An even more fundamental challenge comes from the Uses and Gratification theorists, who see power lying in the hands (or eyes and ears) of the audience rather than the media. However, the most interesting challenge to all the above perspectives occurred during the 1970s with the Encoding/Decoding approach developed at the Birmingham Centre for Contemporary Cultural Studies. It is this fifth approach which will now be introduced.

The Birmingham Centre for Contemporary Cultural Studies (BCCCS), originally led by Stuart Hall, was influenced by Gramsci's concept of 'hegemony'. The theory of 'hegemony' is that ideological domination can never be complete but is a continuous struggle in which the media are crucial. Media studies within this paradigm is therefore concerned with how the media 'manufacture consent' to the dominant order. Theorists at the BCCCS explicitly opposed *Screen* theory, which dominated thinking in Britain during the 1970s. They argued that this structuralist approach is inadequate because it fails to explore the relationship between texts and actual audiences. It fails to examine whether people actually accept the subject position offered to them and, if they do, whether that necessitates accepting the ideological content of the film (Morley, 1980: 153). *Screen* theory, critics argue, gives little acknowledgement to diversity between viewers in how they may 'read' the media. The encounter between text and reader is viewed in isolation from all social and historical structures and without regard to audiences' actual, diverse experiences. Some of this criticism of the classic early *Screen* approach comes from within film theory. For example, the way in which Mulvey, and many of her followers, theorize 'the male gaze' has been criticized for neglecting differences between viewers, such as their sexual identity (Stacey, 1988), and for privileging gender differences in a way which actively suppresses recognition of race (hooks, 1992: 123). Other challenges come from outside film theory and question the approach for failing to recognize that readers come to texts already constituted as subjects, with their own preferences, identities, and opinions.

The foundations for developing an alternative approach were laid by Stuart Hall's influential paper, 'Encoding and Decoding the TV Message' (1973). This stresses the need to take the communicative process as a whole—with the moment of programme making at one end and the moment of audience reception at the other. Hall argues that texts are 'polysemic', being open to more than one reading, and that there is no necessary correspondence between the message encoded by the film or programme maker and that decoded by audiences. Hall proposes three hypothetical positions from which decodings of a televisual discourse might be constructed: the dominant, the negotiated, and the oppositional. The dominant-hegemonic position was where the viewer 'takes the connoted meaning from, say, a television newscast or current affairs programme full and straight, and decodes the message in terms of the reference code in which it has been encoded, we might say that the viewer is *operating inside the dominant code*' (Hall, 1973: 101). The negotiated position involves accepting the legitimacy of the dominant framework in the abstract, but negotiating the application of this framework to 'local conditions'. For example, a worker may accept a news broadcast's hegemonic definition of the economic necessity of freezing wages in 'the national interest' in order to avoid inflation but still be willing to oppose such measures at the level of the shopfloor. The oppositional position, by contrast, challenges the broader hegemonic framing of the problem—questioning whether wage freezes do indeed serve the 'national interest' or only the interest of the dominant class.

Hall's distinction between 'encoding' and 'decoding' highlights the possibility that 'meaning' does not lie in the text alone. Researchers cannot accurately predict how audiences will relate to and interpret a particular cultural product simply by analysing headlines and photographs, camera angles, lighting, sound track, and scripts. Paying attention to the process of decoding also opens up questions of audience diversity and allows that 'other discourses are always in play besides those of the particular text in focus—discourses . . . brought into play though "the subject's" placing in other practices—cultural, educational, institutional' (Morley, 1980: 163). In other words, people are not blank slates who approach a film without any pre-existing identity, experience, or resources. They come to the cinema (or TV set) with sets of prior opinions, views, and ideas of themselves. In order to understand the role of the media it is therefore, Hall argues, imperative to discover how different groups respond to and interpret any particular programme, to explore the resources they bring to bear on their interpretation and the discourse to which they have access.

On the surface, this approach might seem to converge with the Uses and Gratifications perspective. Both approaches acknowledge that texts can have multiple meanings and that the text-reader relationship takes the form of a negotiation. Both think about audiences as 'active' and watching television as a social process. Certainly, some of the work inspired by Hall is reminiscent of earlier work. Remember, for example, the women (from a variety of age and income brackets) in Herzog's 1941 study, who took different messages from the same radio serial. However, there are some crucial differences between the theories developed at BCCCS and the Uses and Gratifications research paradigm as it has become established over time. Whatever the implications of individual pieces of work (and Herzog's study is worth rereading in this respect) the U&G tradition has focused on how individuals use the media to satisfy their needs and achieve their goals. It tends to exaggerate audience 'freedom' and 'choice' and rely on a psychological conception of human personality which focuses narrowly on the media's function for the individual. The work at the BCCCS, by contrast, relies on a social theory of subjectivity and meaning construction. Hall's argument is that the range of different interpretations are not free-floating or individual readings but are influenced by the social context. Rather than thinking about perception as personal or private, Hall argues that audience research should be in the business of locating 'significant clusters' of meaning and linking these to the social and discursive positioning of readers. He is interested in 'inking in the boundaries of various interpretative communities', drawing up a 'cultural map' of the audience, and relating these to social and political processes.

It was this understanding which laid the ground for a flowering of sociologically informed and in-depth empirical work with actual audiences during the 1980s and 1990s. One of the first, and most influential, of these studies was David Morley's work on people's responses to the popular current affairs programme *Nationwide*. David Morley and Charlotte Brundson had already conducted a textual analysis of the programme. Morley then decided to study ordinary viewers' interpretations. His aim was to produce a typology of different responses and examine how these related to people's various socio-economic positions. To this end, he showed video recordings of an episode of *Nationwide* to 29 groups of people including managers, students, apprentices, and trade unionists. The video showings were followed by group discussions.

Morley's work confirms Hall's theory that there are at least three possible readings of a text—the dominant reading (accepting the preferred reading of the text), a negotiated reading, and an oppositional reading. His findings show that people differed in their critique of the style of the programme and their critique of the content/framework and that this was related to class. For example, managers objected to the style of *Nationwide* but accepted the content, whereas trade unionists did the opposite. However, Morley also found that many people across a range of groups were well aware of the 'preferred' meanings embedded in the programme and that 'awareness of the construction by no means entails the rejection of what is constructed' (Morley, 1980: 140). He also found that class alone was inadequate to explain the diversity of audience responses. There were differences between working-class people active within the trade union movement and those who were not. There were also additional cross-cutting differences to do with age, gender, and ethnicity.

Moving on from this study Morley became increasingly interested in the context of consumption. He was concerned about the 'unnatural' settings in which his study of *Nationwide* audiences had been conducted. His research participants might never have chosen to watch *Nationwide* in the first place, and were unlikely to have engaged in such in-depth discussion and analysis of the programme in the normal course of events. He also hypothesized that the reading a shop steward makes in company with other shop stewards may be very different from the interpretation he might make at home in conversation with his partner, the most usual viewing situation. Morley's next study therefore focused on how people actually watched television at home and he subsequently went on to scrutinize the impact of the media *as technological hardware*, e.g. the effect of having television in the home alongside other technologies such as the computer or phone (Morley and Silverstone, 1991). It is this approach to audience reception analysis—the analysis of the process of consumption itself—that is introduced in more depth in the next chapter, Chapter 11. This is followed by a discussion of another key branch of theorizing about audience—theorizing about audience pleasures and diverse interpretations. The final chapter, Chapter 13, then returns us to the question of media influence and examines the evidence of media 'effects' drawing on the work of the Glasgow Media Group.

Figure 10.1 Glued to the set?

Chapter Eleven

Consuming the Media: Communication Technology and Audience Choice

Examining how people actually consume cultural products (e.g. how they watch television or listen to the radio) has become a thriving area of media research. In previous chapters, we discussed the potential impact of technological changes on the *form* and *nature* of messages (from the development of photography to the technologies which allowed for constant live coverage of the Gulf War). But concerns about the effect of such changes are not confined to the message content. As different media and technologies have come on line, questions are also asked about the impact on family and cultural life. Just as women's cinema attendance attracted disapproval at the turn of the century (see Chapter 2) so the attractions of the original daytime radio soaps rang warning bells for some critics. The psychiatrist Louis Berg claimed that listening to radio serials caused: 'acute anxiety states, tachycardia, arrythmias, increase in blood pressure, profuse perspiration, tremors, vasomotor instability, nocturnal frights, vertigo, and gastro-intestinal disturbances'. He based this claim on subjecting himself to an intensive listening period (quoted in Allen, 1985: 21). Concern was also expressed about the effect of the new media on the welfare of children. Some critics worried that women might 'evade' their maternal responsibility and use television and radio as electronic baby-sitters (it was this concern which led to the introduction of *Listen with Mother* and *Watch with Mother*, conceived in order to involve women in their children's media consumption). Television in particular, regardless of programme content, has been accused of reducing literacy, destroying the art of conversation, and interrupting proper child development (Winn, 1977). Critics such as Winn depict children being turned into zombies: 'the child's facial expression is transformed. The jaw is relaxed and hangs open slightly; the tongue rests on the front teeth (if there are any). The eyes have a glazed vacuous look' (quoted in Root, 1986: 10). From a different perspective other writers are alarmed by television's stranglehold on leisure time. They argue that this serves the interests of the dominant class—consuming energies which might otherwise be mobilized in political actions. The average viewing time among adults in Britain is 26 hours per week, the heaviest in Europe (Golding, 1994). This is a disappointment to some left-wing commentators, who point out that the class struggle to increase autonomy and reduce working hours was not intended simply to free up empty leisure time, 'filled for better or worse by the programmed distractions of the mass media and the oblivion merchants' (Gorz, cited in Lodziak, 1986: 146).

Such concerns have been countered by those who argue that television is not simply 'peddling oblivion' and that such reactions are symptomatic of political arrogance or Luddite 'techno-fear'. Rather than adopting a technological deterministic approach (assuming that technologies carry with them inevitable fixed consequences), researchers such as Morley and Silverstone (1991) argue for empirical investigations of how people actually use technologies. They examine what technologies people buy and why, and how they use them in everyday life—from the positioning of television sets in the home to the use of the remote control device. Such research points to the fact that people are not passive consumers at the mercy of technological instruments but active users of different technologies and mediums.

Just because the average television is switched on for several hours a day does not mean it is being avidly watched. Indeed, surveys asking about actual viewing practices suggest that, for most viewers, 'watching telly' is usually combined with a whole range of other activities (see Gunter and Svennevig, 1988). This is confirmed by in-depth interviews, spy cameras and participant observation in people's homes which show that TV viewers are often not 'viewing' the television at all. People may simply have the TV on for company and pay little attention to the visual images. They may play cards with their backs to the screen, fight, talk, cook, or do their homework (McQuail et al., 1972; Collet and Lamb, 1986; Palmer, 1986: 63).

Rather than colonizing creative leisure time, television viewing may be used to recuperate from work and simply replace 'doing nothing' (Curran and Tunstall, 1973). Rather than 'taking over' it may be integrated into people's day-to-day lives and serve particular purposes in the social organization of the home. 'Housewives' may use the radio (or a soap opera or women's magazines) to structure the repetitious and monotonous nature of their working day (Hobson, 1980; Modleski, 1984; Winship, 1987). Watching television may be used to calm a tired and fractious child (Brodie and Stoneman, 1983) or as an opportunity to sit down and have a cuddle. Alternatively, people may switch on the television because they want to 'switch off' from interacting with other people (Lull, 1980, 1990; Bausinger, 1984) and, in a crowded home, TV viewing may 'function as a way of avoiding conflicts, of lessening tensions in lieu of spatial privacy' (Lindlof and Traudt, 1983).

Far from destroying 'the art of conversation', it is argued, television may actually serve as a social glue. Programmes provide a conversational resource. Soap operas, for example, provide a sort of 'virtual community', creating a shared virtual reality in which moral and personal dilemmas may be explored. Soaps are discussed in the home while they are being broadcast and also provide common topics for discussion with friends, colleagues, or even complete strangers ('Did you see . . .' is a routine opening gambit).

Technology such as the video machine can also allow audiences to take more control over their viewing practices and shared video-watching can be used as a social event in itself (Gray, 1987). It can also be a way of gaining access to cultural resources unavailable on mainstream programming (or only shown unsociably late at night). Gillespie, for example, shows how viewing Asian film videos acts as a forum for the negotiation of British Asian identity (Gillespie, 1989; 1995). Indeed, Ang argues that the use of video by groups of migrants all over the world (e.g. Indians, Chinese, and Turks)

offers opportunities of new forms of bonding and solidarity, new ways of forging cultural communities . . . The circulation and consumption of ethnically specific information and entertainment on video serves to construct and maintain crossnational 'electronic communities' of geographically dispersed peoples. (Ang, 1990*a*: 255)

Research into the practical and social aspects of audience interactions with the television set (and other media such as books or the radio) identifies the ability of audiences to use media technologies in their own interests. It provides an important correction to naïve assumptions about the nature of that relationship (assumptions explicit in phrases such as 'telly addicts', 'soap junkies', and 'couch potatoes'). This research, presents the one-eyed monster lurking in the corner of the living room as more a cuddly ET than a threatening Frankenstein creation.

Interest in the use of media technologies and the process of consumption also opens up new questions about power, not the power of the media *per se*, but the social power structures within which consumption is embedded. One extension of this line of inquiry involves examining the television set itself as a cultural object which carries symbolic meaning. For example, one's choice of media hardware can indicate status, disposable income, and taste (or the lack of it). The appearance of satellite dishes in a particular street is used by estate agents to signal that an area is going 'downmarket', but possessing a flat-screen high-definition television implies high standards and discriminating tastes (Morley, 1995). In fact, media technologies may carry meaning independent of their usual use. In a community in Sri Lanka richer villagers often display television sets as the centrepiece of their personal collections of 'wealth signifiers' despite the fact that the lack of electricity supply makes the sets inoperable, in any narrow functional sense (Gell, 1986; cited in Morley, 1995: 314–15).

Within the home itself, media technologies are also an important site of 'living room politics' (Cubitt, 1985). Men and women, adults and children compete over the media hardware: who has a TV in their bedroom or who gets the small black and white set. They also struggle over its use: what, when, and how to watch television and what counts as acceptable or unacceptable, high-status or low-status programmes. Research in this sphere often reveals a depressing picture in which, for example, men tend to monopolize the remote control and priorltize their programme preferences, while women are expected to interrupt their viewing to take care of children and cooking (Morley, 1986).

However, such research is often also concerned with identifying sites of resistance. In particular, much of this work explores the creative way in which women use reading, television viewing, or radio listening in the context of traditional family life. Coming from a background in literary studies, Radway showed how women used the romantic novel to create space away from their 'duties' as wives and mothers (Radway, 1984). Others have documented how 'addiction' to soap opera may be employed by women to establish time where they are not available and attentive to the needs of others (Brunsdon, 1981; Hobson, 1982; Seiter *et al.*, 1989). Hobson's work even suggests that women may use soap watching as a way to 'kick against patriarchal domination' because they know their husbands despise it (Fiske, 1991: 75). The practice of viewing (or reading or listening) is thus a weapon in gender skirmishes around the structure of social relations in the home and, more broadly, may be an assertion of a woman's independence.

The 'domestic technology' approach to theorizing about audiences thus focuses on the actual practice of consumption and uses of media technologies. It focuses on how people view or read the media and the meanings they make from these processes. Through this lens, TV watching is seen to be about much more than consuming media messages; it is a way of negotiating social relationships, identities, and desires.

Some scholars argue that this is the cutting edge of media studies, the way forward for theorizing about media audience. According to proponents such as Ang, this approach enables us to conceive of 'the ideological operations of television in a much more radical way than has hitherto been done'. It allows us to see that

If television is an 'ideological apparatus' . . . this is not so much because its texts transmit certain 'messages' as because it is a cultural form through which those constraints [on structuring social relationships, identities, and desires] are negotiated and those possibilities take shape. (Ang, 1989: 109)

Examination of media consumption processes has certainly introduced important new perspectives into media studies. The insights coming from this line of research should never be ignored. However, there are costs in prioritizing this approach and many problems in some of the research which is pursued under the rubric of the 'domestic technology' paradigm. There are also dangers in how existing studies are interpreted, abstracted, and marshalled to create a celebratory image of 'active consumption' that misrepresents the actual power relations between the media and their audiences. Before concluding this chapter, it is therefore necessary to unpack some of these problems.

First, it should be noted that there are some clear limitations in the existing focus of enquiry. For example, while purporting to be about the 'media', such work routinely concentrates on the television set and virtually ignores the press. There is little acknowledgement that a TV news bulletin, for example, is just one form of a story released through a series of different media, including newspapers.

Secondly, although claiming to be about how media are consumed 'in everyday life', most of these studies focus on the moment of consumption within the traditional nuclear family to the virtual exclusion of all other contexts. Most also fail to explore the practical consequences of an 'empowered' consumption process. Important exceptions to this include Brown's work on gossip networks (Brown, 1994) and Bobo's work on black women's reception of the film *The Color Purple* (Bobo, 1988).

Thirdly, there is the danger in some 'domestic technology' work of indulging in endless vacuous discoveries of audience activity. Some researchers seem to be pursuing ever 'thicker' and more in-depth ethnographies which foreground the banal practicalities of television viewing as if they were major revelations rather than important background information. There is nothing very earth-shattering about the observation that people may knit or mend a puncture while watching *EastEnders*. However, such behaviour is treated with great amazement and even reverence by some researchers. One can only suppose they have spent far too long in the dark conducting decontextualized textual analysis. They seem to emerge blinking into the daylight of actual viewing situations with a wide-eyed, naïve surprise which lacks a critical perspective.

Fourthly, related to the above point, some of this work indulges in uncritical celebration of audience 'uses' of television. Some of the less sophisticated versions of this work imply that audience 'use' of the media for their own ends is *ipso facto* A Good Thing. However, as the in-depth work with families makes clear, it is misleading to celebrate an individual's 'use' of the television set without looking at how that operates in power relations with other people. If a man uses the TV to 'switch off' from any responsibility for housework or child care this cannot simply be celebrated as free-wheeling consumer sovereignty. It must be understood within the gender and generation politics of the household.

The more sophisticated work on consumption within the traditional family clearly challenges such assumptions but can commit its own 'error of optimism'. Some of this work overexaggerates the transformatory potential of alternative practices—as if revolution could be found in a woman watching a soap opera which her husband despises and 'freedom' meant channel-grazing with the remote control. Gender skirmishes within the home should not be confused with challenges to actual power relations in society as a whole. Nor is 'active consumption' a substitute for the ability to intervene in the press or broadcasting industry. The power to switch the television on or off, or integrate the set creatively into your life, is not comparable with the power to produce or influence programme content. Nor should a concern with how people 'appropriate' and 'use' technologies lose sight of the politics of production and distribution. People's access to media hardware is subject to material inequalities and the design and development of these technologies are shaped by economic and political forces (Golding and Murdock, 1990: 40; McGuigan, 1992: 160).

All four of the above criticisms can be dismissed as mere issues of emphasis or interpretation compared with the fifth, and most fundamental criticism. This criticism is that the domestic technology approach focuses on the *medium* at the expense of the *message*. It thus loses sight of the question which is unique and central to media studies—the question of the meanings conveyed via the press, radio, or television. Many of the studies of consumption processes fail (except perhaps in the final paragraph) to theorize the implications of their findings for the transmission of meanings via the television set. The understandings that people take away from what they hear and see has become subordinated (linguistically and/or conceptually) to the details of the consumption process. Although many of the researchers cited above *do* consider the meaning of texts, the 'domestic technology' approach as a whole is becoming increasingly diverted from such questions. Indeed, some media researchers are now pursuing the power struggles within families in ways which entirely neglect the content of programmes. The television is treated as an item of domestic technology equivalent to the microwave and watching television is studied as if it were no more and no less than other types of consumption. Many of these analyses of television watching could, for example, be applied equally to the process of food consumption: who cooks, who carves the joint, what people do while they are eating, the rituals, cultural meanings, and power struggles over food.

More worrying still is when such studies do not simply ignore questions of ideological effect, but seem to equate active audience use and control of the television with audience power and freedom from media influence. Some of these equations are implied by the deceptive use of language. As Seaman (1992) points out, these theorists say that viewers *use, employ,* or *exploit* the soap opera to make sense of real-life situations. However, one might equally state that people *rely* on it to do so. Similarly theorists who celebrate audience 'active consumption' argue that the television provides conversational *resources*. However, one could equally argue that people are *dependent* on, and restricted by, the discourse provided by the television. Seaman concludes that

If, as Morley would have it, television 'is being used to provide the reference points, the ground, the material, [and] the stuff of conversation' (Morley, 1986: 22), then in light of the sorts of information and views that we know are systematically excluded from the medium, we ought to find such 'uses' quite alarming ... (Seaman, 1992: 305)

It is crucial not to assume that the range of alternative activities that viewers perform while watching television necessarily undermine media power. Fiske, for example, although acknowledging that such studies 'do not tell us about the meanings that viewers make of television', goes on to argue that they do show that viewers 'are rarely dominated or controlled by it as so many of its critics would claim' (Fiske, 1991: 73). Such conclusions are only warranted if dominance and control are to be measured by the intensity of a viewer's engagement with 'the box'. It tells us little about the role of television as a conduit for information and ideas (or identities and desires). Alternatively, such conclusions rely on the assumption that inattentive audiences are less susceptible to media power. However, as we shall show later, the opposite may be true. The fact that people view or listen inattentively may simply reduce their chance of engaging critically with the media. It may also actually reinforce the power of dominant messages and undermine the influence of 'deviant' voices. The inattentive audience, then, is not inoculated against media influence and audience 'activity' in the physical sense (whether this is doing the ironing or turning cartwheels) should not be confused with conceptual activity.

The challenge for those interested in media consumption and power is to address both the meanings generated by the 'event' of consumption *and* the meanings read into and taken away from the text itself. This challenge was acknowledged by some of the original scholars who introduced a concern with the consumption process. However, it seems to have been evaded by subsequent researchers. The strength of Radway's work, for example, is that she holds on to the potential tensions between different strands of meaning generated by reading a romantic novel. On the one hand, she examines how such reading is used by women to create space for themselves and enjoy 'escapism'. On the other hand, she explores how romance literature promotes discourses antithetical to women's liberation. Radway shows how women use their reading of romantic fiction both to protest against and to escape temporarily from the limited roles prescribed for them. However, she also demonstrates how the romances paradoxically make those roles seem desirable (although she does this primarily through analysis of the text rather than reader responses). Radway argues that these books rationalize male violence as overwhelming desire or loss of control and help to keep women trapped by providing merely fantasy resolutions to female discontent. She highlights, for example, how the romance narrative includes the feminization of the hero. During the course of these books the arrogant, cruel, and unfeeling man becomes sensitized to the heroine's finer feminine sensibility. In this sense Radway is clear that, whatever the potential resistance in the act of reading, the books themselves propose a utopia which 'can be realised within the framework of existing, patriarchal power relations between men and women—an imaginary "solution" totally at odds with the feminist scenario' (Ang, 1985: 122).

To conclude, the insights emerging from work on TV as an item of domestic technology or the act of 'reading' (or viewing or listening) as a cultural activity have usefully enlarged the sphere of media studies.

They open up important new questions about the role of audiences and the operation of media power. Sensitive examination of these questions allows for a fuller exploration of the meanings of a romantic novel, a soap opera, a news bulletin, or a cartoon. However, while these insights should be incorporated into media studies, they should not be explored to the exclusion of examining the meanings understood from the text itself.

Chapter Twelve

Appropriating Pleasure: Diverse Interpretations and Audience Rereadings

How people watch television or read a book is not the only question which has attracted the attention of media researchers in recent years. An equally important and overlapping question is *why* people consume the media and what they get out of it. Central to that question is the issue of audience pleasure. This issue has been addressed primarily through studies of entertainment programmes and, in particular, through studies of female audiences. A key contribution to this area of enquiry was made during the 1980s by a group of women academics working at the Birmingham Centre for Contemporary Cultural Studies. In addition to drawing on Hall's distinction between encoded and decoded meaning, these academics were influenced by critical cultural theory—in particular, studies of leisure, style, and consumption. Male colleagues, such as Willis (1977) and Hebdige (1979), both of whom worked at the BCCCS, had examined 'sub-cultures' such as those of working-class lads, hippies, Rastafarianism, and punk. They challenged pervasive views of these youth cultures as delinquency or social pathology and, instead, examined them as evidence of symbolic resistance to the dominant culture. This approach was developed by writers on women's cultural consumption who shared a desire to counter perceptions of the media as bearers of dominant ideology invading the consciousness of the masses. Instead, they sought to emphasize popular resistance––demonstrating how oppressed groups create a meaningful world for themselves, 'using the very stuff offered to them by the dominant culture as raw materials and appropriating it in ways that suit their own interests' (Ang, 1990*a*: 246).

The writing on women's cultural consumption, however, is distinguished from previous work on 'youth culture' by adding in a gender analysis of this process. Authors such as Angela MacRobbie (who wrote about magazines and 'the culture of femininity'), Terry Lovell (who wrote about *Coronation Street*), Ien Ang (who studied *Dallas*), and Dorothy Hobson (who studied *Crossroads*) rejected the class and gender condescension displayed toward 'mass female culture' (magazines, romance, and soap opera). They also challenged specific academic neglect of 'the domestic' (female sphere) in preference for 'street culture' (where men and boys predominated). In particular they dissented from the predominant dismissal of female media genres as beneath serious critical attention. In this, their work acknowledges the way in which social hierarchies of 'good taste' and 'quality' versus 'popular' culture are socially constructed—an idea most closely associated with the French sociologist Pierre Bourdieu. Bourdieu draws attention to the close correspondence between socio-economic position and patterns of taste in art and music. Instead of simply accepting that the middle and upper classes have 'better taste' than the working class Bourdieu argues that hierarchies of cultural and aesthetic judgement are a way of defining and legitimating social difference. 'Taste', he argues, is an important 'cultural capital' that serves to maintain and reinforce inequalities (Bourdieu, 1986). Feminist researchers have taken a similar approach to the status given to 'masculine' taste (sports, 'hard' news, action movies) over 'feminine' taste (soaps, 'soft' news, romance). Instead of reifying such distinctions and accepting them as natural, many researchers into women's viewing practice were concerned to explore the 'feminine' skills brought to the consumption of female genres (women's underrated cultural competencies). They also, often, acknowledged their own enjoyment of such genres. Indeed, rather than positioning themselves as 'the critical outsider committed to condemn the oppressive world of mass culture', many of these writers consciously declared themselves as 'fans' alongside the subjects of their research and saw their role as 'giving voice to and celebrating audience recalcitrance' (Ang, 1990*a*: 246).

Examining why such genres were sources of pleasure was an essential part of this research agenda. The focus on pleasure was in clear opposition to mainstream Marxist thinking (as promoted by theorists such as Adorno and Horkheimer), in which pleasure was dismissed as manipulation. It was also a response to the success of Thatcherism in Britain during the 1980s, a success which 'had much to do with how it worked upon real conditions and desires, addressing ordinary people's material aspirations and stressing the sense of personal freedom and choice engendered by the market' (McGuigan, 1992: 113). In addition, for many researchers, a concern with pleasure was also part of a dialogue with feminism. As Janice Winship wrote about her study of women's magazines:

I felt that to simply dismiss women's magazines was also to dismiss the lives of millions of women who read and enjoyed them each week. More than that, *I* still enjoyed them, found them useful and escaped with them. And I knew I couldn't be the only feminist who was a 'closet' reader. (Winship, 1987: xiii; italics in original)

From the very start of second-wave feminism, popular culture was a key target of criticism (see Hermes, 1995). Betty Friedan, who wrote *The Feminine Mystique* (1963), was herself a former editor of women's magazines. She attacked mass media images of 'happy housewives' to which, she argued, women struggled to conform and by which they were condemned to a perpetual sense of failure. 'I helped create this image,' she wrote, '. . . but I can no longer deny my knowledge of its terrible implications' (Friedan, 1963: 59).

Feminist theory not only identified media misrepresentation of women's lives and the reality of female discontent, but also questioned women's pleasures. Pleasure (whether it came from reading romantic novels or pornography, wearing high-heeled shoes, or luxuriating in a real fur coat) became the subject of heated debate. Germaine Greer wrote, in *The Female Eunuch* (1971), that women's pleasure in the idealized romantic hero was evidence of women 'cherishing the chains of their bondage' (Greer, 1971: 176) and Susan Brownmiller's classic *Against Our Will* (1975) presented female fantasies of being ravished or 'taken' as 'a product of male conditioning' and 'a mirror-image female victim psychology' reflecting women's subordination (Brownmiller, 1975: 324).

One response to the feminist critique of popular culture and women's pleasure was to seek to 'imagine radically new forms of pleasure' and develop 'a political refashioning of the economies of pleasure' (Parker and Pollock, 1987: 54). Some feminists sought to do this through structural-social change and consciousness raising: talking about their own pleasure and pain, seeking to understand these 'subjective' and 'private' experiences in a political context and to reconstruct them in the light of this new perspective. Others set about developing innovative cultural forms: feminist films, magazines, photography, and art.

An alternative approach pursued by some feminists (sometimes the *same* feminists) was to engage actively with existing female pleasures and women's genres. These activists were concerned that structural-social change on its own was slow or insufficient, that consciousness raising had too restricted an appeal and that feminist art-forms were incomprehensible to most women. They argued that 'refashioning the economies of pleasure' ignored 'ordinary women' and were hopelessly idealistic and 'puritanical'. Retreating from simple opposition to mainstream culture or the attempt to create avant-garde alternatives, these feminists argued that it was important to explore and even celebrate women's enjoyment of mainstream culture. This should be done, they asserted, even when this culture might, at first glance, seem to operate against women's own interests, or to conflict with their political consciousness. Modleski, for example, challenged the idea that 'feminist artists must first of all challenge this [mainstream/masculine] pleasure and then out of nothing begin to construct a feminist aesthetics and feminist form'. This, she argued,

is a mistaken position. . . . [F]eminist artists don't have to start from nothing; rather, they can look for clues to women's pleasure which are already present in existing forms, even if this pleasure is currently placed at the service of patriarchy. (Modleski, 1984: 104)

It was against such a theoretical and political background that researchers began to study popular genres and, in particular, to conduct in-depth empirical work with female audiences. In order to illustrate the nature of such work, it is worth looking at specific research projects in detail. Here, we have chosen to focus on two studies—one conducted by Dorothy Hobson at the BCCCS, the other by Ien Ang at the University of Amsterdam.

Dorothy Hobson: Audience Reception of Crossroads

Hobson studied *Crossroads*: 'the most maligned programme on British Television' (Hobson, 1982: 36). At that time, this soap opera was attracting audiences of around 13 million, mainly female, viewers. Hobson went to women's homes to watch *Crossroads* with them and to discuss their enjoyment of the programme. She found that although *Crossroads* was broadcast during the early evening—a time of frantic activity for women involved in cooking tea and dealing with children coming home from school—they went to great efforts to watch, or at least listen to, this soap. Watching *Crossroads* was a considerable source of pleasure (Hobson, 1982: 115). For one woman, isolated with a young baby on the ninth floor of a tower block (an isolation that led her sometimes to kill time by counting cars as they passed below), the serial gave her 'something to look forward to the next day' (Hobson, 1982: 117). For others, it was a source of speculation and discussion—women enjoyed hypothesizing about the future actions of characters and would engage in sophisticated games with soap opera characters, including them in their 'gossip' even though fully cognizant of their fictional status. Above all, *Crossroads* was enjoyed for its 'emotional realism'. The acting might be poor and the situations implausible, but the emotional dilemmas were, in the words of one viewer, 'close to home' (Hobson, 1982: 109). Far from being meaningless escapism, in the sense of running away from problems and seeking diversion, Hobson argues that *Crossroads* was enjoyed because it focused on women's everyday difficulties (Hobson, 1982: 34).

Hobson also maintains that far from being passive, women were actively involved in bringing meaning to the programme by drawing on experiences in their own lives. She, herself, was sometimes surprised by how the women she studied reacted to particular episodes. For example, one story-line explored 'Glenda's frigidity and inability to have sexual intercourse with Kevin after they returned from honeymoon'. Hobson assumed that the elderly widow who participated in her research would not enjoy this storyline—but her assumption proved incorrect. The woman responded positively to this theme and talked to Hobson about sex when she was first married:

We used to say we were frightened of our husbands putting their trousers on the bedrail, you know, we had no pill, we had nothing. I mean . . . we were terrified really, if the man got anything out of it it's right, but you were too frightened to let yourself go. (Hobson, 1982: 135)

Such examples lead Hobson to conclude that viewers 'work with the text and add their own experience and opinions to the stories in the programme', a process which is actively encouraged by the serial format. Indeed, Hobson asserts that all soap opera is 'progressive' because of the work the audience contributes to the understanding of the drama. Soap opera, she argues, 'is one of the most progressive forms on television because it is a form where the audience is always in control'. According to Hobson, it does not matter how a specific dilemma is resolved—whether an abortion is considered a reasonable option, the husband suffers for having an affair, or the romance ends in marriage— the point is that the issue is raised for debate. The conclusion of the storyline is almost irrelevant because the serial format, in which the dilemma is discussed, allows audiences to incorporate their own perspectives. Hobson states: 'The production can include whatever solutions it wishes, the viewer *always knows best*. They will always reinterpret the ending and make allowances for the dramatic needs of the programme, or the ignorance of reality on the part of the producers' (Hobson, 1985; cited in McGuigan, 1992: 144). Attending to audience pleasure and acknowledging their active engagement with the text, challenges traditional analyses of media content. Hobson concludes:

> To look at a programme like *Crossroads* and criticize it on the basis of a conventional literary/media analysis is obstinately to refuse to understand the relationship which it has with its audience . . . To try to say what *Crossroads* means to its audience is impossible for there is no single *Crossroads*, there are as many different *Crossroads* as there are viewers. (Hobson, 1982: 135–6)

Ien Ang: Audience Reception of *Dallas*

Hobson's approach is echoed, at least superficially, by a study conducted by Ien Ang looking at the American soap *Dallas*, set in the home of a rich Texan oil family. Like *Crossroads*, this was a much-despised programme. Unlike *Crossroads*, it attracted international audiences. Indeed, during the 1980s it was the most widely viewed television programme in the world. In spring 1982, for example, over half the population of the Netherlands were watching *Dallas* every week—an unprecedented popularity which led to the programme being identified as the 'symbol of American cultural imperialism' (Sontag, cited in Ang, 1985: 2). Ang's work took place in the context of debates not only about 'female culture' but also about 'global culture', commercialization, and the threat to national identity and boundaries. Ang argues, however, that a political stance against the increasing commercialization of broadcasting at the level of policy should not 'preclude the recognition, at a cultural level, of the real enjoyment people take in commercially produced media material'. Her study was designed to explore 'the ways in which people actively and creatively make their own meanings and create their own culture, rather than passively absorb pre-given meanings imposed upon them' (Ang, 1990a: 242). Ang placed an advertisement in a Dutch women's magazine identifying herself as a fan of *Dallas* and inviting people to write to her about what they liked or disliked about the programme. Like Hobson, she found that

> there is not just one 'reason' for the pleasure of Dallas, which applies for everyone; each has his or her own more or less unique relationship to the programme. What appeals to us in such a television serial is connected with our individual life histories, with the social situation we are in, with the aesthetic and cultural preferences we have developed and so on. (Ang, 1985: 26)

For fans of *Dallas*, a large part of their pleasure came from the way in which the programme facilitated fantasy. Ang argues that rather than seeing such soaps as 'misrepresenting' reality, academics should acknowledge that these programmes are intended to be fiction and are recognized as such by their audiences. For example, 'feminist common sense', Ang declares,

> would undoubtedly ascribe the Sue Ellen character [in *Dallas*] to the realm of negative images, reflecting a traditional, stereotyped or trivialised model of womanhood. However, this approach . . . implies a rationalistic view of the relationship between image and viewer (whereby it is assumed that the image is seen by the viewer as a more or less adequate model of reality), it can only account for the popularity of soap operas among women as something irrational. In other words, what the role/image approach tends to overlook is the large emotional involvement which is invested in identification with characters of popular fiction. To counteract this attitude, we first of all need to acknowledge that these characters are products of fiction and that fiction is not a mere set of images to be read referentially, but an ensemble of textual devices for engaging the viewer at the level of fantasy. (Ang, 1990b: 83)

Like Hobson, Ang also argues that enjoyment of *Dallas* is based on its *emotional* rather than its *literal* realism. The complicated plot and over-the-top events of the *Dallas* melodrama are, she argues, regarded by fans as 'symbolic representations of more general living experience'. The dizzying round of infidelity, fires, memory loss, and discovery of long-lost relatives is undeniably unrealistic but, for *Dallas* enthusiasts, 'what is recognized as real is a subjective experience of the world: "a structure of feeling" '. It is this emphasis on feeling which is highlighted in the programme text—for example by the frequent use of close-up facial shots. Indeed, where the cliff-hanging ending of an action serial traditionally shows the hero literally clinging to the cliff by his finger-nails, the final freeze-frame shot of each episode of *Dallas* usually showed a close-up of a face signifying a psychological cliffhanger.

Ang argues that in order to enjoy such a programme it is therefore necessary to have certain cultural competencies:

> the tragic structure of feeling suggested by *Dallas* will only make sense if one can and will project oneself into, i.e. recognise, a melodramatic imagination. Viewers must therefore have a certain cultural competence or orientation to understand and evaluate *Dallas* in a melodramatic way. (Ang, 1985: 79)

In this, she echoes the assertion by Brunsdon that enjoying soap operas

> calls on the traditionally feminine competencies associated with the responsibility for 'managing' the sphere of personal life . . . sensitivity, perception, intuition and the necessary privileging of the concerns of personal life . . . Just as a Godard

film requires the possession of certain forms of cultural capital on the part of its audience to 'make sense' . . . so too does . . . soap opera. (Brunsdon, cited in Ang, 1985: 79)

Audience Diversity and Deviant Readings

Such investigations of women's viewing pleasures and cultural competencies are paralleled by other studies of cross-national and cross-cultural reception. These confirm that different people may enjoy programmes and interpret their meaning in quite diverse ways. They also demonstrate that the export of American films and television programmes is not a simple process of 'cultural colonization'. Katz and Liebes's study of the reception of *Dallas*, for example, found that Russian Jews, newly arrived in Israel, read *Dallas* as capitalism criticizing itself, while a Moroccan Jew 'learned' from the series that Jewishness was the right way to be—because it was clear that non-Jews lived messy and immoral lives (Katz and Liebes, 1985).

Within a single country, different cultural interpretations may also produce quite distinct 'readings' of a single film or programme. A study of women's reactions to representations of violence against women reports that a group of British Asian women 'learned' from *The Accused* (a film about a gang rape and the subsequent trial) that drinking and flirting was dangerous:

they seemed to view the film almost anthropologically as a report upon the wider society. . . . their reading of the film validated their differences, showing how their culture could operate to protect them from danger. (Schlesinger *et al.*, 1992: 164)

Other minority or oppositional social/political groups within a dominant culture may adopt a similar 'anthropological' gaze. A lesbian or gay man, for example, may enjoy *Blind Date* as a showcase for some of the more absurd heterosexual rituals and as confirmation of the superior socio-sexual skills evident in lesbian and gay communities.

It is clear then that audiences are not passive absorbers of preordained meaning. Indeed, the 'active viewer' may appropriate unexpected pleasures from the most mainstream of texts. The diversity of ways in which this operates is amply illustrated by studies of one particular mainstream genre: the 'cowboy and Indian' film. Such films routinely present stereotypical accounts of 'how the West was won'—casting cowboys as heroes and 'Indians' as savages. They are, therefore, rejected by some Native Americans, who identify with the 'Indian' characters, are critical of the stereotypes and inaccuracies in the films, and refuse to enter into the story (Shively, 1992: 725). However, such films are also actively enjoyed by many Native Americans. Why is this? One study by JoEllen Shively found that a group of 'full-blooded Sioux' men from a reservation did not identify with the 'red Indians' at all but identified with John Wayne—'the good guy' (and hater of 'Indians'). In this way, their response to the film was very similar to the Anglo respondents included in the study. However,

although both Anglos and Indians responded in similar ways to the structure of oppositions in the narrative, the two groups interpreted and valued characteristics of the cultural product differently once they 'entered the narrative'. (Shively, 1992: 729)

The Anglo men emphasized that they enjoyed the film as an 'authentic portrayal of the Old West' whereas the Sioux men emphasized their pleasure in the portrayal of the cowboys' way of life. 'Westerns', they said, 'relate to the way I wish I could live,' 'The cowboy is free,' 'He's not tied down to an eight-to-five job day after day,' 'He is his own man.' One Native American bartender summed up his enjoyment of the film, stating: 'Indians today are the cowboys.' By this, Shively says, he meant that it is contemporary Native Americans (not Anglos) who preserve a commitment to an autonomous way of life that is not fully tied to industrial society (Shively, 1992: 732).

Rather than simply either rejecting such images or appropriating pleasures from such programmes, viewers may also 'borrow' from a media portrayal and apply the message to new contexts. Staying with the genre of 'cowboy and Indian' films, it is worth drawing attention to a study by Hodge and Tripp (1986). They found that Australian Aboriginal children, watching a cowboy and Indian film, identified with the Native Americans rather than John Wayne, and drew links between their own oppression and that of the 'Indian' underdogs in the film. They thus demonstrate 'the ability of a subculture to make its own sense out of a text that clearly bears the dominant ideology' (Fiske, 1991: 70).

A study by Gillespie found that *Neighbours* (an Australian soap featuring an all-white cast) attracted young 'British Asians' who perceived it as offering 'a complex metaphor for their own social world' (Gillespie, 1995: 207). *Neighbours* explores the tensions which exist between families and their neighbours in a way which resonated with those young people's experiences of their communities (Gillespie, 1995: 164). Viewing *Neighbours* and talking about it in the peer group also, Gillespie argues, enables young people in Southall to 'compare and contrast their family lives and neighbourhood with "white culture on the box" '

(Gillespie, 1995: 174). These young Punjabi Londoners, she says, 'draw on the soap as a cultural resource . . . as they attempt to construct new modes of identity for themselves' (Gillespie, 1995: 143).

Advertisements can be used in a similar way. In fact, people can consume commercials 'independently' of the products advertised (Nava and Nava, 1992). Some of the most sophisticated and expensive advertising is constructed in ways intended to exploit this. When an advertising slogan enters everyday talk ('It's the real thing', 'Pure Genius', 'I bet he drinks Carling Black Label'), this is a success for the industry. However, this can also be seen as audience creativity and appropriation. For example, Coca-Cola adverts were very popular among the teenagers studied by Gillespie. These adverts, she argues, 'place the product within an idealised world of teenagers, free from parental and other constraints' and represent a 'utopian vision of teenage lifestyle'. She concludes:

Since the spaces available for public representation of what they see as their generational culture are so limited, and since neither British nor Indian media offer representations which they view as acceptable or appropriate, it is perhaps no wonder that they turn to a third, alternative space of fantasy identification: they draw on utopian images of America to construct a position of 'world teenagers' which transcends those available in British or Indian cultures. (Gillespie, 1995: 197)

Research into children's use of mainstream media has yielded similarly interesting results. Studies of *Prisoner: Cell Block H*, the Australian soap set in a woman's prison, found that school students strongly identified with the prisoners and that working-class children appropriated meaning from this programme and 'used it subversively against the rule-bound culture and institutions of the school' (Curthoys and Docker, 1989). The programme provided Australian school students with language and cultural categories with which to think through their experiences: teachers were given nicknames from the cast of prison guards and the children used the programme as a way of understanding and articulating their powerlessness (Palmer, 1986).

Indeed, pleasures, confirmation, and meaning are often quite consciously 'poached' from mainstream texts and this may be especially true for viewers who are marginalized within mainstream texts, or within society (e.g. by gender, age, culture, or national or ethnic identity). Lesbians and gay men in particular are skilled practitioners in, and have theorized at length about, such creative viewing (Dyer, 1986; Doty, 1993; Jay and Glasgow, 1992; Griffen, 1993; and Wilton, 1995). *Prisoner: Cell Block H* is not only a favourite with Australian schoolchildren. It also has a strong lesbian following (along with other series dominated by female casts such as *Cagney and Lacey* and *The Golden Girls*). Gay fan clubs celebrate productions ranging from *The Wizard of Oz* to *Strictly Ballroom*, from *Star Trek* to *Dynasty*, from Doris Day's *Calamity Jane* to almost any Judy Garland film. Some stars gain a gay following because of rumours about their off-screen sexuality (Whatling, 1994), others because they challenge gender role stereotypes or 'camp it up', but pleasures may be snatched from the most traditional of genres or formats. Lesbian viewers describe self-consciously imposing themselves into film or television texts, well aware that they are uninvited guests in the narrative structure. For example, a set piece in a mainstream Indian film involves the male lover singing to his heterosexual object of desire. In the film *Razia Sultan*, however, the love song is performed by a woman to a woman (even though the singing is interspersed with shots of the male lover). This scene is recalled as a particular moment of poached pleasure by an Asian lesbian (Florence, 1993). A lesbian may identify with both the film hero and heroine or insert herself between the two. It is this process, familiar to many marginalized viewers, which is captured by Deborah Bright, in her photographic exhibition showing her own image inserted into film stills: photographs which place her between Spencer Tracy and Katherine Hepburn, or show her popping up beside Vanessa Redgrave and catching the eye of Glenda Jackson (Whatling, 1994). Alternatively, a viewer may even take pleasure in identifying with the villain. Some lesbians say they enjoy identifying with the evil lesbian queen in *Red Sonja* or the bisexual ice-pick murderer in *Basic Instinct* or even finding alternative role models in vampire movies! One lesbian describes how vampires provided her with positive models of defiance during a time of intense isolation and alienation as a teenager. Her family treated her as an outsider, abnormal and therefore potentially dangerous. '[A]ll my adolescent rebellion and loneliness', she writes, 'coalesced around that figure [of the vampire] on screen':

I knew I was supposed to feel relieved when the vampire got staked. I didn't. . . . I knew I was supposed to find vampires frightening, and my home, family and their expectations of me comforting, safe. I didn't. I identified with the vampires. *They* were the rebels I wanted to be. They didn't have elders bugging them. I dreamed of independence and revelled in the vampires' anarchic force: they spurned families, marriage and other social conventions. . . . Although loners themselves, they found others like them and were united by a shared difference against the mass of humanity. (Garland, 1991: 36)

All these examples illustrate how people actively engage with books, films, radio and television programmes within the context of their own lives. The discovery of 'active audiences' in the studies outlined above challenges more traditional understandings of the mass media and 'the masses'. It disrupts old assumptions about how texts convey meaning and raises important new theoretical issues. Even if the extent to which these insights are 'new' is disputed (see Curran, 1990) it is still worth highlighting the three main ways in which this recent research is often distinguished from other approaches.

First, work on the 'active audience' often prioritizes the issue of pleasure, trying to understand, instead of ignore, people's enjoyment of mass culture. This work seeks to locate the sources and nature of such delight instead of merely dismissing it as evidence of gullibility or proof of effective media manipulation. The relationship between people and texts has been found to be much more complicated than previously assumed. Pleasure is not simply determined by identifying with the appropriate characters or messages. Audience enjoyment may depend on 'perverse' or 'inverted' identification. It may be due to pleasure in 'gossip' or in fantasy. It may even be located in the format of a programme which allows viewers to know more than the characters in the drama, to anticipate events and exercise their 'cultural competencies' or 'melodramatic imagination'.

Secondly, much of the work with audiences disrupts assumptions about the homogeneity of the viewing/listening public. Many researchers exploring audience reception now attend to differences between people's 'readings' on the basis not only of class, but also of ethnic identity, nationality, gender, and sexual identity. Insofar as audience reception research acknowledges overlapping social and political locations this work has fed into, and drawn upon, perspectives developed within, for example, feminist and black theory and experience. In this sense, academia is 'catching up' with the cultural criticism developed from explicitly political perspectives—although it does not always take on the political sharpness of such analysis and might even be said to dull its radical edge. Compare, for example, the theorizing discussed in this chapter and the grass-roots cultural criticism described by bell hooks, recounting her experiences growing up in an ordinary black family:

Cultural criticism has historically functioned in black life as a force promoting cultural resistance, one that enabled black folks to cultivate in everyday life a practice of critique and analysis that would disrupt and even deconstruct those cultural productions that were designed to promote and reinforce domination. In other words, a poor black family, like the one I was raised in, might sit around watching *Amos 'n' Andy*—enjoying it even as we simultaneously critiqued it— talking about the way this cultural production served the interests of white supremacy. . . . Within the context of an apartheid social structure where practically every aspect of black life was determined by the efforts of those in power to maintain white supremacy, black folks were incredibly vigilant. . . . Then there was no passive consumption of images. How indeed could black viewers passively consume a film like *Birth of a Nation* when we lived daily with the threat of lynchings and the reality of racial murder. How could little black girls growing in a segregated south so charged with sexualised violence . . . not feel the sexual terrorism that is an underlying tension in *Immitation of Life*. Our gaze was not passive. The screen was not a place of escape. It was a place of confrontation and encounter. (hooks, 1991: 4)

Thirdly, and most crucial of all, work with audiences challenges textual determinism. It discredits the assumption that the text alone determines audience response. It demonstrates that viewers and listeners will not necessarily adopt the perspective intended by the film producers, script writers, or journalists: people do not automatically take on the subject position, or ideological meaning, inscribed in the text. Audiences seize pleasure and meaning that may be quite different from that accessible by a formal content analysis of the text alone. Empirical work with audiences throws up unexpected interpretations, unanticipated pleasures, and a complex interweaving of diverse audience appropriations and reactions. So, for example, as Modleski declares: 'The price women pay for their popular entertainment is high, but they may still be getting more than anyone bargained for' (Modleski, 1984: 34).

Such recognition has meant a reassessment of audience reception processes and the end of uncontested condescending portraits of women (or 'the working class' or any other subordinate group) as 'cultural dupes', victims of the dominant cultural order, swallowing pre-digested ideological tracts which promote ideas and values which are against their own interests. It allows us to recognize that

consumption, despite its overdetermination by the market and the unequal distribution of access to economic and cultural capital . . . is not a passive process but an expressive and productive activity . . . Thus, in order to understand the effectivity of TV we need to study not only its images and narratives but what the consumer 'makes' or 'does' with them . . . (Gillespie, 1995: 13)

Such insight has, over the last ten or fifteen years, opened up whole new fields of enquiry and ways of thinking about text–audience relations. It has also led to an unprecedented expansion in ethnographic work with readers and viewers: the blossoming of in-depth studies exploring audience pleasures and interpretations.

But is this blossoming entirely a good thing or have we now reached a point where innovation has been replaced by endless banal replication whereby, as Meaghan Morris argues, 'thousands of versions of the same article about pleasure, resistance, and the politics of consumption are being run off under different names with minor variation' (Morris, 1988: 20)? The 'new paradigm' of audience research emerging out of the discovery of 'active audiences' certainly opens up fresh questions but does it also *close down* possible areas of investigation? And, above all, what can such work tell us about the operation of power? What is the relationship between 'oppositional' cultural consumption and political change? If people wrest 'pleasure' or positive meaning from a text which might otherwise be alienating or offensive, is this necessarily 'liberating'? And if audiences read texts 'in their own way', does this mean that the media are powerless to convey ideology?

The answers to all these questions are not straightforward. Although many of the original studies cited *do* address these questions, derivative work and the broader research paradigm evolving out of these roots seems to assume that the answers are self-evident and in the affirmative. Some recent work even dismisses such questions as irrelevant. Indeed, 'active audience theory' seems to be hardening into a new theoretical orthodoxy within cultural and media studies. This is an orthodoxy which dismisses questions of media power by focusing on audience activity and interpretative capabilities. It is an orthodoxy which revises old ideas about the media's power to convey ideology— sometimes it revises them out of existence. This orthodoxy, sometimes known as the 'new revisionism' (because of the way it revises old ideas about power and ideology), is dangerous. It is certainly misleading to assume, as some 'new revisionist' authors seem to, that pleasure is inherently revolutionary and 'oppositional' readings can be equated with 'liberation' in the real world (for critiques see McGuigan, 1992; Seaman, 1992; Kitzinger and Kitzinger, 1993). Some authors seem to adopt an uncritical 'cultural populism' which suggests that popular readings are, by definition, 'good' and that mass audiences can be trusted to exercise an almost instinctive capacity to 'resist'. Others imply that the text is so 'unstable' and 'polysemic', open to so many interpretations, that it really has no meaning at all (for critiques see Corner, 1991; Gitlin, 1991; McGuigan, 1992).

The enthusiasm for discovering 'active audiences', celebrating 'cultural populism', and documenting textual instability can lead to a failure to engage constructively in many of the central contemporary debates about media power in Britain (and across the world) such as those addressed so far in this book. It has led to a form of cultural relativism which often seems to do no more than produce apologies for mass culture and ends up 'valorizing each private act of consumption as oppositional and resistant and positing dominant classes that have somehow lost control of their messages' (McLaughlin, 1993: 614). The new revisionist paradigm is disengaged from debates about the content of media representation and the 'political economy' of the media system. It tells us a great deal about audiences as 'consumers' but very little about 'citizenship'. Theorists ensnared by the new revisionism have been incapacitated from expressing concern about North American cultural imperialism and have been silent in the altercations about 'quality television' and campaigns to create cultural products which 'break the mould'. As Seiter points out,

the popularity of US television programmes on export around the world should not make us forget that other forms of television might also please (and possibly, please better). In our concern for audiences' pleasures in such programmes, we run the risk of continually validating Hollywood's domination of the worldwide television market. (Seiter et al., 1989: 5)

The focus on celebrating pleasure in popular culture as it currently exists creates a premature 'full-stop' to the development of cultural innovation. Like the Duchess's baby in *Alice in Wonderland*, we are told that 'he likes what he gets and he gets what he likes.' But just because the mass media attract mass audiences with their current menu does not mean that other diets might not be even more popular while simultaneously including original or challenging content.

Most disturbing of all, the new revisionism, intentionally or not, plays into the hands of those seeking to build up monopolies and capitalize on a 'free market' in media institutions. McGuigan points out that Hobson's work on *Crossroads* has been used to argue for the popular usability of commercial television and attack the need to defend the ideal of public service broadcasting (McGuigan, 1992: 164). The theories propagated by new revisionists and 'cultural populists' are echoed, in form at least, in speeches by modern media moguls. Rupert Murdoch regularly gives speeches in which he expresses populist sentiment, challenging the stuffiness of British public service and Establishment values, and attacking elitist and patronizing attitudes toward the public (see McGuigan, 1992: 183). The original impetus to understand and dignify the activity of 'the masses' and to explain the attractions of consumerism, the joys of popular culture, and the success of Thatcherism has thus become distorted. It has disintegrated into complicity and the abnegation of critical responsibility. As McGuigan concludes: 'a pact has been made, overtly or covertly, with economic liberalism, rediscovering the virtues of the market as a cultural provider and incitement to pleasure' (McGuigan, 1992: 173).

At the same time the 'new revisionist' paradigm has become increasingly detached from broader political and sociological concerns. Critiques of the racist or sexist content of a programme are dismissed because they are assumed to characterize audiences as compliant zombies—victims of the text. At the same time, programmes which are popular with minority groups are celebrated as inherently revolutionary (for a critique of this in relation to black viewers' enjoyment of *The Cosby Show*, see Jhally and Lewis, 1992). Concern about the under-representation of ethnic minorities within media institutions is regarded as 'old-fashioned' and boringly empirical, compared to pursuing thrilling explorations of the potential for audience fantasy and creativity. As Jakubowicz *et al.* comment, introducing their study of media racism,

Strongly influenced by French deconstructionist analyses and semiotic studies of the content of media discourse, there has been a growth in a 'new revisionism' in which texts are removed from the process of their industrial production and set in a landscape of ideas and values, without a relationship to any material interest. The subjectivity of the reader is given paramount place, with great attention paid to the discontinuities between author and audience. . . . The reaffirmation of subjective sensibility offers a necessary corrective to . . . theories . . . which removed the opportunities for subversion and adaptation by those at the receiving end of the communication blitz. However, this reaffirmation can also lead to the mass media's uncritical celebration of the popular merely as oppositional and self-consciously subversive. (Jakubowicz *et al.*, 1994: 23)

The focus on 'pleasure' also neglects the role of media coverage of some of the most important contemporary world events (e.g. war in the former Yugoslavia). The enthusiasm for examining the rich variety of audience interpretation leads to a failure to discuss the truth (or falsehood) of media information. A focus on interpretation seems to have blurred concern about media influence. The obsession with audience creativity sidelines questions about audiences' beliefs, comprehension, and understanding. In the rush to document audience resistance, questions of 'meaning' and 'effect' have become unfashionable. A fixation on demonstrating textual polysemy has more or less precluded discussion of the *consequences* of interpreting things in diverse ways or how cultural power might operate through the media. As Corner concludes,

so much effort has been centred on audiences' interpretative activity that even the preliminary theorization of influence has become *awkward*. . . . In certain versions of the reception perspective . . . [there has been] a loss of critical energy, in which increasing emphasis on the micro-processes of viewing relations displaces (though rarely explicitly so) an engagement with the macro-structures of media and society. (Corner, 1991: 267–9; italics in original)

This is a concern shared by some of the key theorists whose work started the trend toward revisionism. Morley himself acknowledges this danger. Responding to the criticism of 'active audience' theory he argues that we must find a way of 'steering between the dangers of an improper romanticism of "consumer freedoms", on the one hand, and a paranoiac fantasy of "global control", on the other' (Morley, 1992: 272). 'The challenge', he proposes, 'lies precisely in the attempt to construct a model of television consumption that is sensitive to both the "vertical" dimensions of power and ideology and the "horizontal" dimension of television's insertion in, and articulation with, the context and practices of everyday life' (Morley, 1992: 276).

We agree with Morley that it is this combined approach that will help toward a greater understanding of media power and reception processes. Attempts to develop such approaches at the Glasgow Media Group are the subject of the next chapter.

Chapter Thirteen

Rethinking Media Influence and Power

Do the media influence what people actually believe? Do television, radio, and press reports affect public understandings and attitudes? Strangely enough these straightforward questions have not been central to the audience reception work discussed so far. The previous two chapters explored the ways in which people exploit media technologies, make their own meanings from media texts, and take pleasure from the available repertoire of programmes. This work has crucial implications for understanding the operation of media effects. However, we have argued that the processes of reception and consumption *mediate*, but do not necessarily *undermine*, media power. Acknowledging that audiences are 'active' does not mean that the media are ineffectual. Recognizing the role of 'interpretation' does not invalidate the concept of 'influence'.

This chapter develops this argument by focusing on an alternative approach to researching audience reception: the work conducted at the Glasgow Media Group. This work presents a quite different perspective on media power. It demonstrates that, although there are variations in audience 'readings' of media reports, there are pervasive common themes in the meanings conveyed to the public. It reveals that even though people may 'resist' the dominant message of a programme, it may still have the power to convey facts and to influence their ideas, assumptions, and attitudes. The Glasgow Media Group research shows that in spite of audience 'activity' in all its forms, the media help to shape perceptions of key social issues. Indeed, the way people reread individual texts or take unexpected pleasures can *reinforce*, rather than undermine, broad media influence over public understandings. The way in which people use the media and incorporate soap opera plots, media stories, or slogans from advertisements into their everyday lives can strengthen, rather than weaken, media power.

The studies introduced here were conducted during the late 1980s and early 1990s and were all topic-based. They examined specific issues including: AIDS (Kitzinger, 1990), industrial disputes (Philo, 1990), sexual violence (Kitzinger and Skidmore, 1995), food scares (Miller and Reilly, 1995), and the conflict in Northern Ireland (Miller, 1994). All the projects explored people's understandings through group discussion rather than naturalistic observation of people in front of their television sets. (For the advantages of this approach, see Kitzinger, 1994a, 1994b.) All also used a specific research technique called the 'news game' or 'scriptwriting exercise'. Rather than showing people videos of actual TV programmes, research participants were actively engaged in trying to write and criticize a media report. They were given sets of still photographs taken from television coverage of the relevant topic and asked to reconstruct or invent an accompanying text. These texts were usually in the style of a news bulletin, hence the nomenclature 'news game'. However, sometimes people were asked to reproduce the dialogue from a soap opera, to reconstruct an advertising slogan, or to write a tabloid newspaper report (see Kitzinger and Hunt, 1993; Henderson, 1996; Philo, 1996; for further discussion of this research technique see Kitzinger, 1990, 1993; Philo, 1990).

This research consistently reveals a clear correspondence between certain recurrent themes in news reporting and what is recalled, understood, and sometimes believed by audience groups. This is true across the whole range of topics explored.

Philo researched the media coverage of the 1984–5 miners' strike, a historic and bitter industrial dispute which lasted a year. His work shows that the media coverage encouraged people to exaggerate the degree of violence on the picket lines and assume that the striking miners were primarily responsible for any disorder (Philo, 1990). Miller studied the reporting of the conflict in Northern Ireland. His work shows how the media coverage led many British people to have inflated fears about visiting Northern Ireland and to accept incorrect 'facts' about particular events. For example, Miller demonstrates that many research participants had absorbed misinformation about a key moment in the conflict: the shooting dead of three IRA members in Gibraltar in 1988. They believed that the three IRA members had been armed, that a bomb had been found, and that a key witness was a prostitute. Each of these ideas were promoted by government propaganda and disseminated through sections of the media. They were designed to justify the actions of the Secret Service and discredit voices of dissent. They all proved to be false (Miller, 1995).

Both the above examples illustrate the power of the media to convey information and construct beliefs. Both studies identify media influence. However, neither promote a simple linear model of media power. It is clear from both pieces of work that people were able to resist dominant messages. In particular, personal experience (e.g. of seeing a picket line or being in Northern Ireland) provided an important counterbalance to media information. Such experiences are, of course, not random. They intersect with people's socio-demographic position, politics, and identity (e.g. being a trade unionist or Irish). Thus it is possible, as Hall argued in his paper on encoding and decoding (1973), to locate 'significant clusters' of meaning and link these to the social and discursive positioning of the readers and their 'interpretative communities'. In this sense the findings echo work by Hall, Morley, and others discussed in Chapter 10. However, the 'interpretative communities' are not coherent and sealed; they are cross-cut by multiple and overlapping experiences (see Morley, 1980). In addition, as we will show later, those experiences may themselves be shaped by the media. Personal experience is not a media-free zone.

The complexity of the reception process and the operation of media power can be best illustrated by looking at two studies in more depth. This allows closer examination of the exact influence of different elements in media reporting. It also permits more detailed exploration of the way in which audience reception is mediated by people's own pre-existing identities and perspectives. Here we focus on two of the most extensive studies of audience reception: the first on AIDS, the second on child sexual abuse.

The AIDS Media Research Project

The 'AIDS Media Research Project' examined the production, content, and reception of media messages about AIDS (ESRC grant XA4420006). It was conducted by a team of four researchers, each of whom was responsible for investigating different strands of the communication process. Miller and Williams conducted in-depth investigation of source strategies and the actions of journalists in relation to AIDS (Miller and Williams, 1993), Beharrell concentrated on content analysis (Beharrell, 1993), and Kitzinger took main responsibility for exploring audience reception (Kitzinger, 1993). The audience reception work was based on discussions with 52 different groups. The research participants discussed their beliefs, talked about their sources of information, described their changing perceptions of the problem, and wrote their own news scripts about AIDS.

Kitzinger found widespread similarities in how people understood the coverage of AIDS and identified significant media influence. The press, television, and radio coverage provided people with facts and figures (e.g. about the threat of HIV to heterosexuals). It familiarized them with a vocabulary (such as 'safer sex', 'body fluids', or 'the heterosexual community'). It introduced a new set of images (e.g. of death from immune deficiency-related illness). The group discussions were permeated with information, phrases, and images explicitly gleaned from the media. Parts of the media coverage were shown to influence people's views: helping to establish different classes of 'AIDS victims' (the guilty and the innocent); associating the virus with perverse or unnatural behaviour, and relegating people with HIV to the status of 'walking time bombs' (Kitzinger, 1993, 1995).

Kitzinger's analysis highlights the way in which different elements in the media coverage influence public opinion and how misunderstandings could be encouraged by particular terminology and images. For example, there were frequent media references to body fluids containing HIV and warnings that 'mixing body fluids' or 'the exchange of body fluids' may result in the transmission of infection. This terminology had stuck in people's minds, sometimes with misleading consequences. It was this phrase which led some people to believe that saliva is highly dangerous ('because it's a body fluid') in spite of this being contrary to orthodox scientific opinion.

Images are just as important as language. One of the most powerful images from the AIDS media coverage is 'the face of AIDS': the portrait of a haggard, painfully thin person with jutting bones, sunken eyes, and a listless expression of despair. This image was vividly recalled by research participants. It was a source of fear; it also dehumanized 'AIDS victims' and it could undermine crucial health education messages. In particular, Kitzinger found that such representations could undercut the health promotion advice that people with HIV can look perfectly well for years. In fact, television and newspaper representations are, for many people, the lens through which they view the reality of AIDS. Media images of the visible ravages of disease thus form the template for their perceptions of the world and of the people in it. They may have friends or acquaintances who are seropositive but be unaware that this is so because the person 'looks OK' and does not disclose his or her antibody status. On the other hand, they may meet people who look very ill and then assume that they have AIDS. In fact, when one of the male prostitutes who participated in the research protested that he had seen some information saying that people with the virus might *not* look ill, another young man countered with the statement:

A guy came up last night, his eyes were all black under there, his face all stinging, his face was all red there, wee scabs, his lips were all scabby . . . they *do* look different! (cited in Kitzinger, 1995: 63)

The man's face resembled a photomontage of all those images of AIDS in the press and on television; the young man therefore assumed that this client must have the virus (an assumption which, in turn, reinforced his belief in the media image). The media portrait of 'the face of AIDS' is thus self-reinforcing; it can define 'real-life encounters' which, in turn, carry more credibility than might be accredited to media images on their own.

The powerful image of 'the face of AIDS' could also alter how people 'read' health education advertisements. Indeed, one health education advertisement, which was designed to inform people that you cannot tell who is infected just by looking, was entirely misread by some research participants. This misreading was due, in part, to their pre-existing familiarity with 'the face of AIDS'. The health education advertisement showed the words 'Two eyes, nose, mouth' arranged on the page, with each word in the appropriate position as if on a face. The caption read 'How to recognise someone with HIV'. The intention was to convey the information that people with HIV look just like anyone else with two eyes, a nose, and a mouth. However, some research participants thought that the message was entirely different. People with HIV, they said, looked very odd indeed: 'their hair drops out', or 'they are all black under the eyes'. The mass media image of 'the face of AIDS' was superimposed over the abstract representation of the 'normal' appearance of someone with HIV (Kitzinger, 1995).

On a more subtle level people's understandings of AIDS can be influenced by the media's use of adjectives and metaphor, their framing of the story and the emerging trajectory of coverage, such as the shift of emphasis from 'risk groups' to the promotion of the heterosexual threat, and back again (Kitzinger, forthcoming). Public interpretation of the coverage is also influenced by broader cultural associations and the underlying logic of the reporting narrative. For example, some of the media coverage of AIDS associated the syndrome with sin and deviation. It was this association which led some people to assume that lesbians must be 'a high-risk group'. This belief was widespread: about two-thirds of the population believed that lesbians are 'greatly' or 'quite a lot' at risk from AIDS (Brook, 1988: 75). This is in spite of the fact that very few women are thought to have become infected as a result of lesbian sex and scientific evidence suggests that sex with women is generally safer than sex with men. When beliefs about lesbian risk status were explored in the focus groups it became clear that perceptions of lesbians as 'high risk' were not usually directly due to statements in the media (the media is generally silent or vague on this topic). However, such perceptions were encouraged by the underlying association of AIDS with 'perversity'. Lesbians, according to some research participants, must be at high risk because, as one person stated, 'they are leading the same life as what two men are' and this life is 'unnatural' or 'sinful'. This point was reiterated in other groups. One research participant commented: 'the point is this—biologically your body is not made for either homosexuality or eh, or eh, lesbianism.' Another declared: 'God made two kinds of sex, male and female. They go together. He didn't mean males to go with males and females to go with females. And that's how they got it [AIDS].'

Clearly, then, the way in which the media feeds into public opinion is not deducible from straightforward content analysis of the surface meaning. It is also necessary to explore implicit associations. In addition, the power of any particular media message depends on how it taps into, and builds on, people's pre-existing perceptions. Public reactions to the media coverage of AIDS are influenced by assumptions that predate the epidemic, including ideas about homosexuality (such as those illustrated above) and ideas about sexually transmitted diseases, illegal drug use, gender, sexuality, class, and race. Another clear example of this was evident in group discussion about the origins of the virus. Most people thought that it came from Africa, the origin theory promoted most widely in the media. For most white research participants this origin theory was easy to accept, not least because it fitted neatly into long-established racist images of 'the dark continent' (notions which were often subtly reiterated in the media reporting of AIDS). In talking about Africa as the 'cradle' and 'hotbed' of HIV infection many white research participants drew on images of Africa as a disaster zone, a continent riddled with death and disease and a place of primitive and excessive sexuality. By contrast, many black research participants rejected media portrayals of 'African AIDS', dismissing it as typically racist (Kitzinger and Miller, 1992).

Finally, it is important to note that media power does not operate in a social vacuum. The dissemination of any particular message is also a social process involving the exchange of information and ideas between friends, relatives, and colleagues. The influence of any particular message will therefore relate to its 'social currency': the value of a particular item of information or a specific story in a social context and people's willingess to reiterate what they have read or seen.

The operation of such 'social currency' was evident in the lively exchange of some phrases, stories, and jokes in the group discussions.

For example, when some research participants talked about saliva being dangerous, others countered by declaring that one would need intimate contact with a great deal of saliva before transmission could occur. Someone would need, they said, to 'bathe in it, while covered in open sores' or to drink 'a thousand gallons'. When asked how they knew this to be true, some research participants cited newspaper reports, television programmes, or health education advertisements. Certainly such statements are evident in some (albeit a minority) of the publicity surrounding AIDS. According to one newspaper article, for example, 'you'd have to drink saliva by the gallon to run any significant risk of acquiring the HIV virus' (*Scotsman*, 29 December 1989). However it is also important to note that such information was not simply directly communicated from the media to individuals. Many people had heard about it from friends and such statements were readily repeated between people in conversation. The discussions about body fluids in the groups caused a great deal of hilarity. It would appear that such half-fascinating, half-repellent images are ensuring that this particular message enters everyday talk—it is recalled and repeated between friends, family, and colleagues, thus reinforcing and increasing exposure to the original media version.

The same process operated in some groups for a series of other phrases, items of information, or ideas. For example, many of the groups spontaneously exchanged tales of 'the vengeful AIDS carrier': the man or woman who deliberately infects their partner, perhaps leaving the message 'Welcome to the AIDS club' scrawled in lipstick on the mirror. The influence of such tales lies both in the ubiquity of such stories in the media and also in their social currency. In fact the tale of 'the vengeful AIDS carrier' has become an urban myth. It was not just a story read in a newspaper; in several groups it was described as a real event which had actually happened to a friend of a friend. Such stories serve as cautionary tales which carry the attractive frisson of the thriller plot and as articulations of different fears and moral positions (such as the dangers of anonymous sex). The plausibility of such tales is bound up with negative attitudes toward the traditional risk groups (as irresponsible and antisocial) and the logic of some health education advice (which focuses on individual responsibility and in some cases positions the audience as the recipient of infection from 'the other'). Revenge tales also have a reactionary function: they were used in group discussions to justify draconian measures against those with the virus, measures such as incarceration or branding.

The 'reading' and 'rereading' acceptance or rejection, reiteration or dismissal of media messages is thus a complex interaction which involves both text and audiences. When such information is supposed to influence actions (as is the case with safer-sex advice) the process becomes even more complex (see Kitzinger, forthcoming). On the one hand such complexity means that some messages are interpreted in entirely unexpected ways or rebuffed altogether. On the other hand, some messages may be embraced and take on a life of their own. Either way, it is clear that media messages are not simply directly injected into the hearts and minds of a passive public.

In addition it is important to note that the media are not people's sole source of information. Research participants also received information from their doctors, friends, and neighbours, or the observed behaviour of professionals. In some cases they drew on personal experience of being HIV antibody positive or knowing other people with the virus, being gay or having gay friends, or their own knowledge of illegal drug use or the sex industry. In other cases a critical perspective was informed by, for example, black consciousness, identifying themselves as Scottish, or simply because of their own involvement in stories which had attracted media (mis)representation.

Nevertheless, people do absorb assumptions, often without even realizing it. This is true even when the facts or ideas being promoted do not accord with their own preferred political position. Although people often express routine scepticism about the media, in practice, in the absence of other sources of data, most of us, most of the time, go along with what the media tells us to be the case. This may even be true when our politics or identity might otherwise lead us to resist. There were many examples in the group discussion where people were surprised to realize that they had accepted certain ideas without critically reflecting on them. Thus, even some of those who saw themselves as 'liberal', 'anti-racist', or 'permissive' accepted some of the racist representations of 'African AIDS' or the negative association of AIDS with 'unnatural' or 'perverse' behaviour. One young man, for example, realized during the course of the research session that his perception of lesbian sex as high risk did not accord with his understandings of the biology of transmission. In spite of his 'better judgement' he had simply assumed they were high risk because of a residual sense that lesbianism was 'abnormal'. 'It's just, I suppose, the way you've been brought up,' he commented. 'You think that a man and a woman is more normal than two women. I don't know whether, risk of infection-wise, whether that's true or not, it's just the way that you were brought up' (cited in Kitzinger, 1990: 329).

The second section of this chapter shows how such processs operate in relation to the media coverage of a very different issue: child sexual abuse.

Child Sexual Abuse and Media Power

The 'Child Sexual Abuse and the Media Project' shared a common research design with the AIDS Media Research Project. It examined the production, content, and reception of media messages about sexual violence against children (see Kitzinger and Skidmore, 1995a,b; Skidmore, 1995 ESRC grant R00 233675). The work on audience reception was based on group discussions with 49 different groups—they discussed their beliefs, talked about the sources of their information, described their changing perceptions of the problem, and wrote their own news scripts about child sexual abuse.

At a basic level, the research shows that the media played a central role in establishing public awareness of the issue. The media reporting has facilitated major changes in people's thinking on this topic over the last twenty years and helped to establish a broad public consensus that child sexual abuse exists, that it is damaging, and that it is much more common than once thought.

Such a general initial finding may seem to be common sense. However, it is often hard to disentangle the impact of media reporting from broader cultural change. How does one decide what is cause and what is effect? In some cases it can be shown that public opinion changed *before*, rather than in response to, media coverage. For example, it is widely assumed that the North American media played a key role in turning USA citizens against the war in Vietnam. Detailed examination of the pattern of media reporting and public opinion surveys, however, show that the shift in media support for the Vietnam War followed, rather than led, the shifting public consensus (Williams, 1993). In the case of child sexual abuse, however, this does not seem to be the case and research participants clearly identified media events which had altered their point of view. The launch of 'Childline' (a helpline for children) in 1986 accompanied by massive publicity was a key event for many people. The 'Cleveland scandal' which followed shortly afterwards was the formative episode for many others.

At a more specific level one can examine how ideas from the media are mobilized in people's discussions with one another, or seem to have infiltrated their thinking. This form of media power is most evident when one begins to investigate contradictions within people's thinking: cases where people seem to have a split between what they know on one level and what they know on another. This can be illustrated by looking at the research participants' discussions about *where* children are attacked, and by *whom*.

The majority of research participants 'knew' a child was most likely to be abused in domestic or institutional settings. They had been educated in this fact by statistical information presented via the mass media. However, the research participants' day-to-day fear often focused, inaccurately, on external sites such as woodland, park, or wasteland. The source of this fear could be traced, in part, to other aspects of the media reporting. Research participants were influenced by the high quantity of coverage of such cases: one abduction attracts dozens of articles whereas an individual case of sexual abuse within the home often passes unremarked. Indeed, 10 per cent of the tabloid coverage and 5 per cent of broadsheet coverage of child sexual abuse in 1991 concerned such rare incidents. But it is not just a question of the quantity of coverage. Research participants were also influenced by the nature of the reporting: the vivid images, the structure of the story as it developed over time, and their sense of involvement in the case. People described waiting for news of a child who had disappeared, the police reconstructions, the school photograph of the missing son or daughter, the appeals from the parents and the fears of the local community (and indeed all parents across the country) that there was a 'pervert on the loose'. Some research participants also described the expectations established by the searches across wasteland and recalled the low camera angles highlighting the rough ground where the child's body was eventually discovered.

Similar media influence is evident in people's perceptions about *who* is dangerous. Some people, for example, believe, quite falsely, that gay men are a greater threat to children than their heterosexual counterparts. The perception of gay men as child abusers builds on general images of homosexuality which represent homosexuals as predatory and confuse homosexuality with paedophilia. It also builds on media stereotypes of men who abuse children as 'unmanly' and 'perverted' (Watney, 1987). In addition, research participants' perception of gay men (and lesbians) as dangerous to children is influenced by the way in which the media reports 'homosexual' as opposed to 'heterosexual' assaults. For example, during 1991 most media reports of child sexual abuse involved men attacking girls. However, there was no example of an assault or assailant being described as 'heterosexual'. By contrast, there were fifty reports which explicitly identified the assault or the assailants as 'gay' or 'homosexual' (Kitzinger and Skidmore, 1995*b*).

This reporting conforms with a general tendency to identify abusers as 'other'/stranger/deviant. Most research participants knew on an intellectual level that a child was most likely to be sexually abused by someone they knew. However, for many, their fear focused on strangers. Similarly, although most 'knew' that 'it's not just men in dirty macs', abusers were expected to be 'loners', 'dirty', 'obviously mentally unstable', or very specifically, to have 'staring eyes, like Myra Hindley . . . when you see a photo you think, oh, yeah, I can tell.' Often, these images, as the previous quote illustrates, were explicitly drawn from press or television reports. The research participants drew on the media framing of abusers as incarnations of evil or as 'beasts' and 'monsters'. They invoked broader cultural prejudices (e.g. about mental illness) and appealed to photographs they had seen in the press (such as the infamous Myra Hindley photograph).

Such media constructions interact with, and are incorporated into, people's day-to-day reality and social setting. For example, a fear of strangers, rather than fathers, stepfathers and uncles, is in many ways easier to sustain. The possibility of female abusers was acknowledged but seen as much more horrifying and unnatural than abuse by men. Women with children spoke of their need to be able to trust, and rely on, both men and women for childcare. Suspicion of male friends and relatives was viewed as impractical and disempowering for women and insulting to men (especially fathers). Both male and female research participants also discussed how fear of child abduction, rather than incest, fitted into their own experiences of parenting (cross-cut by variables such as class and access to supervised child care or play areas). For example, media stories about abductions may be recalled and reinforced every time your own child is late home from school. As with AIDS, then, media reporting about child sexual abuse informs personal experience and this, in turn, reinforces the power of such media reports.

If the power of the media can be located by looking at contradictions within people's thinking, and how this relates to their daily experience, then it can also be examined by looking at specific case reports in the media, cases of which they have no personal knowledge. How do people recall a particular story? What do they believe? There was one high-profile case which was most consistently mentioned in the group discussions: the Orkney case. This involved disputed allegations of sexual abuse on the Orkney Islands off the Scottish coast. Nine children were taken into care in 1991, amid much publicity, but later returned to their parents. The evidence for or against the allegations was never properly investigated. However, in 1996, the parents received an apology and compensation from Orkney Islands Council.

The media coverage suggested that the parents were accused of some form of 'ritual abuse' around a disused quarry (although the 'ritual' aspect of the allegations was played down by social-work sources). The story was characterized by conflict: the social workers seeking to justify their actions, the parents seeking to discredit them. Content analysis suggested that the parents and their supporters were very successful in getting their point of view into the media; the bulk of the coverage was supportive of them and highly critical of the social-work intervention. Statements in the media compared the actions of social workers to 'some sort of Nazi state' (*The Sun*, 4 March 1991), 'Russia under Stalin' (*The Mail*, 4 March 1991), 'the Gestapo' (*The Guardian*, 5 April 1991), 'the SAS' (*Sunday People*, 10 March 1991), 'the KGB' (*Sunday Times*, 14 April 1991), and fascism generally, e.g. 'the knock on the door at dawn and grim-faced polizei there under the direction of neo-fascistic social workers' (*The Glasgow Herald*, 15 March 1991).

The Orkney case was raised spontaneously in most group discussions (conducted during 1993 and 1994). It was also used as the basis of the 'news game'. Research participants were given nine stills taken from the television news coverage and asked to try to reconstruct a bulletin.

The peak coverage of Orkney occurred in early 1991. The field work with audience groups did not commence until April 1993. Not unexpectedly, the field work revealed that people remembered very little of the facts about the case. Some of the younger research participants were even unaware that there had been any 'Orkney case' at all. However, most people, although unable to recall many facts, were able to remember particular dramatic incidents from the case and produce scripts which closely echoed the atmosphere, feelings, and patterns of interpretation evident in actual TV and newspaper reports from two years earlier. In particular, the news reports produced by the audience groups repeatedly reiterated five aspects of the Orkney story. First, they recreated the image of Orkney as a quiet, sleepy place. As one research participant commented: 'not the sort of place where you would expect this sort of thing to go on'. Secondly, the participants emphasized the horror of children being taken from their home in what were described as 'dawn raids' by social workers. They were less aware of later events, but had powerful (and often exaggerated) memories of the 'raids'. Recalling the fascist metaphors, research participants spoke of: 'Gestapo methods breaking into the house and dragging the children out', 'SAS attack . . . swinging through the windows', and 'dawn raids with shotguns'! Thirdly, they described the trauma experienced by the parents. Fourthly, they often included statements about the shock experienced by 'the close-knit community'. Fifthly, they often stated that events in Orkney were a repeat of 'the Cleveland scandal' or other similar cases already widely accepted as examples of professional misconduct and false suspicions of abuse.

All five of these themes reflected the language, perspectives, ideas, and emotions reiterated by the parents and their supporters in Orkney. By contrast, the research participants found it hard to represent the perspective of Social Services, who had taken the children into care. One of the stills given to research participants showed the Director of Orkney Social Services. In their news bulletins this was frequently simply captioned: 'The Director of Social Services refused to comment'. This both accurately reflected the stance occasionally taken by Social Services in relation to the media but also, as discussion made clear, reflected the groups' lack of familiarity with the explanations which *were* offered from the social workers' point of view. Another picture showed anatomically correct dolls for use in interviewing children. It showed the dolls lying on a table along with some children's books. However, some audience groups employed this instead to represent the toys discarded by the children as they were snatched from their homes. The picture was used to accompany reconstructed news bulletin statements such as 'Homes, desolate since the 4 a.m. raid by social workers', or provoked comments in group discussion such as:

They've been taken away. You can picture it yourself, somebody coming in and the weans' [children's] toys and photos and his mother upset and, you know, the house is quiet.

In fact, the limitations in how people interpreted the pictures or their 'misreading' of them were highly instructive. One of the pictures from the 'news game' showed a family shot from the back (to preserve anonymity) with the children holding hands with their mother on one side and their father on the other. The original news text which actually accompanied this scene stated: 'Orkney families reunited . . . jubilant parents . . . believe their 5-week nightmare is over' (ITV, 22.00, 4 April 1991). Many research participants produced very similar statements in their scripts and made comments such as 'you can see they are jumping for joy.' However, some saw it quite differently and assumed the adults were social workers taking children into care: 'It looks as if the children are being dragged along the street doesn't it, looks as if they're not going very freely.'

The way in which research participants reconstructed these bulletins shows the power of certain aspects of the reporting to stick in people's minds. It confirms findings from other research work (such as Miller's work on Northern Ireland) that the initial framing of a story may be crucial. Certainly the reporting of the Orkney crisis in the first few weeks seemed to have made the most impact on audiences, both because it established a framework for understanding later events and because many research participants quickly 'switched off' from the Orkney coverage—ignoring later reports. They were often unaware, for example, whether or not any Orkney children had been returned home. In addition, very few knew that Social Services had won an appeal against the judgment which returned the children to their parents.

The bulletins constructed by research participants also demonstrate the influence of four aspects of coverage: first, creating an atmospheric context for a story; secondly, the power of establishing certain associations; thirdly, the importance of reiterating key phrases; and fourthly, the influence of identification.

The atmospheric '*placing*' of the story was crucial. Scenes of Orkney were used by the media in ways which constructed it as a peaceful idyll. One newspaper picture, for example, showed parents looking out over Orkney scenery with the caption 'PARADISE LOST' (*Mail on Sunday*, 3 March 1991). This idyllic imagery was recalled by the audience groups. It is notable that, when working with a news game photograph which showed the harbour (Figure 13.1), people happily talked of Orkney as a beautiful and innocent place. However, when they came to the alternative image, the more unusual shot showing a deserted quarry (Figure 13.2), they were often baffled and unable to incorporate it into their news bulletin reconstructions. This picture, shot close to the ground and showing a burnt-out barrel, was often seen as 'biased', 'sinister', and 'sordid'. Several also commented that the photograph conveyed an especially threatening impression because it was shot from 'child height' (although no one commented that all the other images were shot from at least five feet above the ground—the 'grown up' perspective of most camera angles is taken for granted).

The power of *association* was also highly significant. Participants' discussion of the Orkney case showed that it had been successfully associated in their minds with 'the Cleveland scandal' or 'the Rochdale case'—two cases already seen as evidence of professional malpractice and unnecessary interference in family life. Some research participants stated that they had no clear memories of the Orkney case itself, but simply constructed the bulletin along familiar lines. The idea that Orkney was 'just like Cleveland' was promoted by the parents and their supporters, who repeatedly drew attention to the failure of Orkney Social Services to follow the guidelines drawn up after Cleveland. The similarity between the two cases was explicitly denied by Orkney Social Services. However, headlines at the time linked Orkney both with Cleveland and with the Rochdale case. Indeed, 19 per cent of all newspaper reports about the Orkney case in 1991 also mentioned either Cleveland or Rochdale.

Figure 13.1 and 13.2 Two images of Orkney – the quiet rural idyll and the sinister quarry

The third aspect of the coverage which proved to be important was the *reiteration* of particular key phrases. Other researchers have noted how labels such as 'smart bombs' or phrases such as 'a war on drugs', 'the drift back to work, or 'Winter of Discontent' help to set up ways of thinking about and remembering events from the news (McLeod *et al.*, 1991; Philo, 1990). Within the Orkney reporting, the phrase 'dawn raid' played a similar role. The phrase itself reoccurred throughout the coverage and was used in a total of 56 headlines in the national and Scottish press during 1991. Indeed, some papers used the term as a shorthand for the Orkney case, e.g.: 'Unhappy Letters of Dawn Raid Children' (*The Mail*, 3 March 1991): 'Dawn Raid Boss "Had Not Read Vital Report" ' (*The Mail*, 30 August 1991). In the group discussions, the phrase itself was echoed in 31 of the 40 groups who could remember anything at all about the Orkney case (and others talked of 'dawn swoop' or 'snatch'). Mention of the phrase was often greeted with cries of recognition from other members of the group. The phrase acted as a trigger for memory ('it's all coming back to me now') and conjured up images of armed raids to arrest suspected terrorists and, in particular, drugs raids. The phrase thus not only told them what to remember but added layers to those memories and influenced *how* people recalled the incidents in Orkney. As one person commented: 'It was a swoop, it was a swoop, I don't know why I never got that down [in the news bulletin] because that's the word that always comes into my mind when I'm thinking about the Orkney trials . . . it was like a drug bust to me,' or as a participant in another group remarked: 'It was like a drugs raid. That is the image it gave me,' a comment to which her colleague responded: 'Yeah, in my mind it is exactly of a drugs raid . . . that kind of thing when you go in with a hammer and hurtling up the stairs and just sort of taking the children. That is the sort of image I have.'

The fourth aspect of the coverage which proved crucial was the influence of *identification*. People tended to recall the parts of the story with which they could identify. They often imagined how they would feel if they were the Orkney parents and some spoke of their own sense of vulnerability to social-work interference. As one women commented: 'you do identify if you're a mother, that's the first thing you would do, think about how you would feel in that position. I think it's every woman's fear . . . that someone's going to come in and take your kids away.' A point also made by the research participant who simply commented: 'it sticks in your mind because it could be the social workers up the 'morrow going and lifting *your* kiddies.' This fear was explicitly invited in media reporting at the time, for example, by the unusual use of dramatic reconstructions on TV news and specific statements in the press:

It is dawn and you are woken by the sound of hammering at the front door. Opening it, you find two social workers. They say they have come to take away your children. And they do. (*Today*, 29 March 1991)

Ostensibly, media coverage and public discussion of the Orkney case focused on the intervention procedures rather than judging the parents' guilt or innocence. The latter issue, however, was usually part of the agenda in the research groups (and was at least implicit in most of the media coverage). People's actual beliefs about whether or not the Orkney parents were innocent of the allegations against them were complex and cannot simply be 'read off' from their news bulletins. It was only in the surrounding debate that one could examine whether people actually believed in the version of the story they had recreated. So, for example, it was only in discussion that it was possible to explore whether images of South Ronaldsay as an island influenced people's acceptance or rejection of the abuse allegations and how representations of social workers affected their judgement. In most cases, these images and representations *were* accepted and did form part of people's belief systems, guiding them toward thinking that the social workers acted totally without justification. Research participants commented that they just couldn't believe that sexual abuse could go on in an idyllic place like the Orkney Islands, or that they found the idea that social workers had acted totally without foundation entirely plausible because they already had such a low opinion of the profession; after all, 'look at what happened in Cleveland.' However, such responses were not inevitable and there was evidence of diverse audience interpretations and 'resistance' to the dominant message of the coverage.

One source of resistance lay in the contradictory messages available in other parts of the media. For example, although the coverage of the Orkney case generally emphasized an idyllic image of the islands, people also drew on a quite different cultural iconography about island life as backward, ridden with strange customs and, as one person declared, 'an ideal place for witchcraft'. Research participants referred to films such as *The Wickerman* (about devil worship in the Western Isles) and made comments about the insular nature of 'primitive' island living: 'It's like *Lord of the Flies*, you develop your own rules.'

Another way in which people resisted the dominant media message in support of the parents was to combine the elements of the story outlined above in quite unexpected ways. For example, as already stated, associating Orkney with Cleveland helped to establish the parents' innocence because, as one man commented: 'social workers are *always* picking on innocent people.' However, sometimes this association could be used by research participants to reach quite different conclusions. The very fact that Orkney Social Services were reported to have repeated errors made in Cleveland led some people to be *more* likely to accept that Social Services must have had good evidence. Otherwise, people asked, why would they have risked 'putting themselves on the line again'? Thus it is quite possible for the message presented by a source with the intention of promoting one conclusion, to have quite the opposite effect. (For other examples of such 'boomerang effects' see Curran, 1987.)

These forms of 'resistance' were intertwined with variations in the socio-demographic and personal experience of the research participants. Gender, parenthood, class, age, sexual, ethnic, and national identity were all sources of variation in audience reception. Responses to the media coverage were also influenced by whether or not people had been to the Orkney Islands, their politics (including prior attitudes to sexual violence, the family, and social workers), and their own knowledge about child abuse. However, the most important source of resistance to many of the dominant media messages outlined above was personal experience of sexual abuse—either one's own or the abuse of one's child, sister, or brother. Research participants who spoke about such experiences were more likely fully to accept that abuse could occur in the family home and be perpetrated by a close relative. They were also more likely to *reject* the idea that abusers looked different from anyone else, and to do so completely and without reservation. Some of the research participants who talked about having been sexually abused themselves also related quite differently to the Orkney story and viewed the stills from the news coverage in a very different light. For example, although most people identified with the parents, many abuse survivors identified with the children. Thus, whereas one woman, as already quoted, commented that the Orkney case stuck in her mind 'because it could be the social workers up the 'morrow going and lifting *your* kiddies', another recalled the Orkney case through the lens of her own childhood. She had been sexually abused by her father and run away from home, only to be forcibly returned to her assailant by the police. For her, the picture of the children 'reunited' with 'jubilant parents' was deeply disturbing.

The research discussed here shows that media messages are not simply translated into audience beliefs. Information or ideas intended by a source agency to lead to one conclusion may lead some people to quite another point of view. A dominant message in one story may be counteracted by pre-existing messages from other cultural forms and, in any case, reporting on a story is never homogeneous and individual journalists may struggle to assert distinct perspectives. Most important of all, people's own experiences may lead them to challenge dominant accounts or identify with a story from a different point of view.

However, such evidence of resistance and variation in interpretation does not mean that the media are without influence. The Orkney coverage did have a powerful impact in particular ways and did influence public beliefs. For the parents protesting their innocence, the media coverage was a success—although not completely so. For Social Services, however, it was a public relations disaster. This PR disaster had effects which reached beyond the particular case in dispute. The public presentation of the Orkney case created a 'collective memory' of dawn raids and fear of social-work malpractice. This was true even for those research participants who were critical of the 'bad press' received by social work. Indeed, people often protested about the 'scapegoating' of social workers and argued against 'tarring the whole profession with the same brush'. However, such a critique of the media coverage could co-exist with ways of thinking about social workers that drew on precisely those media representations that they rejected. At a basic level, people did not have access to explanations which might, for some people, have justified some of the actions of social workers. For example, there was very little reporting of Social Services' rationale for taking the children from their homes before the school bus arrived in the morning, when the families were most likely to be together. It is interesting to note that the subsequent inquiry into the removal of the children from Orkney did severely criticize social-work actions. However, the report also concluded that

The conduct of the workers in the removal of the children was efficient and supportive . . . the timing of the removals was beyond serious criticism. (Clyde, 1992: 349)

Such statements (which received minimal publicity) seem incomprehensible in the light of most people's image of 'the dawn raids', even those who wished to see social workers in a more favourable light.

It is also important to note that sometimes participants' memories of events placed social workers in a worse light than was explicit in the actual reporting at the time. For example, some research participants remembered the earlier Cleveland case as a 'social-work scandal'. They made no mention of the medical professional at all and several thought that the doctor who was the focus of press reports at the time (Dr Marietta Higgs) was actually a social worker. In addition, the negative coverage helps to create a particular image of social work. Many people saw Social Services as a last resort rather than as part of the investigation or support process. During the course of one research session, two women discovered that they both had long-standing concerns about a child that they knew. However, neither of them had ever discussed this before or sought help from Social Services. As one woman explained: 'you'd have to be absolutely certain [before approaching Social Services]. You don't want kids whipped away for nothing.' There was, in fact, a widespread assumption that children suspected of being abused would immediately be removed from the home by legal order. This accords with the image presented by the bulk of media coverage but does not accord with usual practice: this would only happen in about 3 per cent of cases (Gibbons *et al.*, 1995). The concrete effect of such representations for some abused children was summed up by one teenage girl who was sexually abused by her stepfather. She was discouraged from seeking help for several years because of her fear of Social Services, a fear she found to be unjustified when she eventually did speak out. 'I used to think I'd get sent away if I told', she said. '[Journalists] . . . make social workers out to be big and bad . . . they sort of put a barrier up' (Kitzinger and Skidmore, 1995*a*: 11).

Conclusion

The research on audience reception discussed in this chapter illustrates the operation of media power. It identifies the precise way in which elements of media coverage of different issues 'worked' or failed to work. It also identifies both the potential and the limits of people's ability to deconstruct and 'resist' media accounts. Personal experience, political consciousness, and socio-demographic position can alter people's trust in, and reading of, specific press, television, and radio reports. However, experience and identity are not created in a media-free space. The media play a part in how people classify, recall, or interpret events in their own lives, the way in which they see themselves and locate themselves in society.

The model of media influence developed here takes account of what people bring to their 'reading' of the media, and what they take away from it. It recognizes the pleasure people gain from the media, the social currency of different phrases or stories, and the way in which media messages are incorporated into day-to-day conversation. Acknowledging these levels of complexity is not incompatible with theorizing about the influence of the press, films, television, and radio. The diversity and multi-layered reactions of individuals should not act as a smokescreen to obscure media power. Instead, we need to recognize that such power is not absolute, nor does it exist in isolation. The media do not operate as a single force in a hermetically sealed ideological conspiracy. It is all much more messy and contradictory than that. If there is one thing that this book has tried to show, it is that mass media and power in modern Britain is a site of contest and conflict. It involves struggles over media ownership, state intervention, advertising, propaganda, and media representation. It also encompasses debate about the use of media technologies, audience pleasure, interpretation, and public understandings. It is these struggles that make engaging with the media worth while: as journalists, pressure groups, source agencies, critics, audiences, and as citizens.

Bibliography

ALLEN, R. (1985), *Speaking of Soap Operas* (Chapel Hill, NC: University of North Carolina Press).

ANG, I. (1985), *Watching* Dallas: *Soap Opera and the Melodramatic Imagination* (New York: Methuen & Co.).

—— (1989), 'Wanted: Audiences. On the Politics of Empirical Audience Studies', in E. Seiter, H. Borchers, G. Kreutner, and E. Warth (eds), *Remote Control: Television, Audiences and Cultural Power* (London: Routledge).

—— (1990*a*), 'Culture and Communication: Towards an Ethnographic Critique of Media Consumption in the Transnational Media System', *European Journal of Communication*, 5: 239–60.

—— (1990*b*), 'Melodramatic Identifications: Television Fiction and Women's Fantasy', in M. E. Blumler and E. Katz (eds), *The Uses of Mass Communications* (Beverly Hills, Calif.: Sage).

ANGELL, N. (1922), *The Press and the Organisation of Society* (London: Labour Publishing Society).

AULICH, J. (1992) (ed.), *Framing the Falklands War. Nationhood, Culture and Identity* (Buckingham: Open University Press).

BARKER, M. (1984) (ed.), *Video Nasties* (London: Pluto Press).

—— (1992), 'Stuart Hall: Policing the Crisis', in M. Barker and A. Beczer (eds), *Readings into Cultural Studies* (London: Routledge).

BARNETT, S., and CURRY, A. (1994), *The Battle for the BBC: A British Broadcasting Conspiracy* (London: Aurum).

BAUSINGER, H. (1984), 'Media, Technology and Daily Life', *Media, Culture and Society*, 6: 343–51.

BBC (1992), *Extending Choice* (London: BBC).

BCCCS WOMEN'S STUDIES GROUP (1978), *Women Take Issue* (London: Hutchinson).

BEHARRELL, P. (1993), 'AIDS and the British Press', in J. Eldridge (ed.), *Getting the Message* (London: Routledge).

BERGER, J. (1972), *Ways of Seeing* (London: BBC/Penguin).

—— (1980), *About Looking* (London: Writers & Readers).

—— and Jean, M. (1975), *A Seventh Man* (Harmondsworth: Penguin).

—— and MOHR, J. (1982), *Another Way of Telling* (London: Writers & Readers).

BIRNBAUM, N. (1971), 'Monarchs and Sociologists: A Reply', in N. Birnbaum, *Towards a Critical Sociology.*

BLAND, L. (1985), 'Cleansing the Portals of Life: The Venereal Disease Campaign in the Early Twentieth Century', in M. Langan and B. Schwarz (eds), *Crises in the British State 1880–1930* (London: Hutchinson).

BLUMLER, J., and KATZ, E. (1974) (eds), *The Uses of Mass Communications* (Beverly Hills, Calif.: Sage).

Bibliography

Bobo, J. (1988), '*The Color Purple*: Black Women as Cultural Readers', in D. Pribram (ed.), *Female Spectators: Looking at Film and Television* (London: Verson).

Bourdieu, P. (1986), 'The Aristocracy of Culture', in R. Collins, J. Curran, N. Garnham, P. Scannell, P. Schlesinger, and C. Sparks (eds), *Media, Culture and Society: A Critical Reader* (London: Sage).

Bourke, M. (1994), *Working Class Cultures in Britain 1890–1960* (London: Routledge).

Boyce, D. (1987), 'Crusaders without Chains', in J. Curran, A. Smith, and P. Wingate (eds), *Impacts and Influences* (London: Methuen).

—— Curran, J., and Wingate, P. (1978) (eds), *Newspaper History* (London: Constable).

Brendon, P. (1982), *The Life and Death of the Press Barons* (London: Secker & Warburg).

Briggs, A. (1961), *The History of Broadcasting in the United Kingdom. Vol. 1: The Birth of Broadcasting* (Oxford: Oxford University Press).

—— (1965), *The History of Broadcasting in the United Kingdom. Vol. 2: The Golden Age of Wireless* (Oxford: Oxford University Press).

—— (1995), *The History of Broadcasting in the United Kingdom. Vol. 5: Competition* (Oxford: Oxford University Press).

British Broadcasting Corporation (1994), *The Future of the BBC, Serving the Nation, Competing World-Wide* (London: HMSO).

Broadcasting Committee (The Sykes Report) (1923) (London: HMSO).

—— (Crawford Report) (1925) (London: HMSO).

—— (Ullswater Report (1936) (London: HMSO).

—— (Beveridge Report (1951) (London: HMSO).

—— (Pilkington Report (1960) (London: HMSO).

—— on Financing the BBC (Peacock Report) (1986) (London: HMSO).

—— on the Future of Broadcasting (Annan Report) (1977) (London: HMSO).

Brody, G., and Stoneman, Z. (1983), 'The Influence on Television Viewing on Family Interactions—a Contextualist Framework', *Journal of Family Issues*, 14: 329–48.

Brook, L. (1988), 'The Public's Response to AIDS', in R. Jowell, S. Witherspoon, and L. Brook (eds), *British Social Attitudes: The 5th Report* (Aldershot: Gower).

Brown, J., and Schluze, L. (1990), 'The Effects of Race, Gender and Fandom on Audience Interpretations of Madonna's Music Videos', *Journal of Communication*, 40: 88–102.

Brown, M. E. (1990) (ed.), *Television and Women's Culture: The Politics of the Popular* (London: Sage).

—— (1994), *Soap Opera and Women's Talk: The Pleasure of Resistance* (London: Sage).

Browne, D. (1985), 'Radio Normandie and the IBC Challenge to the BBC Monopoly', *Historical Journal of Film, Radio and Television*, 5: 3–18.

Brownmiller, S. (1975), *Against Our Will: Men, Women and Rape* (New York: Bantam Books).

Brunsdon, C. (1981), '*Crossroads*: Notes on Soap Opera', *Screen*, 22: 32–7.

—— (1989), 'Text and Audience', in E. Seiter, H. Borchers, G. Kreutzner, and E. Warth (eds), *Remote Control: Television, Audience and Cultural Power* (London: Routledge).

—— and Morley, D. (1979), *Everyday Television: Nationwide* (London: BFI).

BRUNT, R. (1992), 'Engaging with the Popular: Audience for Mass Culture and What to Say About Them', in L. Grossberg, C. Nelson, and P. Treichler (eds), *Cultural Studies* (London: Routledge).

BUCKINGHAM, D. (1987), *Public Secrets: Eastenders and its Audiences* (London: BFI Publishing).

BURNS, T. (1977), *The BBC: Public Institution, Private World* (London: Macmillan).

CALLINICOS, A. (1989), *Against Postmodernism: A Marxist Critique* (Cambridge: Polity Press).

CAMERON, J. (1985), *Point of Departure* (Glasgow: Collins).

CAREY, J. (1992), *Intellectuals and the Masses* (Harmondsworth: Penguin).

CARR, E. H. (1971), *What is History?* (Harmondsworth: Penguin).

CHRISTIE, I. (1994), *The Last Picture Show* (London: BFI Publishing).

CLYDE, J. (1992), *The Report of the Inquiry Into the Removal of Children from Orkney in February 1991* (Edinburgh: HMSO).

COCKERELL, M., HENNESSY, P., and WALKER, D. (1985), *Sources Close to the Prime Minister* (London: Macmillan).

COCKETT, R. (1989), *Twilight of Truth: Chamberlain, Appeasement and the Manipulation of the Press* (London: Weidenfeld & Nicholson).

COHEN, S. (1987), *Folk Devils and Moral Panics: The Creation of the Mods and Rockers* (Oxford: Blackwell).

—— and Young, J. (1981) (eds), *The Manufacture of News: Social Problems, Deviance and the Mass Media* (London: Constable).

COLLETT, P., and LAMB, R. (1986), *Watching People Watching Television*. Report to the Independent Broadcasting Authority (London: IBA).

CONNELL, I. (1988), 'Fabulous Powers: Blaming the Media', in L. Masterman (ed.), *Television Mythologies: Stars, Shows and Signs* (London: Comedia).

COOPER, L. (1932), *The Rhetoric of Aristotle* (New York: Appleton-Century Company).

CORNER, J. (1986), 'Codes and Cultural Analysis', in R. Collins *et al.* (eds), *Media, Culture and Society: A Critical Reader* (London: Sage).

—— (1991), 'Meaning, Genre and Context', in J. Curran and M. Gurevitch (eds), *Mass Media and Society* (London: Edward Arnold).

CORRIGAN, P. (1983), 'Film Entertainment as Ideology and Pleasure: Towards a History of Audiences', in J. Curran, and V. Porter (eds), *British Cinema History* (London: Constable).

CRANFIELD, G. (1978), *The Press and Society* (London: Longman).

CUBBITT, S. (1985), 'The Politics of the Living Room', in L. Masterman (ed.), *Television Mythologies* (London: Comedia).

CURRAN, J. (1977*a*), 'Capitalism and Control of the Press 1900–1975', in J. Curran, M. Gurevitch, and J. Woollacott (eds), *Mass Communications and Society* (London: Edward Arnold).

—— (1977*b*), 'Mass Communication as a Social Force in History, Unit 2', Open

Bibliography

University course in Mass Communication and Society (Milton Keynes: Open University).

—— (1987), 'The Boomerang Effect: The Press and the Battle for London 1981–6, in J. Curran, A. Smith, and P. Wingate (eds), *Impacts and Influences* (London: Methuen).

—— (1990), 'The New Revisionism in Mass Communication Research: A Reappraisal', *European Journal of Communication*, 5: 135–64.

—— and SEATON, J. (1991), *Power without Responsibility: The History of Press and Broadcasting* (London: Methuen/Routledge).

—— TUNSTALL, J. (1973), 'Mass Media and Leisure', in M. Smith, S. Parker, and C. Smith (eds), *Leisure and Society in Britain* (London: Allen Lane).

CURTHOYS, A. and DOCKER, J. (1989), 'In Praise of *Prisoner*', in T. Tullock and G. Turner (eds), *Australian Television: Programmes, Pleasures and Politics* (London: Allen & Unwin).

CURTIS, L. (1984), *Ireland: The Propaganda War* (London: Pluto).

DANGERFIELD, S. (1961), *The Strange Death of Liberal England* (New York: G. Putnams and Son).

DEWE-MATHEWS, T. (1994), *Censored: The Story of Film Censorship in Britain* (London: Chatto and Windus).

DOTY, A. (1993), *Making Things Perfectly Queer: Interpreting Mass Culture* (London: University of Minnesota Press).

DYER, R. (1986), *Heavenly Bodies* (London: Macmillan).

ECO, U. (1976), *A Theory of Semiotics* (London: Macmillan).

—— (1994), *Apocalypse Postponed* (London: British Film Institute).

ELDRIDGE, J. (1993) (ed.), *Getting the Message: Essays from Glasgow University Media Group* (London: Routledge).

ELLIOTT, P. (1977), 'Reporting Northern Ireland: A Study of News in Britain, Ulster and the Irish Republic', in UNESCO (ed.), *Media and Ethnicity* (Paris: UNESCO).

EVANS, H. (1983), *Good Times, Bad Times* (London: Hodder & Stoughton).

—— (1984), *Good Times, Bad Times*, 2nd edn. (London: Hodder & Stoughton).

FERGUSON, E. (1995), 'Goodbye to All That', *Observer*, 19 Nov.

FEUER, J. (1989), 'Reading *Dynasty*: Television and Reception Theory', *The South Atlantic Quarterly*, 88: 443–60.

FISKE, J. (1989), 'Moments of Televison: Neither the Text nor the Audience', in E. Seiter, H. Borchers, G. Kreutzner, and E. Warth (eds), *Remote Control: Television, Audience and Cultural Power* (London: Routledge).

—— (1991), *Television Culture* (London: Methuen).

FLORENCE, P. (1993), 'Lesbian Cinema, Women's Cinema', in G. Griffin (ed.), *Outwrite: Lesbianism and Popular Culture* (London: Pluto Press).

FRANKLIN, B. (1994), *Packaging Politics: Political Communications in Britain's Media Democracy* (London: Routledge).

FRIEDAN, B. (1963), *The Feminine Mystique* (London: Penguin).

FRITH, S. (1983), 'The Pleasures of the Hearth: The Making of BBC Light Entertainment', in T. Bennett *et al.* (eds), *Formations of Pleasure* (London: Routledge).

GARLAND, R. (1991), 'Suburban Vampire', *Trouble and Strife*, 20: 35–40.

GARNHAM, N. (1989), 'Has Public Service Broadcasting Failed?', in N. Miller and C. Norris (eds), *Life after the Broadcasting Bill* (Manchester: Manchester School of Education), 17–33.

—— (1990), *Capitalism and Communication* (London: Sage).

GERARD, D. (1982), 'The Impact of the First Newsmen in Jacobean London', *Journalism Studies Review*, 7: 32–4.

GERBNER, G. (1973), 'Cultural Indicators: The Third Voice', in G. Gerbner, L. Gross, and W. Melody (eds), *Communications Technology and Social Policy* (New York: Wiley).

GIBBONS, J., CONROY, S., and BELL, C. (1995), *Operating the Child Protection System* (London: HMSO).

GILLESPIE, M. (1989), 'Technology and Tradition: Audio-Visual Culture among South Asian Families in West London', *Cultural Studies*, 3: 226–39.

—— (1995), *Television, Ethnicity and Cultural Change* (London: Routledge).

GILROY, P. (1987), *There Ain't No Black in the Union Jack* (London: Hutchinson).

GITLIN, T. (1991), 'The Politics of Communication and the Communication of Politics', in J. Curran, and M. Gurevitch, *Mass Media and Society* (London: Edward Arnold).

GLASGOW UNIVERSITY MEDIA GROUP (1976), *Bad News* (London: Routledge & Kegan Paul).

—— (1980), *More Bad News* (London: Routledge & Kegan Paul).

—— (1985), *War and Peace News* (Milton Keynes: Open University Press).

—— (forthcoming), *Dying of Ignorance: AIDS, the Media and Public Belief* (London: Sage).

GOFFMAN, E. (1976), *Gender Advertisements* (London: Macmillan).

GOLDING, P., and MURDOCK, G. (1990), 'Screening Out the Poor', in J. Willis, and T. Wollen (eds), *The Neglected Audience'* (London: BFI).

GOLDING, P. (1994), 'Telling Stories: Sociology, Journalism and the Informed Citizen', *European Journal of Communication*, 9: 461–84.

GOLDMAN, R. (1992), *Reading Ads Socially* (London: Routledge).

GRAY, A. (1987), 'Behind Closed Doors: Video Recorders in the Home' in H. Baehr, and R. Dyer (eds), *Boxed In: Women and Television* (London: Pandora).

GREER, G. (1971), *The Female Eunuch* (New York: McGraw-Hill).

GRIFFEN, G. (1993), (ed.), *Outwrite: Lesbianism and Popular Culture* (London: Pluto Press).

GRIPSRUD, J. (1995), *The Dynasty Years* (London: Routledge).

GUNTER, B. and SVENNEVIG, M. (1988), *Attitudes to Broadcasting Over the Years* (London: Libby).

HAGEN, I. (1994), 'Expectations and Consumption Patterns in TV News Viewing', *Media, Culture and Society*, 16: 415–28.

HALL, S. (1973), 'Encoding and Decoding the TV Message', CCCS mimeo, University of Edinburgh.

—— (1980), 'Encoding/Decoding', in S. Hall, D. Hobson, A. Lowe, and P. Willis (eds), *Culture, Media, Language* (London: Hutchinson).

—— and JEFFERSON, T. (1976) (eds), *Resistance through Rituals: Youth Subcultures in Post-War Britain* (London. Hutchinson).

Bibliography

HALL, S. , CRITCHER, C., JEFFERSON, T., CLARKE, J., and ROBERTS, B. (1978), *Policing the Crisis. Mugging, the State and Law and Order* (London: Macmillan).

HARRIS, R. (1983), *Gotcha! The Media, the Government and the Falklands Crisis* (London: Faber and Faber).

—— (1990), *Good and Faithful Servant: The Unauthorised Biography of Bernard Ingham* (London: Faber and Faber).

HARRISON, S. (1974), *Poor Men's Guardians* (London: Lawrence and Wishart).

HARTLEY, J., GOULDEN, H., and O'SULLIVAN, T. (1985), *Making Sense of the Media*, Block 2, Unit 3, 'Media Institutions' (London: Comedia).

HEATH, S. (1977), 'Notes on Suture', *Screen*, 18: 48–76.

HEBDIGE, D. (1979), *Subculture: The Meaning of Style* (London: Methuen).

HENDERSON, L. (1996), *The Issue of Child Sexual Abuse in TV Fiction: Audience Reception of Channel 4 Brookside* (London: Channel 4).

HERMES, J. (1995), 'A Perfect Fit: Feminist Media Studies', in R. Buikema and A. Smelik (eds), *Women's Studies and Culture: A Feminist Introduction* (London: Zed Books).

HERZOG, H. (1941), 'On Borrowed Experience: An Analysis of Listening to Daytime Sketches', *Studies in Philosophy and Social Science*, 9: 65–95.

HMSO (1988), *Competition, Choice and Quality* (London: HMSO).

HOBSON, D. (1980), 'Housewives and the Mass Media', in S. Hall, D. Hobson, A. Lowe, and P. Willis (eds), *Culture, Media, Language* (London: Hutchinson).

—— (1982), Crossroads: *The Drama of a Soap* (London: Opera Methuen).

—— (1989), "Soap Operas at Work', in E. Seiter, H. Borchers, G. Kreutzner, and E. Warth (eds), *Remote Control: Television and Cultural Power* (London: Routledge).

HODGE, R. and TRIPP, D. (1986), *Children and Television* (Cambridge: Polity Press).

HOOKS, B. (1991), *Yearning: Race, Gender and Cultural Politics* (London: Turnaround).

—— (1992), *Black Looks: Race and Representation* (London: Turnaround).

HORRIE, C., and CLARKE, S. (1994), *Fuzzy Monsters: Fear and Loathing at the BBC* (London: Heinemann).

HUGHES, R. (1980), *The Shock of the New: Art and the Century of Change* (London: BBC).

HUTTON, W. (1995), 'A State of Decay', *Guardian*, 18 Sept.

JAKUBOWICZ, A., GOODALL, H., MARTIN, J., MITCHELL, T., RANDALL, L., and SENEVIRATNE, K. (1994), *Racism, Ethnicity and the Media* (St Leonards, Australia: Allen and Unwin).

JAY, C., and GLASGOW, J. (1992) (eds), *Lesbian Texts and Contexts: Radical Revisions* (London: Onlywomen).

JENSEN, Klaus B. (1990), 'The Politics of Polysemy: Television News, Everyday Consciousness and Political Action', *Media-Culture and Society*, 12: 57–77.

JHALLY, S., and LEWIS, J. (1992), *Enlightened Racism*: The Cosby Show, *Audiences and the Myth of the American Dream* (Oxford: Westview Press).

JONES, Stephen G. (1987), *The British Labour Movement and Film, 1918–39* (London: Routledge & Kegan Paul).

KATZ, E., and LAZERSFELD, P. (1955), *Personal Influence: The Part Played by People in the Flow of Mass Communications* (New York: Free Press).

—— and LIEBES, T. (1985), 'Mutual Aid in Decoding *Dallas:* Preliminary Notes for a Cross-Culture Study', in P. Drummond and R. Paterson (eds), *Television in Transition* (London: British Film Institute).

KITZINGER, J. (1990), 'Audience Understandings of AIDS Media Messages: A Discussion of Methods', *Sociology of Health and Illness*, 12: 319–35.

—— (1993), 'Understanding AIDS: Media Messages and What People Know about AIDS', in J. Eldridge (ed.), *Getting the Message* (London: Routledge).

—— (1994*a*), 'Focus Groups: Method or Madness?, in M. Boulton (ed.), *Challenge and Innovation: Methodological Advances in Social Research on HIV/AIDS* (London: Taylor & Francis).

—— (1994*b*), 'The Methodology of Focus Groups: The Importance of Interactions between Research Participants', *Sociology of Health and Illness*, 16: 103–21.

—— (1995), 'The Face of Aids', in I. Marcova and R. Farr (eds), *Representations of Health and Illness* (Chur: Harwood Academic Publishers).

—— (forthcoming), 'Resisting the Media', in Glasgow University Media Group, *Dying of Ignorance: AIDS, the Media, and Public Belief* (London: Sage).

—— and HUNT, K. (1993), *Evaluation of the Zero Tolerance Campaign* (Edinburgh: Edinburgh District Council Women's Committee).

—— and KITZINGER, C. (1993), ' "Doing it": Representations of Lesbian Sex', in G. Griffin (ed.), *Outwrite: Lesbianism and Popular Culture* (London: Pluto Press).

—— and MILLER, D. (1992), 'African AIDS: The Media and Audience Beliefs', in P. Aggleton, P. Davies, and G. Hart (eds), *AIDS: Rights, Risk and Reason* (London: Falmer Press).

—— —— (1995*a*), *Child Sexual Abuse and the Media: Summary Report to the ESRC* (Glasgow: Glasgow Media Group).

—— and SKIDMORE, P. (1995*b*), 'Playing Safe: Media Coverage of Child Sexual Abuse Prevention Strategies', *Child Abuse Review*, 4: 47–56.

KNIGHTLEY, P. (1982), *The First Casualty: The War Correspondent as Hero, Propagandist and Mythmaker* (London: Quartet Books).

KOESTLER, A. (1947), *Darkness at Noon* (Harmondsworth: Penguin).

LEAPMAN, M. (1986), *The Last Days of the Beeb* (London: Allen & Unwin).

LEE, A. (1976), *The Origins of the Popular Press 1850–1914* (London: Croom Helm).

LEHMAN, D. (1991), 'Oh No, [de] Man Again!', *Lingua Franca*, 1(4): 26–33.

LENNON, P. (1994), *Foreign Correspondent: Paris in the Sixties* (London: Picador).

LEWIS, P., and BOOTH, J. (1989), *The Invisible Medium: Public, Commercial and Community Radio* (London: Macmillan).

LINDLOF, T., and TRAUDT, P. (1983), 'Mediated Communication in Families', in M. Mander (ed.), *Communications in Transition* (New York: Praeger).

LINTON, M. (1995), 'Sun-Powered Politics', *Guardian*, 30 Oct.

LIVINGSTON, S. (1990), 'Interpreting a Television Narrative: How Different Viewers See a Story', *Journal of Communication*, 40: 72–85.

LODZIAK, C. (1986), *The Power of Television* (London: Frances Pinter).

LULL, J. (1980), 'The Social Uses of Television', *Human Communication Research*, 6: 198–209.

Bibliography

LULL, J. (1990), *Inside Family Viewing: Ethnographic Research on Television's Audiences* (London: Routledge).

MacCABE, C. (1980), *Godard: Images, Sounds, Politics* (London: BFI).

McCULLIN, D. (1995), *Sleeping with Ghosts: A Life's Work in Photography* (London: Vintage).

McGUIGAN, J. (1992), *Cultural Populism* (London: Routledge).

McINTYRE, I. (1994), *The Expense of Glory: A Life of John Reith* (London: HarperCollins).

McLAUGHLIN, L. (1993), 'Feminism, the Public Sphere, Media and Democracy', in *Media, Culture and Society*, 15: 599–620.

McLEOD, J., KOSICKI, G., and PAN, Z. (1991), 'On Understanding and Misunderstanding Media Effects', in J. Curran and M. Gurevitch (eds), *Mass Media and Society* (London: Edward Arnold).

McLUHAN, M. (1973), *Understanding Media* (London: Abacus).

McQUAIL, D. (1972) (ed.), *Sociology of Mass Communication* (Harmondsworth: Penguin).

—— BLUMLER, J., and BROWN, J. (1972), 'The Television Audience: A Revised Perspective', in D. McQuail, *Sociology of Mass Communication* (Harmondsworth: Penguin).

McROBBIE, A. (1982), 'Jackie—An Ideology of Adolescent Femininity', in B. Waites, T. Bennett, and G. Martin (eds), *Popular Culture: Past and Present* (London: Croom Helm).

—— (1991), *Feminism and Youth Culture* (London: Macmillan).

Manchester, W. (1989) (ed.), *In Our Time: The World as Seen by Magnum Photographers* (London: André Deutsch).

MARZAROLI, O. (1984), *One Man's World: Photographs 1955–84* (Glasgow: Third Eye Centre).

MATTELART, A. (1991), *Advertising International: The Privatisation of Public Space* (London: Routledge).

MERTON, R. (1946), *Mass Persuasion: The Social Psychology of a War Bond Drive'* (New York: Harper Brothers).

MILLER, D. (1993), 'The Northern Ireland Information Service: Aims, Strategy and Tactics', in J. Eldridge (ed.), *Getting the Message: News, Truth and Power* (London: Routledge).

—— (1994), *Don't Mention the War* (London: Pluto).

—— (1995), 'The Media and Northern Ireland: Censorship, Information Management and the Broadcasting Ban', in G. Philo (ed.), *Glasgow Media Group Reader. Vol. 2: Industry, Economy, War and Politics* (London: Routledge).

—— and REILLY, J. (1994), 'Food and the Media: Reporting of Food "Risks" ', in S. Henson and S. Gregory (eds), *The Politics of Food* (Reading: Reading University).

—— —— (1995), 'Making an Issue of Food Safety: The Media, Pressure Groups and the Public Sphere', in D. Maurer and J. Sobal (eds), *Eating Agendas: Food, Eating and Nutrition as Social Problems* (New York: Aldine De Gruyter).

—— and WILLIAMS, K. (1993), 'Negotiating HIV/AIDS Information: Agendas,

Media Strategies and the News', in J. Eldridge (ed.), *Getting the Message: News, Truth and Power* (London: Routledge).

MILLS, C. W. (1956), *The Power Elite* (Oxford: Oxford University Press).

MODLESKI, T. (1984), *Loving with a Vengeance: Mass-Produced Fantasies for Women* (London: Methuen).

—— (1986), *Studies in Entertainment: Critical Approaches to Mass Culture* (Bloomington, Ind.: Indiana University Press).

MOORES, S. (1988), 'The Box on the Dresser: Memories of Early Radio and Everyday Life', *Media, Culture and Society*, 10: 23–40.

—— (1990), 'Texts, Readers and Contexts', *Media, Culture and Society*, 12: 9–29.

—— (1993), *Interpreting Audiences: The Ethnography of Media Consumption* (London: Sage).

MORLEY, D. (1980), *The* Nationwide *Audience: Structure and Decoding* (London: BFI).

—— (1986), *Family Television: Cultural Power and Domestic Leisure* (London: Comedia).

—— (1992), *Television, Audiences and Cultural Studies* (London: Routledge).

—— (1995), 'Theories of Consumption in Media Studies', in D. Miller (ed.), *Acknowledging Consumption: A Review of New Studies* (London: Routledge).

—— and SILVERSTONE, R. (1991), 'Communication and Context: Ethnographic Perspectives on Media Audiences', in K. Jenson, and N. Jankowski (eds), *A Handbook of Qualitative Methodologies* (London: Routledge).

MORRIS, M. (1988), 'Banality in Cultural Studies', *Block*, 14: 15–25.

MULVEY, L. (1975), 'Visual Pleasure and Narrative Cinema', *Screen*, 16(3): 6–18.

MURDOCK, G. (1992), 'Citizens, Consumers and Public Culture', in M. Skovmand and K. C. Schroder (eds), *Media Cultures* (London: Routledge).

—— and GOLDING, P. (1978), 'The Structure, Ownership and Control of the Press, 1914-76', in D. Boyce, J. Curran, and P. Wingate (eds), *Newspaper History* (London: Constable).

NAIRN, T. (1988), *The Enchanted Glass: Britain and its Monarchy* (London: Hutchinson).

NAVA, M., and NAVA, O. (1992), 'Discriminating or Duped? Young People as Consumers of Advertising/Art', in M. Nava (ed.), *Changing Cultures: Feminism, Youth and Consumerism* (London: Sage).

PALMER, P. (1986), *The Lively Audience: A Study of Children around the TV Set* (Sydney: Allen & Unwin).

PARKER, R., and POLLOCK, G. (1987), 'Fifteen Years of Feminist Action: From Practical Strategies to Strategic Practices', in R. Parker and G. Pollock (eds), *Framing Feminism: Art and the Women's Movements 1970–1985* (London: Pandora).

PEARSON, G. (1983), *Hooligan: A History of Respectable Fears* (London: Macmillan).

—— (1984), 'Falling Standards: A Short, Sharp History of Moral Decline', in M. Barker (ed.), *Video Nasties* (London: Pluto Press).

PEGG, M. (1983), *Broadcasting and Society* (London: Croom Helm).

PHILLIPS, M., and HENRY, G. (1993), 'A Game of Courts and Camps', *Guardian*, 13 Jan.

Bibliography

PHILO, G. (1990), *Seeing and Believing* (London: Routledge).

—— (1995), 'Political Advertising and Popular Belief', in G. Philo (ed.), *Glasgow Media Group Reader. Vol. 2: Industry, Economy, War and Politics* (London: Routledge).

—— (forthcoming) (ed.), *The Media and Mental Distress* (London: Longman).

POSTMAN, N. (1987), *Amusing Ourselves to Death* (London: Methuen).

POTTER, D. (1994), *Seeing the Blossom* (London: Faber).

PRONAY, N., and SPRING, D. W. (1982) (eds), *Propaganda, Politics and Film 1918–45* (London: Macmillan).

RADWAY, J. (1984), *Reading the Romance: Feminism and the Representation of Women in Popular Culture* (Chapel Hill, NC: University of North Carolina Press).

REITH, J. (1924), *Broadcast over Britain* (London: Hodder & Stoughton).

RICHARDS, J. (1984), *The Age of the Dream Palaces* (London: Routledge).

RITCHIN, F. (1989), 'What is Magnum?', in W. Manchester (ed.), *In Our Time: The World as Seen by Magnum Photographers* (London: André Deutsch).

ROBERTSON, J. (1985), *The British Board of Film Censors: Film Censorship in Britain, 1896–1950* (London: Croom Helm).

ROBINS, K. (1994), 'Forces of Consumption: From the Symbolic to the Psychotic', *Media, Culture and Society*, 16: 449–68.

RODGER, G. (1995), *Humanity and Inhumanity: The Photographic Journey of George Rodger* (London: Phaidon).

ROOT, J. (1986), *Open the Box* (London: Comedia).

ROZENGREN, K., WENNER, L., and PALMGREEN, P. (1985) (eds), *Media Gratifications Research* (Beverly Hills, Calif.: Sage).

SCANNELL, P., and CARDIFF, D. (1976), 'The Social Foundations of British Broadcasting', supplementary material, units 1–6, Open University Mass Communications and Society course (Milton Keynes: Open University).

—— —— (1991), *A Social History of British Broadcasting. Vol. 1: 1922–1939* (Oxford: Blackwell).

SCHLESINGER, P. (1987), *Putting 'Reality' Together: BBC News*, 2nd edn. (London: Methuen).

—— (1991), *Media, State and Nation: Political Violence and Collective Identities* (London: Sage).

—— MURDOCK, G., and ELLIOTT, P. (1983), *Televising 'Terrorism': Political Violence in Popular Culture* (London: Comedia).

—— DOBASH, R., and WEAVER, K. (1992), *Women Viewing Violence* (London: BFI).

SEAMAN, W. (1992), 'Active Audience Theory: Pointless Populism', *Media, Culture and Society*, 14: 301–11.

SEITER, E., BORCHERS, H., KREUTZNER, G., and WARTH, E. (1989) (eds), *Remote Control: Television and Cultural Power* (London: Routledge).

SEYMOUR-URE, C. (1991), *The British Press and Broadcasting since 1945* (Oxford: Blackwell).

SHAWCROSS, W. (1992), *Rupert Murdoch: Ringmaster of the Information Circus* (London: Chatto & Windus).

SHILS, E., and YOUNG, M. (1953), 'The Meaning of the Coronation', *Sociological Review*, 1: 63–82.

SHIVELY, J. (1992), 'Cowboys and Indians: Perceptions of Western Films among American Indians and Anglos', *American Sociological Review*, 57: 725–34.

SILBER, L., and LITTLE, A. (1995), *The Death of Yugoslavia* (London: BBC/Penguin).

SIMPSON, J. (1993), 'Shooting the Messenger', *Guardian*, 17 Sept.

SKIDMORE, P. (1995), 'Telling Tales: Media Power, Ideology and the Reporting of Child Sexual Abuse in Britain', in D. Kidd-Hewitt and R. Osborne, *Crime and the Media* (London: Pluto Press).

SNODDY, R. (1992), *The Good, the Bad and the Unacceptable: The Hard News about the British Press* (London: Faber and Faber).

SONTAG, S. (1983), *A Susan Sontag Reader* (Harmondsworth: Penguin).

SORLIN, P. (1994), *The Mass Media* (London: Routledge).

STACEY, J. (1988), 'Desperately Seeking Difference', in L. Gamman and M. Marshment (eds), *The Female Gaze* (London: The Women's Press).

STAUBER, J., and RAMPTON, S. (1995), 'Democracy for Hire: Public Relations and Environmental Movements', *The Ecologist*, 25(5): 173–80.

STEAD, P. (1989), *Film and the Working Class* (London: Routledge).

STREET, S., and DICKINSON, M. (1985), *Cinema and the State: the Film Industry and the British Government 1927–84* (London: BFI).

STUART, A. (1988), '*The Color Purple*: In Defence of Happy Endings', in L. Gamman and M. Marshment (eds), *The Female Gaze* (London: The Women's Press).

STUART, C. (1975) (ed.), *The Reith Diaries* (London: Collins).

SWEENEY, J. (1995), 'UN Cover-up of Srebrenica Massacre', *Observer*, 10 Sept.

SWINGEWOOD, A. (1975), *Marx and Modern Social Theory* (London: Macmillan).

TAYLOR, P. (1995), *Munitions of the Mind* (Manchester: Manchester University Press).

THOMPSON, E. (1968), *The Making of the English Working Classes* (Harmondsworth: Penguin).

TOMLINSON, A. (1990), 'Introduction: Consumer Culture and the Aura of the Commodity', in A. Tomlinson (ed.), *Consumption, Identity and Style* (London: Routledge).

TUNSTALL, J. (1996), *The Media are American* (Oxford: Oxford University Press).

VULLIAMY, E. (1994), *Seasons in Hell: Understanding Bosnia's War* (London: Simon and Schuster).

WATNEY, S. (1987), *Policing Desire: Pornography, AIDS and the Media* (London: Comedia).

WELLINGS, K. (1988), 'Perceptions of Risk—Media Treatments of AIDS', in P. Aggleton and H. Homans (eds), *Social Aspects of Aids* (London: Falmer Press).

WHATLING, C. (1994), 'Fostering the Illusion: Stepping Out with Jodie', in D. Hamer and B. Budge (eds), *The Good, the Bad and the Gorgeous: Popular Culture's Romance with Lesbianism* (London: Pandora).

WHITAKER, B. (1981), *News Ltd.* (London: Minority Press Group).

WILLIAMS, K. (1993), 'The Light at the End of the Tunnel: The Mass Media, Public Opinion and the Vietnam War', in J. Eldridge (ed.), *Getting the Message: News, Truth and Power* (London: Routledge).

WILLIAMS, R. (1961), *Culture and Society* (Harmondsworth: Penguin).

Bibliography

WILLIAMS, R. (1980*a*), 'Advertising: The Magic System', in R. Williams, *Problems in Materialism and Culture* (London: Verso).

—— (1980*b*), *The Long Revolution* (Harmondsworth: Penguin).

WILLIS, P. (1977), *Learning to Labour: How Working-Class Kids Get Working-Class Jobs* (Farnborough: Saxon Jouse).

WILTON, T. (1995) (ed.), *Immortal Lesbians and the Moving Images* (London: Routledge).

WINN, M. (1977), *The Plug-in Drug* (New York: Penguin Books).

WINSHIP, J. (1987), *Inside Women's Magazines* (London: Pandora).

WINSTON, B. (1986), *Misunderstanding Media* (London: Routledge & Kegan Paul).

YOUNG, J. (1981), 'The Myth of the Drug Taker in the Mass Media', in S. Cohen, and J. Young (eds), *The Manufacture of News: Deviance, Social Problems and the Mass Media* (London: Constable).

Index

Index

Index

U.W.E.L LEARNING RESOURCES